ALASTAIR SAWDAY'S
SPECIAL PLACES TO STAY

BRITISH
HOTELS
INNS AND
OTHER
PLACES

Design: Caroline King

Maps & Mapping: Bartholomew Mapping, a division of HarperCollins, Glasgow

Printing: Canale, Italy

UK Distribution: Portfolio, Greenford, Middlesex

US Distribution: The Globe Pequot Press, Guilford, Connecticut

Published in 2003

Alastair Sawday Publishing Co. Ltd
The Home Farm Stables, Barrow Gurney, Bristol BS48 3RW
Tel: +44 (0)1275 464891 Fax: +44 (0)1275 464887
E-mail: info@specialplacestostay.com Web: www.specialplacestostay.com

The Globe Pequot Press
P. O. Box 480, Guilford, Connecticut 06437, USA
Tel: +1 203 458 4500 Fax: +1 203 458 4601
E-mail: info@globe-pequot.com Web: www.GlobePequot.com

Fifth edition

ISBN 1-901970-38-8 in the UK
ISBN 0-7627-2855-8 in the US

Printed in Italy

The publishers have made every effort to ensure the accuracy of the information in this book at the time of going to press. However, they cannot accept any responsibility for any loss, injury or inconvenience resulting from the use of information contained therein.

A WORD FROM
ALASTAIR SAWDAY

When we first published this pioneering book we were told
that it wouldn't work. Well, each year it has grown and this
year we had to reprint. It is clearly reaching the parts that other
books don't reach.

But things change at bewildering speed. We have dropped
places because they have become over-priced, or pompous,
or out of touch with local people. Laurels are often rested
upon. Let us know what we have missed, and do please let
us know how you get on.

I first travelled in the 1950s, in France, when it was an adventure
just to be there. We expected few comforts because there were
few around and France was still struggling to get back on its feet.
We were tolerant of human frailties and oddities but it was
that very human contact that made it all fun, together with
the simplicity of things and the haunting beauty of France.

I remember such things. That, perhaps, goes some way to
explaining why we are so keen to reveal the human, and
even quirky, side of Special Places – the warm beings who
make things happen. Peoples' memories and expectations
have shifted yet most of us – however 'modern' – still long
to be included and appreciated. However hip, luscious, grand,
stylish or cutting-edge a hotel may be, we nevertheless need
to feel human. Special Places' owners understand that.

My final word is in praise of those whose hard, hectic, work
keeps hotels going against the odds and whose passions are
driving a quiet revolution. 'Things' are getting better out
there – with more hotels supporting their communities
and buying local food. Best of all, the British are becoming
adventurous about taste.

I hope your memories serve you well and that these wonderful
places will nurture them – and you.

Alastair Sawday

ACKNOWLEDGEMENTS

Nicola Crosse created this book, though like many successful people she was standing on the shoulders of others – Tom Bell and Stephen Tate, previous editors whose tenacity and taste established the early editions. But hotel owners can be like clams, closing up when approached, so it takes a rare determination to get through – and Nicola has it. She has a keen eye for people and places that we consider special and has, like the archers at Agincourt, been unwavering. She has included and written about some beautiful traditional country house hotels and some fascinating minimalist hotels, whose owners have proved just as interesting and a smattering of all styles in between.

Jo Boissevain has been, as ever, inventive, methodical and eagle-eyed – never allowing a stylistic or syntactical oddity to slip in without query. Danielle Williams, my PA, is too useful not to be hijacked occasionally and has, with steadfast charm, extracted those all-important last-minute details and photographs from an army of recalcitrant owners. Behind the scenes Julia Richardson's production team has strived to produce a book as handsome as it is varied. And neither could the book exist without its inspectors – I thank them all.

Alastair Sawday

Series Editor:	Alastair Sawday
Editor:	Nicola Crosse
Editorial Director:	Annie Shillito
Production Manager:	Julia Richardson
Web & IT:	Russell Wilkinson, Matt Kenefick
Copy Editor:	Jo Boissevain
Editorial:	Sarah Bolton, Roanne Finch, Jessica Hughes, Danielle Williams
Production Assistants:	Rachel Coe, Paul Groom, Beth Thomas
Accounts:	Bridget Bishop, Sheila Clifton, Jenny Purdy, Sandra Hassell
Sales & Marketing:	Siobhan Flynn, Julia Forster
Writing:	Nicola Crosse, Jo Boissevain
Inspections:	Nicola Crosse, Tom Bell, Jan Adam, Annie Coates, Gillian Charlton-Meyrick, Auriol Marson, Penny Rogers, Robin Williams

A special thank you, too, to the other inspectors who saw just one or two houses for us.
Photos of The Priory Hotel courtesy of The Grimsby Telegraph.

WHAT'S IN THE BOOK?

CONTENTS

england

CONTENTS

channel islands

CONTENTS

scotland

CONTENTS

wales

INTRODUCTION

When I was asked if I would like to edit this book my heart
sank like the fake flaky pastry top on a service station steak and
kidney pie. I've always thought of British Hotels, Inns & Other
Places as a 'Man's Book'. Not least because my predecessors
– intrepid, chunky-knit and Timberland-shod male experts –
have yomped through the office reeling off terrifying facts and
figures about the hotel and pub world.

Chaps who can take off in a car for weeks on end, leap on
and off ferries in the Highlands, or hare around London on a
bicycle, unearthing new treasures by chatting up the locals;
fellows who know about real ale and who can chew the cud
into the wee small hours with hotel owners and landlords;
men who seem instinctively to know which chef has moved
to which kitchen, which pub is 'on the up' and which hotel
has 'gone down'. Men, in other words, with a sixth sense for
the changing scene of Hotels, Inns & Other Places.

My preconceptions and fears weren't eased by colleagues'
reactions to my new project. "Tough book," they'd mutter,
shaking their heads and scratching their chins like builders
eyeing up a Big Job. Still, you can't work at Sawdays and not
pitch in. So this year has seen me careering along country roads
in the LPG-driven car, simmering with dread about meeting
hard-nosed hotel-owners, serious fad-fond foodies and 'mine
hosts', Iris and Donald who, I feared, might want to 'extend
me a warm welcome'.

What I found, though, was a remarkable collection of people.
Charming ex-Londoners with crisp townhouses in the Cotswolds,
young family people growing and cooking organic vegetables,
sourcing local food and running a great restaurant with rooms
above. A dynamic owner who feels so passionately about the
industry and getting good young people to come into it that
she regularly lectures in schools. Some very slick hotels which
nevertheless manage to stay essentially human and some utterly
devoted folk who let you into their own home and spoil you
with Slow Food. Passionate art collectors with a serious gallery
where you can sleep listening to bird song – and some proper
English Inns with flag-stones and cheery staff. People who are
prepared to get up early, stay up late and be courteous and
friendly in between. In short, people who care.

INTRODUCTION

So I take my hat off to all the owners in this book – a hard-grafting bunch – for caring enough to do whatever they do differently. I applaud the owner who asked the local tourist board inspector to leave because he was "unspeakably dull", and I rejoice in the amount of fresh, seasonal and local food that is landing on their chopping boards.

We hope you enjoy using this book as much as I have enjoyed meeting the lovely people in it.

How do we choose our Special Places?

We choose places that we like because we have visited them. It's as simple as that. And then we write them up as honestly as we can so that you can choose what you like and ignore the rest.

Hotels, Inns & Other Places

Hotels

About half the places in the book are hotels. Some of them are swish and large and run like conventional hotels with room service and porters to carry your luggage. Some of them are smaller and things like that are not their style, but they will still be special for one reason or another.

Inns

There are about 60 inns in the book. Some are old and traditional with a good local presence in the bar so that sleeping above it might be difficult if you are not a joiner-in after 10 o'clock – beware! Some others have been labelled 'gastro-pubs' where the main focus is on the food, not the ale and the banter. Neither is likely to put the emphasis on room comforts in the same way as a hotel but you will also find some snappy designer bedrooms in these places.

Other Places

These include restaurants with rooms, which continue to spring up all over the country and where the food should be exceptional. The rooms may not be traditional but perhaps more modern and design-led. They also include some places that defy pigeon-holing at all – people's homes, where the owners are a real presence and their tastes will be reflected.

The diversity in this book allows the reader to choose the type of place they want for a particular stay.

INTRODUCTION

Maps

Each property is plotted on the map and flagged by an entry
number in the map section at the beginning of the book.
Don't use the maps as anything other than a rough guide
or you may get lost.

Bedroom descriptions

In the book we use the following:

Double One bed big enough to be shared by two people.
These will vary in size from standard (135cm wide) to super-
king-size (180cm wide). Do ask when you book if this is
important to you.

Single 90cm is standard.

Twin Two separate single beds.

Twin/double Also known as zip and link, these are two single
beds that can be joined together.

Family/triple These rooms have a mixture of beds. Do ask
when you book.

Four-poster Usually rather grand (and not always short) and
often the best room.

Suite In this book we have assumed that a suite is for two
people and will include either a separate sitting room or
a large sitting area in the room.

Bathrooms

Assume that all bedrooms have their own bathroom (and maybe
shower, too) unless we state that there is a *separate* bathroom
(for your exclusive use but you need to leave your bedroom
to get to it) or a *shared* bathroom (down the corridor and also
used by somebody else).

Prices

The range of prices quoted goes from the cheapest room in low
season to the highest, high season price. Where breakfast is not
included we will say so. Check for deals when you book.

Singles

If owners give a special price for singles occupying a double
room it is quoted after the double room price.

INTRODUCTION

Half-board

The price quoted is per person per night and includes a three-course meal. A minimum length of stay may apply. Check.

Meals

Most places serve breakfast until about 9.30am (sometimes later at weekends) but others are much more flexible and sometimes you can have it brought to you in bed. Check the night before. Where places charge separately for breakfast, we give the price.

Breakfast is usually a feast that can set you up for the day – although in my experience it induces a craving for a Danish pastry by coffee time. Choose the full cooked option if you are on holiday – the bacon and sausages are nearly always local and often organic – and it's not something one tends to bother with at home because of all the washing up. So, fill your boots, then waltz off and leave someone else to do the hard work – hurrah!

If there is a lunch price, it refers to two courses, a dinner price refers to three, unless we say otherwise. Fixed price menus are stated and à la carte gives an average price without wine.

Closed

When given in months this means for the whole of the month.

Symbols

See the inside back cover for the full list.

Children

Our symbol shows which places are happy to welcome children of all ages. That doesn't necessarily mean they have any equipment or toys nor does it mean the children should be anything less than impeccably behaved. We mention in italics at the end of the write-up if places only accept children over a certain age. Early suppers for children can sometimes be arranged in advance.

Pets

Your pet may be allowed to sleep in your room, sometimes for a supplement – but it probably won't be able to roam freely so keep it under control. Check in advance about taking a pet.

INTRODUCTION

Payment

Visa and MasterCard are generally fine. American Express is
sometimes accepted but Diners Club hardly ever. Debit cards
are widely accepted. Some places don't accept credit cards at
all and they are marked with a cash/cheque symbol.

Smoking

Most bedrooms and restaurant dining rooms will either be
smoke-free or have smoking restrictions; some hotels are
completely non-smoking. Let's face it: smoking is no longer
cool. However, there is a move afoot to re-introduce 'smoking
rooms' or humidors in an increasing number of places. Is the
cigar making a comeback?

Disabled/wheelchair access

My sister recently checked into a B&B in France with two
disabled children on the strength of a wheelchair access symbol.
The house did have wheelchair access but it was also at the top
of a very steep hill, so once inside they were virtually trapped.
It ruined their holiday but it needn't have done had they asked
a few questions before they booked.

Practical matters

Booking and cancellation

Most hotels need a deposit by cheque or credit card when
booking. You can lose all, or part of it, if you cancel. Check the
exact terms.

Arrivals and departure

Usually your bedroom will be ready by mid-afternoon and
you will be expected to leave it by about 11am.

Hotel Telephones

Ask for the price per minute before making a call – charges
can be high.

Quick reference indices

At the back of the book is a quick reference guide to help you
find the places that will suit you – whether it be somewhere
with a swimming pool or somewhere that has a sound system
in the room, or rooms at £100 a night, or less, for two.

INTRODUCTION

Environment We try to reduce our impact on the environment by:

- publishing our books on recycled paper
- planting trees. We are officially Carbon Neutral®. The emissions directly related to our office, paper production and printing of this book have been 'neutralised' through the planting of indigenous woodlands with Future Forests
- re-using paper, recycling stationery, tins, bottles, etc
- encouraging staff use of bicycles (they're loaned free) and car sharing
- celebrating the use of organic, home-grown and locally-produced food
- publishing books that support, in however small a way, the rural economy and small-scale businesses
- publishing *The Little Earth Book*, a collection of essays on environmental issues and *The Little Food Book*, a hard-hitting analysis of the food industry. *The Little Money Book* is under way, too. See our web site www.fragile-earth.com for more information on any of these titles

Subscription Owners pay to appear in this guide. Their fee goes towards the costs of inspections and producing an all-colour book. We only include places and owners that we find positively special. It is not possible for anyone to buy his/her way into our guides.

Internet Our web site www.specialplacestostay.com has online pages for all the places featured here and from all our other books — around 3,500 Special Places in Britain, Ireland, France, Italy, Spain and Portugal. There's a searchable database, full details, a taster of the write-ups and colour photos.

For more details see the back of the book.

Disclaimer We make no claims to pure objectivity in choosing our Special Places to Stay. They are here because we like them. Our opinions and tastes are ours alone and this book is a statement of them; we hope that you will share them.

We have done our utmost to get our facts right but apologise unreservedly for any mistakes that may have crept in. Feedback from you is invaluable and we always act upon comments. With your help and our own inspections we can maintain our reputation for dependability.

INTRODUCTION

You should know that we do not check such things as fire alarms, swimming pool security or any other regulation with which owners of properties receiving paying guests should comply. This is the responsibility of the owners.

And finally

We want to hear whether your stay was a triumph or not. If you are unhappy about something then do speak to the owner or the manager while you are there. Many problems are best solved 'on the spot'. Please fill out the report form at the back of the book or e-mail us at britishhotels@sawdays.co.uk. We also value your finds and recommendations – for this, or any other book in the series. Do keep writing. If your recommendation results in the inclusion of a special place in any of our guides we'll send you a free copy.

Whichever Hotel, Inn or Other Place you decide upon, I hope you have a marvellous time.

Nicola Crosse

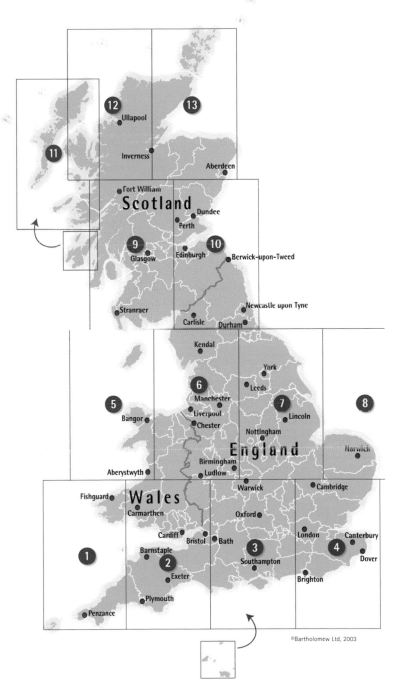

A guide to our map numbers

©Bartholomew Ltd, 2003

©Bartholomew Ltd, 2003

Map 1

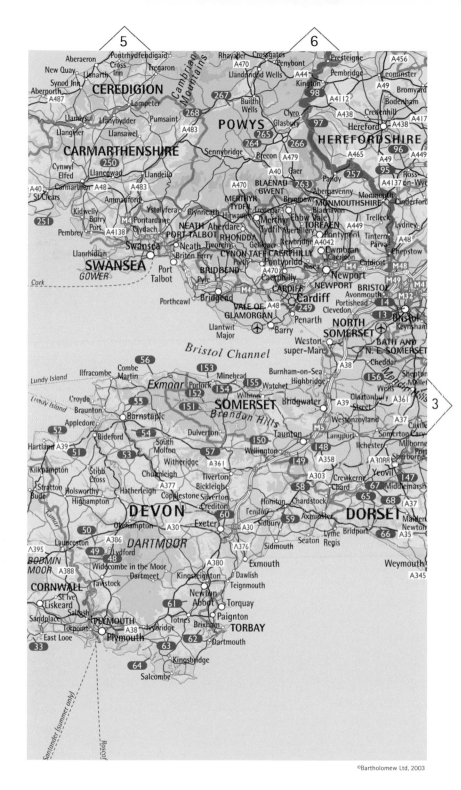

Map 2

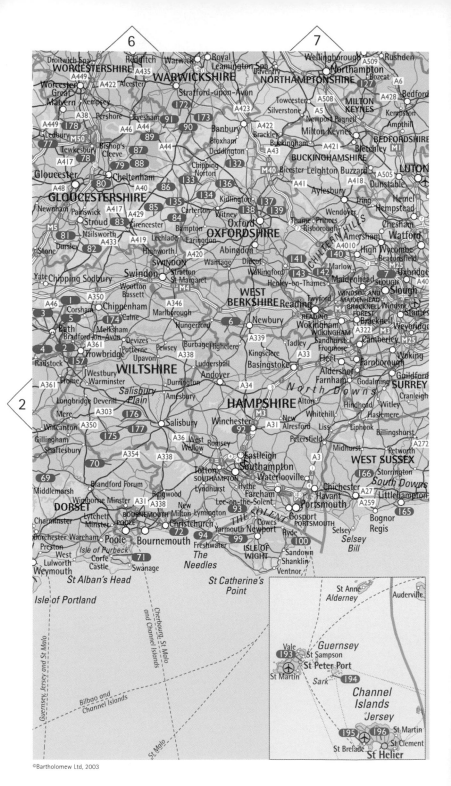

Map 3

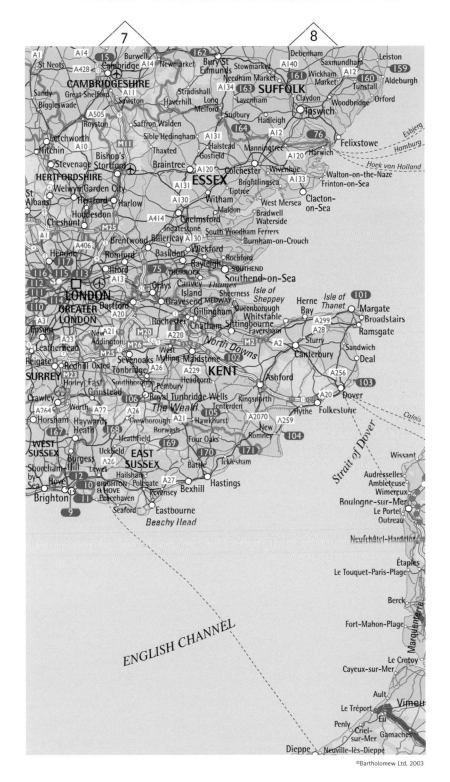

©Bartholomew Ltd, 2003

Map 4

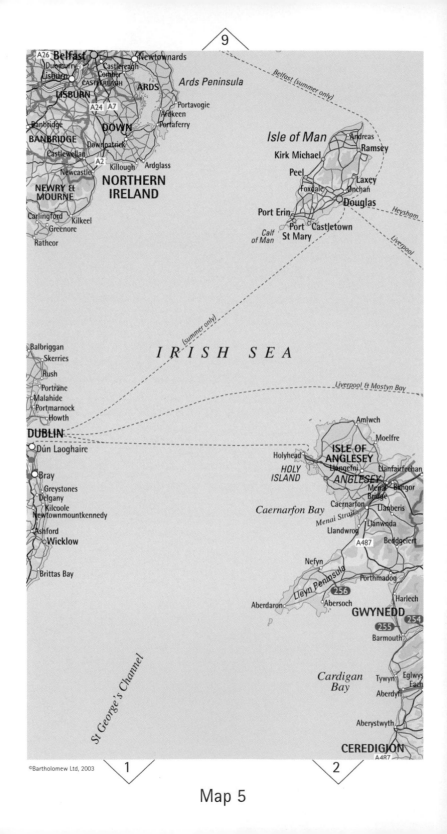

Map 5

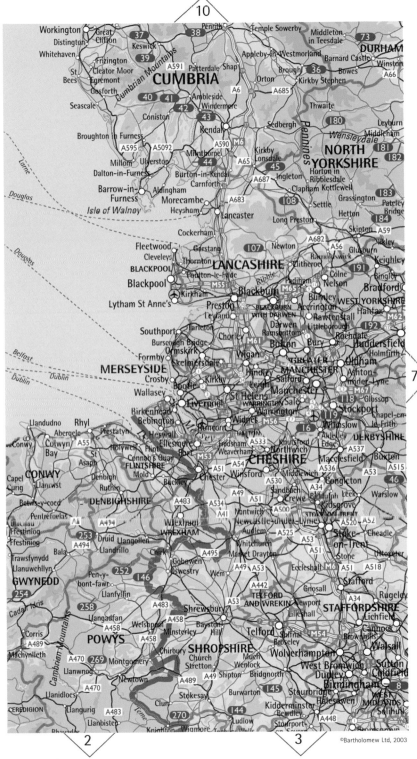

Map 6

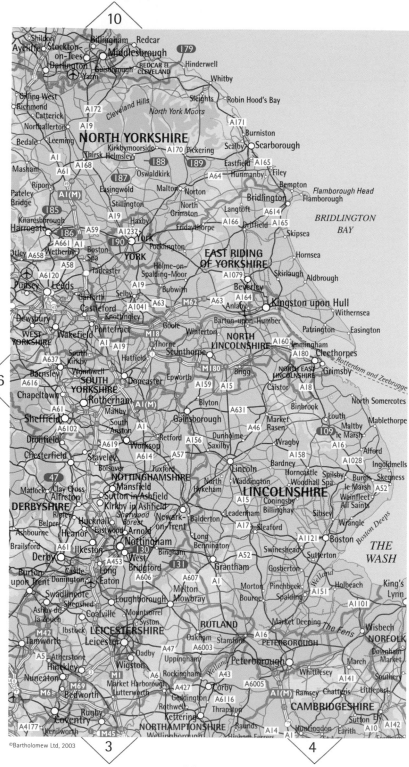

©Bartholomew Ltd, 2003

Map 7

4

Map 8

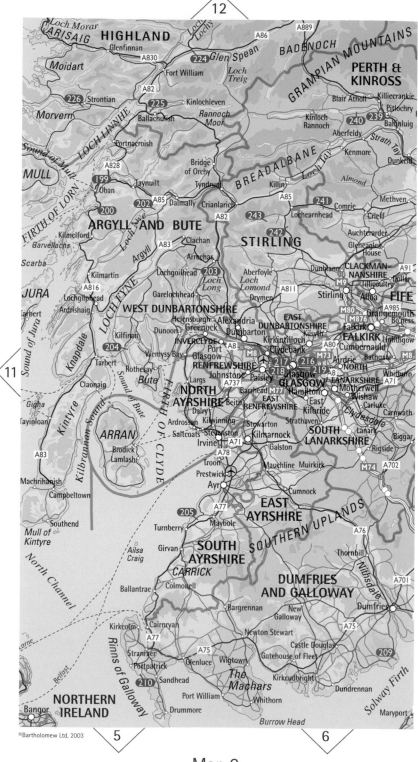

Map 9

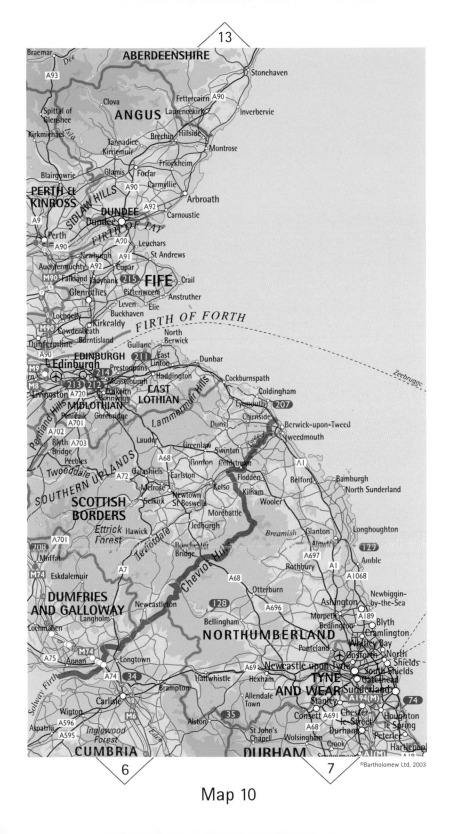

©Bartholomew Ltd, 2003

Map 10

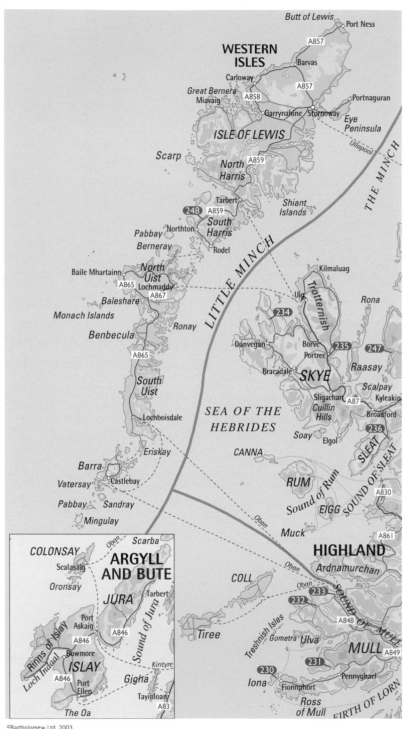

Butt of Lewis
Port Ness

**WESTERN
ISLES**

A857

Barvas

Carloway

A857

Great Bernera
Miavaig

A858

Portnaguran

Garrynahine   Stornoway

ISLE OF LEWIS

Eye
Peninsula

Scarp

Ullapool

North
Harris

A859

THE MINCH

Shiant
Islands

Tarbert

248   A859

South
Harris

Pabbay
Berneray

Northton

Rodel

Kilmaluag

LITTLE MINCH

Uig

Trotternish

Rona

Baile Mhartainn

North
Uist

A865
Lochmaddy

234

A867

Baleshare

Monach Islands

Benbecula

Ronay

Dunvegan

Borve   235   247
Portree

Raasay

A865

Bracadale

SKYE

Scalpay
Kyleakin

South
Uist

Sligachan   A87
Cuillin
Hills

Broadford

236

Lochboisdale

*SEA OF THE
HEBRIDES*

Soay   Elgol

SLEAT

SOUND OF SLEAT

Eriskay

CANNA

Barra

Vatersay   Castlebay

RUM

Sound of Rum

A830

Pabbay   Sandray

EIGG

Oban

Mingulay

Muck

A861

COLONSAY

Oban   Scarba

HIGHLAND

Scalasaig

**ARGYLL
AND BUTE**

Oban   Ardnamurchan

Oronsay

JURA

COLL

Oban   233

SOUND OF MULL

Tarbert

232

Port
Askaig

Sound of Jura

A846

Treshnish Isles   Gometra   Ulva

A848

Rinns of Islay

A846

Bowmore

Tiree

231

MULL

A849

Kintyre

230

Pennyghael

ISLAY

A846
Port
Ellen

Gigha

Iona   Fionnphort

Tayinloan

A83

Ross
of Mull   FIRTH OF LORN

The Oa

Map 11

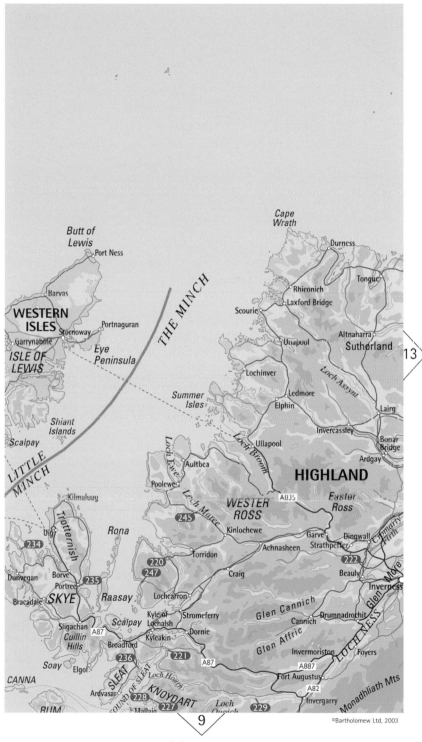

Map 12

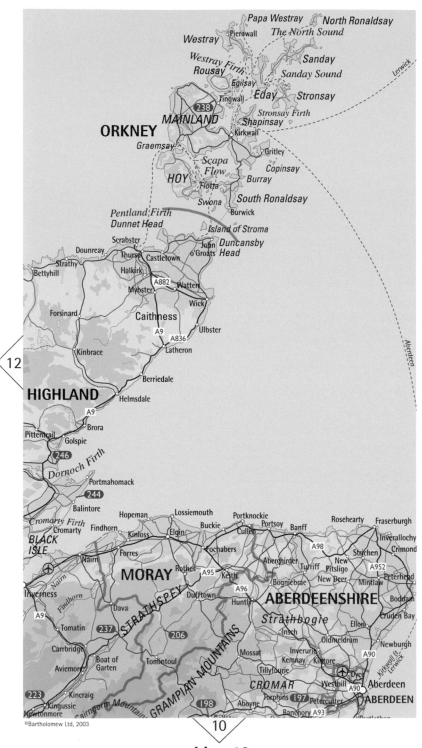

Map 13

HOW TO USE THIS BOOK

explanations

① rooms
Assume all rooms are 'en suite' unless we say otherwise.

If a room is not 'en suite' we say **with separate bath** or **with shared bathroom**: the former you will have to yourself, the latter may be shared with other guests or family member.

② room price
The price shown is for one night B&B for two people sharing a room. A price range incorporates room/seasonal differences. We say when the price is for two.

③ meals
Prices are per person. Meals in B&B's must be booked in advance. If breakfast isn't included we give the price.

④ closed
When given in months, this means for the whole of the named months and the time in between.

⑤ directions
Use as a guide; the owner can give more details.

⑥ map & entry numbers
Map page number; entry number.

⑦ type of place

sample entry

Stein Inn
Stein, Waternish, Isle of Skye IV55 8GA

White cottages bob by the quay in this remote, tiny fishing village, the setting for Skye's oldest inn. Angus stocks 80 single malts, thirst-quenching ales and seasoned opinion behind the bar of this rough-hewn, fire-warmed hostelry. Stand under blackened joists and talk about anything with this affable rogue spirit. In good weather, sit out by the shore of the sea loch: across the water, the headland rises dramatically; to the north, a few low-slung islands lie scattered. Lose yourself with a pint watching locals potter about in their boats against a setting sun. With the sea being so close, the food is really good, too: from your window, watch the catch landed, hauled from the sea to your plate, impossibly fresh. If cosiness comes from contrast and setting, then the clean, closely caved, blue-carpeted and pine-panelled rooms above the bar are perfect. There are moorings for yachts – sailors can ring ahead to have provisions waiting – but… far wiser to spoil yourselves with a couple of nights on land. A little paradise.

⑥ rooms	5. 2 doubles, 2 family, 1 single.
② price	£49-£62. Singles £24.50-£30.
③ meals	Bar lunch from £4.50. Dinner about £13.
④ closed	Christmas Day & New Year's Day.
⑤ directions	From Isle of Skye bridge, A850 to Portree. Follow sign to Uig for 4 miles, left on A850 for Dunvegan for 14 miles. Hard right turn to Waternish on B886. Stein 3.5 miles along loch side.

	Angus & Teresa McGhie
tel	01470 592362
fax	01470 592362
e-mail	angus.teresa@steininn.co.uk
web	www.steininn.co.uk

⑦ Inn

⑧ **⑥** map 11 entry 234

⑧ symbols
See the last page of the book for fuller explanation:

🦽	wheelchair facilities	🐾	pets can sleep in your bedroom
🛏	easily accessible bedrooms	@	internet connection available
👶	all children welcome	🏊	swimming pool
🚭	smoking restrictions exist	🚲	bike hire
💵	cash & cheques only	🚶	walking nearby
🥗	vegetarians catered for with advance warning	🎾	tennis on the premises

england

The Queensberry Hotel & Olive Tree Restaurant
Russel Street, Bath, Bath & N.E. Somerset BA1 2QF

The Queensberry is an old favourite, grand but totally unpretentious and immensely enjoyable. It is rare to find a hotel of this size and elegance still in private hands: owners Laurence and Helen are enthusiastic about their new project and don't plan to make many changes. It's easy to see why. The bedrooms are magnificent – contemporary and dramatic, with bold, inspirational colours and fabrics – and if you feel like spoiling yourself, have breakfast brought up to you: croissants, orange juice, fresh coffee, warm milk and a newspaper. Then pad around in wonderful white bathrobes feeling a million dollars. The bath runs in seconds, the shower imitates a monsoon. At night, pop down to supper and when you get back, your bed will have been turned down, your towels refreshed. As for the home-made fudge after supper… wonderful! All this in a John Wood house in the centre of Bath, a minute's walk from the Assembly Rooms. *Reserved on-street parking.*

rooms	29: 28 twins/doubles, 1 four-poster.
price	£120-£225. Singles from £90.
meals	Continental breakfast included; full English £9.50. Lunch £13.50. Dinner £26.
closed	Rarely.
directions	Into Bath on A4 London Road to Paragon, then 1st right into Lansdown, 2nd left into Bennett Street & 1st right into Russel Street.

Laurence & Helen Beere

tel	01225 447928
fax	01225 446065
e-mail	reservations@thequeensberry.co.uk
web	www.bathqueensberry.com

Hotel

Paradise House

Holloway, Bath, Bath & N. E. Somerset BA2 4PX

The magical 180-degree panorama from the garden is a dazzling advertisement for Bath: the views draw you out as soon as you enter the house. The Royal Crescent and the Abbey are floodlit at night and in summer, hot air balloons float by low enough for you to hear the roar of the burners. Wonderful. Most of the rooms make full use of the view; the best have bay windows. All have a soft, luxurious country feel, with drapes, wicker chairs and good bathrooms. There are also two garden rooms in an extension that planners took six years to approve – it's a remarkable achievement, in keeping with the original Bath stone house, and David is justly proud. The whole place seems to use glass in all the right places; the sitting room has lovely stone-arched French windows that draw in the light. Two doors up on Holloway – the old Roman road into this ancient city – is the old Monastery owned by a music teacher; sit outside with afternoon tea and hear the sound of piano music drift gently across the garden. Further away, the occasional peal of bells. *Seven minutes' walk from centre.*

rooms	11: 4 doubles, 3 twins, 1 family, 3 four-poster.
price	£75–£155. Singles £55–£95.
meals	Restaurants in Bath.
closed	Christmas.
directions	From train station take one-way system to Churchill Bridge. A367 exit from r'bout up hill. After 0.75 miles left at Andrews estate agents. Left down hill into cul-de-sac. On left.

David & Annie Lanz

tel	01225 317723
fax	01225 482005
e-mail	info@paradise-house.co.uk
web	www.paradise-house.co.uk

Hotel

map 3   entry 2

Apsley House
141 Newbridge Hill, Bath, Bath & N. E. Somerset BA1 3PT

Apsley House takes its name from the Duke of Wellington's main London residence which had the mighty address 'No. 1, London'. The Iron Duke is thought to have built this house; the service today is as exemplary as it was then. Claire and Nicholas took two years to find Apsley but they instantly knew this was the place. The house is full of great antique furniture, a grand piano, porter chairs, gilt mirrors and rich Colefax & Fowler fabrics. Take a drink from the bar, then sink into one of the sofas in the drawing room and gaze out through a huge, arched window to the garden. The dining room shares the same, warm elegance, separated by antique screens, with fresh flowers on all the tables and thoughtful touches like jugs of iced water at breakfast (which, by the way, is superb). Most of the pretty bedrooms are large: the four-poster in gleaming carved wood is surrounded by pale blue and white drapes, there are more fresh flowers and bathrooms are a good size too. Morning papers are dropped off at your door, your clothes can be laundered, and there's a car park – precious indeed in this city. *Children over five welcome.*

rooms	10: 3 doubles, 5 twins/doubles, 1 four-poster, 1 family.
price	£75-£140. Singles £60-£85.
meals	Restaurants in Bath.
closed	Christmas.
directions	A4 west into Bath. Keep right at 1st mini-r'bout. On for about 2 miles, then follow 'Bristol A4' signs. Pass Total garage on right. At next lights, branch right. On left after 1 mile.

Claire & Nicholas Potts

tel	01225 336966
fax	01225 425462
e-mail	info@apsley-house.co.uk
web	www.apsley-house.co.uk

Hotel

Dorian House

One Upper Oldfield Park, Bath, Bath & N. E. Somerset BA2 3JX

A cellist with a love of interior design is rare enough, but to find one running a hotel amid the beautiful surroundings of Bath is exceptional. Tim is the London Symphony Orchestra's principal cellist and was once taught by the late and great Jacqueline du Pré: "she played with abandon – she was herself," he says of his tutor. Be yourself in the cosy, spoiling luxury of this converted Victorian house; it feels more home than hotel. Tim and Kathryn have restored everything inside – the original tiled hallway is lovely. Sit with afternoon tea in deep sofas in the lounge, or enjoy one of six types of champagne in comfortable bedrooms all named after cellists; no surprise that the most exquisite – and the most secluded – is du Pré: a huge four poster bed is reached up a flight of stairs. Every room is decorated with beautiful fabrics and Egyptian linen; those on the first floor are more traditional, those on the second more contemporary, with oak furniture and sloping ceilings. Tim and Kathryn's art collection is everywhere, gathered from their travels abroad. Relaxation assured, maybe some music, too.

rooms	11: 3 doubles, 2 twins/doubles, 1 single, 2 family, 3 four-posters.
price	£65–£140. Singles £59–£78.
meals	Restaurants in Bath.
closed	Christmas.
directions	From Bath centre, follow Shepton Mallet signs to sausage-shaped r'bout, then A37 up hill, 1st right. House 3rd on left, signed.

Kathryn & Tim Hugh

tel	01225 426336
fax	01225 444699
e-mail	info@dorianhouse.co.uk
web	www.dorianhouse.co.uk

Hotel

map 3   entry 4

County Hotel

18-19 Pulteney Road, Bath, Bath & N. E. Somerset BA2 4EZ

Maureen and her sister Sandra bought this busy roadside hotel in bustling Bath and dressed the inside in pale creams and lemons with the odd dash of chintz. It is absolutely gleaming and nothing is out of place. Furniture is reproduction but the paintings are original and part of Maureen's art collection. Bedrooms, some smaller than others, are deeply traditional with the occasional piece of French-style white furniture and views over the bowling-green from some. Bathrooms are all a good size and immaculate. There are vases of fresh flowers arranged with flair in the drawing room, reading room and dining room which has a long view over the rugby ground to the Abbey. You will eat well: Maureen arrives at the hotel at 4.45 each morning to start baking the bread and croissants for breakfast, she prefers organic ingredients and eschews the supermarkets. There's a family feel to the County that is downright old fashioned and reassuring; those who don't feel comfortable with stainless steel and smoked glass will settle down happily here. There's plenty of parking but you can walk to everything Bath has to offer.

rooms	22: 18 doubles, 2 twins, 2 singles.
price	£110-£190. Singles £75.
meals	Plenty of restaurants within walking distance.
closed	22 December - 8 January.
directions	M4 Junc 18, A46 to Bath. A36 ringroad to Exeter & Wells. Right towards Holbourne Museum & straight over roundabout. Hotel 50 yds on right.

	Mrs Maureen Kent
tel	01225 425003
fax	01225 466493
web	www.county-hotel.co.uk

Hotel

Crown & Garter

Great Common, Inkpen, Hungerford, Berkshire RG17 9QR

The Crown and Garter lies in a lush paradise just south of the M4 motorway. Quiet lanes dip through fields and woodland, past cottages draped in honeysuckle. The charming bedrooms newly built around a pretty garden are the best surprise of all. Blended voile and Benison fabrics, painted floorboards, recycled furniture and handmade cushions create colourful eclectic rooms – none are the same. The oldest part of the building is the bar area where a huge Inglenook fireplace warms your cockles and deep pink walls are criss-crossed by ancient beams. A wonderful throne-like chair by the front door is part wine box part trapdoor but is often mistaken for an antique. Gill, an ex-university lecturer has had a complete lifestyle change to take over here, aided and abetted by her father (who helps by sitting in the bar chatting) and her son who is, as yet, too young to do much. But it creates a lovely family atmosphere with all generations in attendance. The food's home-made and, afterwards there's excellent walking on Inkpen common. Hard to imagine London is so close.

rooms	8: 5 doubles, 3 twins.
price	£70. Singles £50.
meals	Bar lunch from £6. Dinner from £10. Inn closed for food & drink Mondays & Tuesday lunchtimes.
closed	Rarely.
directions	From M4, junc. 13, A34 Basingstoke; left on A4 for Hungerford. After 2 miles, left for Kintbury & Inkpen. In Kintbury, left opp. corner shop, marked Inkpen Road. Inn on left after 2 miles.

	Gill Hern
tel	01488 668325
e-mail	gill.hern@btopenworld.com
web	www.crownandgarter.com

Inn

map 3　entry 6

Red Roofs at Oldfield

Guards Club Road, Maidenhead, Berkshire SL6 8DN

A dazzling film-set of a house and garden. Built in the 1890s, later home to the Reitlinger Museum and its Egyptian, Persian and Greek artefacts, it now houses Sandy, Colin, a canny collection of Victoriana (if something takes your fancy, you can buy it) and some deeply indulged guests. Bedrooms are packed with gleaming wood, elegant watercolours, vintage fabrics, wooden floors and old knick-knacks; one of the baths has a modesty canopy, and there are fine river views from most. There isn't a reason in the world to feel tense, but just in case you do there's a serious relaxation room for massage, reiki, LaStone therapy and a whole raft of fluffy treatments. The Great Hall with its striking green woodwork and vast windows is a super place to breakfast on local organic sausages and bacon; picnic outside and listen for the swoosh of an oar. The river Thames idles past the bottom of the sweeping lawns and Colin will deliver you by boat to The Waterside at Bray or The Fat Duck for a dinner to die for. How dreamy is that?

rooms	8: 6 doubles, 2 family.
price	Double £85. Singles £70. Family £125.
meals	Available locally.
closed	Christmas.
directions	200 yds off A4 to Maidenhead.

	Colin & Sandy Brooks
tel	01628 621910
fax	01628 638815
web	www.maidenhead.net/redroofsatoldfield

Hotel

entry 7   map 3

Hotel du Vin & Bistro
Church Road, Birmingham B3 2NR

The Hotel du Vin micro-chain's fourth venture converted the disused Birmingham & West Midlands' eye hospital into a five-floored palace of art, style and fun. They've kept the original double staircase, the granite pillars and an oddly-shaped Victorian lift designed to take stretchers but the rest bears the new residents' unmistakable signature: the Parisian-style courtyard, with its bronze statues and palm trees, the cosy cellar bar, with squidgy sofas and quirky lobster art, and the Bubble Lounge, done in the style of Venice's Caffè Florian – it stocks 60 kinds of champagne. As you'd expect, the restaurant is emphatically French: the waiters' uniforms, the Lautrec posters and small tables set comfortably apart transport you to Paris. Minimalist bedrooms please the eye, with Henderson & Redfearn furniture, natural fabrics, huge beds – the biggest measures eight-feet square – and bathrooms with roll-top Edwardian baths and monsoon-like showers. Pamper yourself silly in the health and fitness suite, then relax with a long cocktail. Birmingham is a city on the up and worth re-discovering.

rooms	66: 55 twins/doubles, 11 suites.
price	From £110. Suites from £225.
meals	Breakfast £9.50–£13.50. Lunch & dinner £16–£30.
closed	Rarely.
directions	M6, junc. 6, A38(M) Aston Expressway into city centre. Over flyover, left up slip road, signed Snowhill Station; 2nd exit at r'bout, then 1st left, 3rd right & 1st right into Church Road.

	Michael Warren
tel	0121 200 0600
fax	0121 236 0889
e-mail	info@birmingham.hotelduvin.com
web	www.hotelduvin.com

Hotel

map 6   entry 8

Hotel du Vin & Bistro

Ship Street, Brighton & Hove BN1 1AD

A Hotel du Vin with a seaside twist, yards from Brighton promenade and the cobbled Lanes. No sniffy dress code here, just more of what we've come to expect: funky, ever so luxurious and oozing with class. It's not without a sense of humour either – they've kept the plaque on the front of the building that says 1695, placed there by the Victorian builder responsible for its mock-Tudor façade. Beyond is a vibrant 21st-century hotel, tailored to the original building and its Lanes' setting of twisting alleyways and fascinating little shops. A whacky wrought-iron gate leads to a mediterranean-style courtyard with a vine-covered pergola, a bar with a vaulted ceiling, carved staircases, big, squashy sofas to kick back in. Large Cape Cod style bedrooms will leave you lost for words; some have balconies, others look onto Ship Street through arched, stained-glass windows; all are adoringly done with handmade beds, leather armchairs, woollen carpets, Egyptian linen, embracing towels, and the best bubble-baths known to man. Walk to galleries, cafés and the new Dome Theatre. A snooze in a deckchair is compulsory.

rooms	37: 31 doubles, 3 twins, 3 suites.
price	From £115. Suites from £185.
meals	Breakfast £9.50-£13.50. Lunch & dinner £22-£30.
closed	Rarely.
directions	M23/A23 to Brighton. Right at seafront r'bout opp. pier, 4th right into Middle St then bear right into Ship St. Hotel on right.

Nigel Buchanan

tel	01273 718588
fax	01273 718599
e-mail	info@brighton.hotelduvin.com
web	www.hotelduvin.com

Hotel

Paskins Town House

18/19 Charlotte Street, Brighton & Hove BN2 1AG

Paskins has resolutely cast aside ordinariness in favour of its own values. It is neither grand nor chic, fancy nor smart, just easy-going and genuinely 'green' in outlook. And it is yards from the beach. Paint is used to mask some dilapidation inside, and the colour schemes can be a little overwhelming, but some of the rooms are lovely, with the odd four-poster; all are colourful, with old prints, cabaret posters and modern art on the walls. Spread across two handsome townhouses, the whole place is impeccably clean and snug; it's fun, too. The Art Deco breakfast room is a joy to behold, as is breakfast – some say it's worth travelling to Brighton for: organic tomatoes sprinkled with basil, oak-smoked bacon and many varieties of sausage. Vegetarians are treated royally, too – Paskins claims to serve the best veggie food on the south coast. All the food is organic where available, from local farms if possible. On top of all that, the coffee is Fair Trade, the smellies are free of the taint of animal testing and you're so close to the centre of things – let your excellent room guide point the way. Terrific value.

rooms	19: 6 doubles, 2 twins/doubles, 7 singles, 1 triple, 3 four-posters.
price	£60-£125. Singles £30-£40.
meals	Sandwiches £3.60. Brighton restaurants.
closed	Rarely.
directions	M23/A23 to Brighton. Left at seafront r'bout opposite pier. Hotel 13th street on left.

	Roger Marlow
tel	01273 601203
fax	01273 621973
e-mail	welcome@paskins.co.uk
web	www.paskins.co.uk

Hotel

map 4   entry 10

Blanch House

17 Atlingworth Street, Brighton & Hove BN2 1PL

Dr Who used a phone box and Mr Benn a shop; Chris and Amanda do the same in a Georgian townhouse, transporting your imagination into the realms of luxurious fantasy. Travel back to the days of 70s glam rock chic and the decadent Edwardian house party, or go back even further to the Renaissance. Exotic countries lie behind other doors: stay in an Indian palace, or a Moroccan kasbah. Another two are devoted to roses and champagne. All are lavishly decorated with authentic detail, and no expense has been spared; all come with handmade chocs and hi-tech entertainment systems. The restaurant looks like something out of a 70s sci-fi film, with white moulded chairs, lots of white décor and light flooding through big windows. The menu is ambitious: try salmon cured with jasmine tea, black-leg crab cake, baked fig with a balsamic strawberry turnover. The house may once have been a church, judging by the two-storey arched window. Owners and staff alike are approachable and friendly. Be manicured, pedicured, styled or massaged – all can be done in-house. Cheeky chic and great fun.

rooms	12: 9 doubles, 3 suites.
price	From £125. Suites from £220.
meals	Dinner, à la carte, from £27.50
closed	Christmas.
directions	M23/A23 to Brighton. Left at seafront r'bout opp. pier along Marine Parade to traffic lights, then left, 1st right & 1st right again. Hotel on left.

	Chris & Amanda Blanch
tel	01273 603504
e-mail	info@blanchhouse.co.uk
web	www.blanchhouse.co.uk

Hotel

Claremont House Hotel

13 Second Avenue, Hove, Brighton & Hove BN3 2LL

A prep school during the early part of the last century, this handsome Victorian villa is being gently renovated by its new owners. They're not aiming for opulence, although original 19th-century chandeliers, fireplaces and cornices survive in many rooms and the jazzy black and white entrance steps are worthy of a film set. What Russell and Michael are passionate about is making guests feel welcome and cared for in their home. They're also seriously keen on food, and no special diet is too much trouble. Fresh, local, seasonal food is cooked here daily and that includes the puddings. You can eat out on the back lawn shaded by mature trees and if you need to get an early start, a breakfast tray is no problem. Flowers — outside and in — smell gorgeous. The whole place feels hugely cared for. High-ceilinged bedrooms have good beds and linen, pristine bathrooms, good showers and little extras. Hove is a classically good spot for all sorts at any time of year with nearby castles, seaside, South Downs and, of course, there's opera at Glyndebourne and the Brighton Festival.

rooms	12: 6 doubles, 5 singles, 1 four-poster.
price	£75–£120. Singles £45–£65.
meals	Dinner £17.50, booked in advance.
closed	Rarely.
directions	M23/A23 to Brighton. At seafront r'bout opp. pier, right on A259 Kings Rd/Kingsway for 1.5 miles, then right into Second Ave. Hotel near top of road on right.

Russell Brewerton & Michael Reed

tel	01273 735161
fax	01273 735161
e-mail	claremonthove@aol.com
web	www.claremonthousehotel.co.uk

Hotel

map 4   entry 12

Hotel du Vin & Bistro

The Sugar House, Narrow Lewins Mead, Bristol BS1 2NU

Robin Hutson and his team get better and better as they cover the country with their reinvention of the grand townhouse hotel, turning 'grand' to 'casual' in the process, to the joy of all. Great staff who make everybody feel special however busy they are, fabulous food and a huge choice of wine but it's the inherent good value that's most notable – if they can do such luxury for these prices, then others must look to their laurels. There's lots of space, stone walls, floorboards, rugs, squishy sofas and sandblasted beams. A sprinkling of tables and chairs around a fountain in the courtyard adds further style, as does the fire that shoots up a 100-foot chimney in the glass-fronted lobby, a remnant of the building's warehouse past. Up the steel staircase, spectacular bedrooms have a minimalist Manhattan-loft feel – low-slung furniture, handmade beds, off-white walls, hessian and big bathrooms, with walk-through showers, and baths. But always at the heart of a Hotel du Vin beats the bistro, French to the core, full of life and a great place to be. You can also play billiards or walk into the *humidor* and choose a Havana.

rooms	40: 25 doubles, 5 twins, 10 suites.
price	From £120. Suites £175-£185.
meals	Breakfast £9.50-£13.50. Lunch & dinner £25-£35.
closed	Rarely.
directions	M32 into Bristol, right at lights, follow city centre. Left at big roundabout onto inner ring road. 500 yds on, double back at traffic lights. Hotel on left down small side road after 100 yds.

	Lesley Skelt
tel	0117 925 5577
fax	0117 925 1199
e-mail	info@bristol.hotelduvin.com
web	www.hotelduvin.com

Hotel

The Studio

10 Hensmans Hill, Clifton, Bristol BS8 4PE

An old children's clothes factory in fashionable Clifton converted into two houses, a flat and, on the ground floor, The Studio. Step through a gate in the black iron railings to a little gravelled courtyard and the blue front door. Walk straight in to a large room with pretty windows, solid wooden flooring and plenty of light. Apart from the small, sparklingly bright, white-tiled bathroom, all is here: along one wall, a line of kitchen cupboards with cool blue/grey fronts, a gas hob with electric oven, microwave, fridge/freezer, washing machine and dishwasher. A stylish Conran table and chairs in checked metal sit in one corner and an easy leather chair in the other. Along the other wall there's a firm double bed with modern, pale-wood slatted headboard. That's it! Clifton village life – lots of restaurants and shops – art galleries and the Suspension Bridge are just up the road and you are surrounded by university halls of residence - it's perfect for a stay during graduation. For business folk there is modem access and good public transport to the centre. *Minimum stay two nights.*

rooms	1 double.
price	£70; £350 per week. Singles £50.
meals	Continental breakfast in fridge.
closed	Rarely.
directions	5-minute walk from Clifton Village. Buse: 8 from Temple Meads station.

Anne Malindine

tel	0117 914 9508
fax	0117 914 9508
e-mail	anne@amalindine.freeserve.co.uk
web	www.roseberyhouse.net

Other Place

map 2　entry 14

Hotel Felix

Whitehouse Lane, Huntingdon Road, Cambridge, Cambridgeshire CB3 0LX

It's been a long time coming but Cambridge has finally got the hotel it deserves. Hotel Felix is funky and up to date, a sophisticated country house with a modern twist and just a mile from the charming parts of this historic city. Finding the right site was always going to be difficult, for the university colleges own most of the old buildings, but owners Vivien and Jeremy Cassel knew what they were up against having successfully opened The Grange in York. They've centred the hotel around a Victorian villa in several acres of parkland; home, it's said, to the black squirrel! Two new bedroom wings have been added at right angles to the original building to create a courtyard with statue and plants – that leads to a grand entrance hall. Vivien's bedrooms are luxurious: huge beds, plump cushions, silk fabrics, stone floors in bathrooms with gleaming chrome, and hi-tech equipment that supplies films on demand. Food in the Graffiti restaurant draws on the simple, flavoursome approach of mediterranean and Italian cooking, and there is lots of light, airy space in which to sit and relax. Contemporary style without the attitude.

rooms	52 twins/doubles.
price	£158–£265. Singles from £128.
meals	Continental breakfast included; full English £7.50. Bar meals from £4.95. Lunch about £16. Dinner from £25.
closed	Rarely.
directions	A1 north, then A1307/A14 turn-off onto Huntingdon Road into Cambridge. Hotel on left.

	Shara Ross
tel	01223 277977
fax	01223 277973
e–mail	help@hotelfelix.co.uk
web	www.hotelfelix.co.uk

Hotel

Belle Epoque Brasserie

60 King Street, Knutsford, Cheshire WA16 6DT

Walking round this extravagant 1901 building gives you the sense that it was destined to become something far more indulgent than a temperance hall. The audacity of architect Richard Harding Watt's untethered imagination is a delight. the beamed Arts and Crafts style of a function room upstairs, the wooden-floored private dining room where Georgie Fame and Stephane Grappelli played in the Seventies, and the two massive stone columns in the courtyard hauled by horse and cart from Manchester infirmary; two of the original cartwheels are still propped against the wall. The Mooneys arrived 25 years ago, injecting lots of pazazz and lavish Art Nouveau style. What you see is original: the alabaster clocks, the two blackamoors and the statue of a goddess, arms held skywards. Today, David and Matthew run it with just the same energy as did their parents, Keith and Nerys, who still pop in. They've added a stylish bar and gorgeous, contemporary bedrooms, but pride of place is still the restaurant – an alcove guarded by two Doric columns is special, as is the food.

rooms	6 doubles.
price	£80-£85. Singles £50.
meals	Continental breakfast included; full English £4.95. Bar lunches £4-£7. Dinner, à la carte, £25-£30. Restaurant closed Mondays, Sat lunchtimes & Sun evenings.
closed	Christmas & Bank Holidays.
directions	M6, junc. 19, Knutsford. Enter town, right at r'bout; left at 2nd lights, for Macclesfield. Down hill, 1st left into King St. Halfway up on left.

David & Matthew Mooney

tel	01565 633060
fax	01565 634150
e-mail	info@thebelleepoque.com
web	www.thebelleepoque.com

Restaurant with Rooms

map 6   entry 16

Caradoc of Tregardock

Treligga, Delabole, Cornwall PL33 9ED

Crashing breakers, wheeling gulls, carpets of wild flowers in spring – this place is a dream for artists and a tonic for everyone. Just two fields away from the coastal path, the old farm buildings are set around a grassy courtyard with west-facing patios that catch the setting sun or gathering storm. Some bedrooms look out to sea and all are airy with huge beds, white walls and pretty linen. Caradoc's upstairs drawing room has a magnificent Atlantic view, beams and a woodburner; the farmhouse kitchen with its Rayburn has a large table that seats 12. Janet can stock the fridges with the best of Cornish for your breakfast and point you to good restaurants, some within walking distance along the cliffpath – or hire a chef for special occasions. Caradoc and the cottage are ideal for extended families and special interest groups – guests have use of the 60-foot studio and the Malaysian Summerhouse – for painting or yoga. There are books, music and videos too if staying in seems like a good idea. *July-August: self-catering only. Inclusive yoga breaks £250-£500.*

rooms	Caradoc: 4 twins/doubles or private seaview apartment. Cottage: 1 double, 1 twin.
price	£70-£130. Self-catering £375-£1,400 p.w. Studio £25 a day.
meals	Picnic £8. Cream tea £6. Dinner with wine, by arrangement, £35. Private chef £100 per day.
closed	Rarely.
directions	South from Delabole, after 2 miles right turn to Treligga, 2nd farm road signed to Tregardoc.

	Janet Cant
tel	01840 213300
fax	01840 213300
e-mail	info@tregardock.com
web	www.tregardock.com

Other Place

The Port Gaverne Hotel

Port Gaverne, Nr Port Isaac, Cornwall PL29 3SQ

Having successfully created the relaxed country house, Polsue Manor on the south coast of Cornwall, Graham and Annabelle have turned their attention to overhauling a seaside hotel on the north coast. It's an exciting challenge and very much work in progress but we're confident they have the flair and eye for detail to turn Port Gaverne into a stylish little enclave. The hotel is an old 17th-century inn set back from the rocky, funnel-shaped Port Gaverne near the pretty fishing village of Port Isaac – it's safe to swim. Bedrooms in the oldest part of the building have beamed character, while those in the modern wing have received the Sylvester treatment, and some have access to a small balcony. Down in the warren-like bar, snug cubby-holes are an ideal place to recuperate with a pint after a hike along the coast, or a stroll up an inland valley – both walks start outside. A wonderful stained-glass sailing rigger leads to the formal restaurant. The food has come on in leaps and bounds since they took over, cooked fresh in a modern English style. Come for the sea and quiet relaxation.

rooms	15: 8 doubles, 2 twins, 4 family, 1 triple.
price	£70–£100. Singles £45–£55.
meals	Bar meals from £4.50. Dinner £25.
closed	January–mid-February.
directions	From Wadebridge, B3314, then B3267 to Port Isaac. There, follow road right to Port Gaverne. Inn up lane from cove on left.

Graham & Annabelle Sylvester

tel	01208 880244
fax	01208 880151

Inn

map 1   entry 18

Tregea Hotel

16-18 High Street, Padstow, Cornwall PL28 8BB

Few places have as much going for them as Padstow: pretty quayside, sandy beaches, slate-hung houses on narrow streets, fish restaurants and sailing bustle. And, at the top of the oldest, quietest part of town, the lovely Tregea Hotel. Overlooking the 13th-century church, Tregea – the 'house on the hill' – has deeds going back to 1693 when it was sold for five shillings... New owners Nick and Cazz Orchard, television actors with an eye for a dramatic setting, give you eight wonderful bedrooms (and more rooms planned for 2004) with town or estuary views. Here are natural colours, modern checks, white linen – a clean, metropolitan feel. There's a big sitting room with an open fire to curl up by in winter, and sofas to lounge on after a day at the beach. From sandy Harbour Cove you can watch boats bob and seagulls wheel; in the evening listen out for the gentle snuffle of the deer from the neighbouring Prideaux Manor estate. At breakfast try the daily fish special for breakfast, caught locally... a rare treat. A friendly, civilised place to stay, and wonderfully near the beaches of Daymer and Polzeath.

rooms	8: 6 doubles, 2 twins/doubles.
price	£82-£98.
meals	Restaurants in Padstow.
closed	Christmas & New Year.
directions	From Wadebridge, A389 west to Padstow. Pass turn to town centre & docks, then right after fire station, signed Prideaux Place. 2nd left into Tregirls Lane, then immed. right into High St. Hotel 200 yds on left.

Mr Nick Orchard

tel	01841 532455
fax	01841 533542
e-mail	tim@tregea.co.uk
web	www.tregea.co.uk

Hotel

Number 6

Middle Street, Padstow, Cornwall PL28 8AP

If you dream of the Mediterranean, but don't want to leave the country, pack your bags and head to beatific Number 6. It's the sort of place you'd hope to stumble upon in the back street of an unspoilt fishing village in the south of France. Brenda and Paul came to live by the sea and fulfil the dream. Small, informal and beautifully decorated, it is not a place to come looking for spa baths and room service; it's more about style without pretension, and superb fish landed by local trawlermen, laid on your plate the same day. Eat in the light, fresh, almost Bauhaus style restaurant with its checkerboard floor, white-painted brickwork, wooden blinds and plants, or outside in a tiny courtyard full of pots and passionflower. The restaurant is well known and extremely popular locally so book early if you do want to dine here. Upstairs, the three bedrooms vary in size but not charm: good beds, the best linen, piles of pillows, coir matting, maybe a stainless steel propeller fan, and wonderful bathrooms that bring the beach to you... all bang in the middle of Padstow.

rooms	3 doubles.
price	£90-£120.
meals	Dinner from £25.50.
closed	Occasionally in winter.
directions	From Wadebridge, A389 west into Padstow. With inner harbour on right, right at T-junc., then immed. left. Left into Middle Street, 100 yds on right. Drop bags off at door; parking 5-minute walk.

Brenda & Paul Harvey

tel	01841 532093
fax	01841 532093
web	www.number6inpadstow.co.uk

Restaurant with Rooms

map 1   entry 20

Molesworth Manor

Little Petherick, Nr Padstow, Cornwall PL27 7QT

Art, wine and rugby make a refreshing combination at this friendly, down-to-earth old rectory. Geoff and Jessica have given up the treadmill of London to bring up their small child in the country, buying this family hotel from her parents; apart from the odd hankering for a curry, and Geoff's beloved London Irish, they haven't looked back, adding their own touches slowly. Both love trawling local galleries and auctions for art and interesting antiques. Geoff is also a modest wine buff with a good cellar; the local Camel Valley vintage isn't bad. The huge drawing room pulls in the morning sun; the music room with log fire blazing suits the evening. A carved staircase – no insert is the same – leads to bedrooms that vary in style and size: two at the front are grand, ones in the eaves are bright and beamed. Three in a converted barn across the courtyard are fabulous. The rectory garden is as you'd expect – mature, well-tended and peaceful. Breakfast in the gorgeous tropical-style conservatory – the freshly-made muffins are superb. You'll eat well in Padstow, too.

rooms	13: 9 doubles; 1 double, 1 twin, 1 family, all with separate shower; 1 single with separate bath.
price	£50-£85. Group rates for whole house.
meals	Restaurants in Padstow.
closed	November-January. Open off-season by arrangement.
directions	From Wadebridge, A389 for Padstow for 4 miles. Road dips into Little Petherick, then climbs again. House up hill on right, signed.

Geoff French & Jessica Clarke
tel 01841 540292
e-mail molesworthmanor@aol.com
web www.molesworthmanor.co.uk

Hotel

Tregawne

Withiel, Wadebridge, Cornwall PL30 5NR

Restored with style and multi-starred comfort, the early-18th-century farmhouse sits in a hidden valley overlooking the river Ruthern. There's a meadow for ponies, hills for sheep, a pond, a croquet lawn and a pool you can dine alongside in summer. Antiques, good paintings, tumbling cushions, fresh flowers – country-house elegance at its best. Fun, too, thanks to Peta and David who run it all with unflappable friendliness and love to entertain; delicious, accolade-winning dinners are served at the long oak table. The bedrooms in the main house are big enough to have sofas; gorgeous patterned curtains match padded headboards, walls are sunny yellow, bathrooms seduce with oodles of towels. Two cottages, set slightly apart, have been charmingly converted to provide more rooms for B&B (they're kitted out for self-catering, too). There are art courses in the next village, the Eden Project is a 20-minute drive, and golf courses at St Enodoc and Trevose are within 12 miles. David is a member of both and is delighted to take guests to play.

rooms	8: 6 twins/doubles, 2 twins (for children).
price	£80–£100. Singles £60.
meals	Dinner £27.50.
closed	Rarely.
directions	A30 past Bodmin, over roundabout, after 2 miles right to Withiel. Through Withiel following Wadebridge sign, right at T-junction House 0.25 miles, on left.

David Jackson &
Peta Marchioness of Linlithgow

tel	01208 831552
fax	01208 832122
e-mail	tregawne@aol.com
web	www.tregawne.com

Other Place

map 1   entry 22

Manor Cottage
Tresillian, Truro, Cornwall TR2 4BN

Don't let the slightly shabby exterior of this unpretentious restaurant with rooms put you off – locals break out in nostalgic smiles at the mere mention of the place, their memory jogged by some sublime dish that Carlton once whisked up. This is a small, relaxed operation and everything you come across is the work of either Carlton or Gillian; they painted the yellow walls, polished the wooden floors, hung the big mirror, arranged the flowers and planted the plumbago and passionflower that wander on the stone walls in the conservatory where you eat. Carlton cooks from Thursday to Saturday – the restaurant is closed for the rest of the week, presumably to let him indulge his other talents. He even put in the bathrooms; they're excellent, some with hand-painted tiles. Bedrooms are small but, for their price, superb and full of pretty things. You might have a Heal's of London bed, a hint of Art Deco or scented candles. Wonderful old farm quilts hang on the banister – grab one and roast away till morning. Noise from the road could disturb those who are not used to it so bring your ear plugs, it's worth it.

rooms	5: 2 doubles; 1 double with separate shower; 1 twin, 1 single sharing shower.
price	£55-£75. Singles £28-£45.
meals	Dinner £29.95. Please book in advance. Restaurant closed Sundays-Wednesdays.
closed	Christmas.
directions	From Truro east A390, for about 3 miles. House on left when entering village, signed.

Carlton Moyle & Gillian Jackson
tel 01872 520212
web www.manorcottage.com

Restaurant with Rooms

One Sea View Terrace
St Ives, Cornwall TR26 2DH

Sea-loving style-seekers look no further. This is a perfect seaside place to stay run by gentle, charming John who, until recently, ran the perfect country-house hotel. Meticulous attention to detail has made this magnificent, Edwardian, end-of-terrace house what it is – delicious; minimalist bathrooms have organic soaps and shampoos, there's a little hidden fridge in your room and fresh fruit in a white bowl. There are just two bedrooms for guests – one on the ground floor, one above – and in each, a bay window, two armchairs and a table set with a vase of flowers; perfect for breakfasts. The feel is luxurious and contemporary, colours are muted and pebble-pale, and the captivating harbour views will launch dreams of living by the sea. Modern oak beds are dressed in crisp cotton and soft grey wool, the morning light slants in through wooden-slatted blinds. Leave the car here and stroll down to the Tate and the town... Breton markets line the harbour in summer and the branch railway line follows the glorious coast all the way to Penzance.

rooms	2 doubles/twins.
price	£90. Singles £70.
meals	Restaurants & pubs in St Ives.
closed	Rarely.
directions	From Carbis Bay, on to St Ives. At Porthminster Hotel, continue left until Dunmar Hotel; sharp left, then 1st right to Sea View Terrace. Private parking.

John Charlick

tel	01736 798001
fax	01736 791802
e-mail	oneseaviewterrace@hotmail.com
web	www.seaview-stives.co.uk

Other Place

map 1   entry 24

The Summer House Restaurant with Rooms

Cornwall Terrace, Penzance, Cornwall TR18 4HL

After trawling through the hotels of Britain to find ones to include in this book, we consider the Summer House a glittering catch: stylish, imaginative, bustling, informal, and so, so colourful. Sunshine yellows and strong Tuscan shades bring a dreamy sense of the Mediterranean to the bustling industry of Penzance. Linda and Ciro, English and Italian respectively, run the place with energy and warmth. Food is a celebration here – dishes are fresh, simple and cooked with flair. Linda describes it as "a gentle meander through Provence and Italy", with fish bought daily from nearby Newlyn market. Clusters of shells decorate tables in the restaurant, local artists' work hangs on the walls. Outside, a walled garden of terracotta pots and swishing palm trees is a magical setting for dinner at night; *al fresco* breakfasts in good weather are just as good. Unwind on squashy sofas in a drawing room with Gothic carvings and exotic houseplants, and talk away to other guests – most do. Bedrooms combine beautiful 'collectables' and family pieces with resourceful dabs of peppermint, or lemon stripe; some look over the garden. Fairytale luxury.

rooms	5: 4 doubles, 1 twin/double.
price	£75–£95. Singles from £70.
meals	Packed lunch from £7.50. Dinner £23.50. Restaurant closed Sundays.
closed	January–February.
directions	With sea on left, along harbourside, past open-air pool, then immediate right after Queens Hotel. House 30 yds up on left.

	Linda & Ciro Zaino
tel	01736 363744
fax	01736 360959
e-mail	summerhouse@dial.pipex.com
web	www.summerhouse-cornwall.com

Restaurant with Rooms

Penzance Arts Club

Chapel House, Penzance, Cornwall TR18 4AQ

Amusing, quirky and original… the Arts Club has brought a little fun to old Penzance. Belinda has created an easy-going but vital cultural centre. Fall into bed after a combination of poetry and jazz in the bar — or an intimate meal in the downstairs restaurant. The bar is a riot of paintings, ever-changing as most are for sale. There are fireplaces at either end and comfortable sofas hug an ancient wooden floor that fills with people as the laid-back party atmosphere warms up — invariably it does! Presiding over all in his unassuming way is Dave the barman, ready to pour a pint; the local organic beer is superb. Upstairs, charming bedrooms are as flamboyant as the bar is raffish. The house was the Portuguese embassy in the town's more prosperous days — a little garden and balcony off the bar look over the harbour. Not luxurious but good value and one of the most individual places in this book. A must for the open-minded — and for those who dream of waking up to the sound of seagulls.

rooms	7: 2 doubles; 1 double with separate bath; 1 double, 3 family, all with shower, sharing wc.
price	£60–£100. Singles £30–£45.
meals	Lunch & dinner £15–£20. Restaurant closed Sundays, plus Mondays in winter.
closed	Rarely.
directions	Along harbourside with sea on left. Opp. docks, right into Quay St. (by Dolphin pub). Up hill; house on right opp. St Mary's Church.

Belinda Rushworth-Lund

tel	01736 363761
fax	01736 363761
e-mail	reception@penzanceartsclub.co.uk
web	www.penzanceartsclub.co.uk

Other Place

 map 1   entry 26

The Cornish Range Restaurant with Rooms

6 Chapel Street, Mousehole, Cornwall TR19 6SB

The Spanish Armada wasn't a complete failure – they sacked Mousehole. Blissfully oblivious, the Range ploughs on with its wonderful fish meals, a beacon in the darkness. The dining room is attractive but unremarkable, with straightforward furniture and a view onto the little street. But there is a bustle and purpose to it, a determination to serve excellent fish straight from the sea. Richard and Chad, old mates and ex-rugby players, have only just bought it and they're engagingly keen and open-minded. They've inherited a terrific reputation and some superb bedrooms. Although above the restaurant and with the same limited views, the rooms are beautifully designed, with local handmade furniture. There are exquisite wooden headboards, cane chairs, wood-and-wrought-iron bedside lights and handsome wooden cupboards – all very striking. Bathrooms are almost as good and there's a tiny sitting room with books. There's even a garden with subtropical whimsy, a charming and unexpected touch. Mousehole is delightful and the harbourside is only yards away.

rooms	4 doubles with bath.
price	£70–£85.
meals	Dinner, 2 courses, from £20.
closed	Rarely.
directions	In Mousehole follow road along harbour and straight ahead past the Ship Inn. After two sharp bends, Cornish Range on right.

Richard O'Shea & Chad James

tel	01736 731488
fax	01736 732173
e-mail	info@cornishrange.co.uk
web	www.cornishrange.com

Restaurant with Rooms

Trengilly Wartha Inn

Nancenoy, Constantine, Falmouth, Cornwall TR11 5RP

It's hard to believe the River Helford is navigable up to this point, simply because it's hard to navigate a car down the narrow, steep lanes to this deeply rural hideaway. It's worth the effort. Trengilly started life as a simple crofter's house before a small bar was added to supplement a previous owner's meagre farming income. The pub has grown organically ever since, winning lots of awards along the way, from 'Pub of the Year' to 'Best Dining Pub in Cornwall'. Expect honourable ales, comfy wooden settles and good meals; all the locals come here. Wine is important, too; Nigel knows his grapes, learning much from female wine writers – they're considered better at telling good from bad! Those wanting a less boisterous atmosphere can eat in a restaurant of conservative pastel colours and families can use a no-smoking conservatory. A small, cosy sitting room away from the buzz of the bar has an open fire and lots of books. Country-cottage-style bedrooms are well done: those above the bar have more character than ones in an annexe; all bar one have valley views. In summer, the six-acre garden fills with a happy throng.

rooms	8: 5 doubles, 1 twin, 2 family.
price	£78–£96. Singles £49.
meals	Bar meals £4–£15. Dinner, 2 courses, £21.50; 3 courses, £27. No meals on Christmas Day. Restaurant closed New Year's Eve.
closed	Rarely.
directions	Approaching Falmouth on A39, follow signs to Constantine for about 7 miles. On approach to village, inn signed left, then right.

	Michael & Helen Maguire, Nigel & Isabel Logan
tel	01326 340332
fax	01326 340332
e-mail	reception@trengilly.co.uk
web	www.trengilly.co.uk

Inn

map 1   entry 28

Driftwood Hotel

Rosevine, Portscatho, Cornwall TR2 5EW

Perfectly positioned and full of curiously vibrant design, Driftwood is a welcome change from the formula beach hotel. It's said the original owner of this 1930s beach villa wandered all over the Roseland Peninsula for the right spot and chose here. The view is wonderful: the sun rises over Nare Head, Portscatho village peeks from a small inlet, and boats criss-cross the bay. Fiona and Paul are relaxed hosts who make the place feel more like a home. The refreshing Cape Cod style is clean but not clinical, full of texture, natural colours and lots of light; all puts you at ease. The restaurant is an expanse of white and wooden floor, with simply-laid tables and driftwood 'fish' on the wall. Food is fresh and often from the sea; their chef has cooked in the best London restaurants. There's a bar with comfy window seats and a lounge with handsome driftwood lamps, luxurious sofas and a log fire. Bedrooms are simply done with neutral fabrics in sand, white and pale blue; views from the cabin for two are superb. Sit outside on the decked balcony for breakfast and candlelit dinner, or take a hamper to the private beach — you may see a hairy snail.

rooms	11: 7 doubles, 3 twins, 1 cabin.
price	£140–£190.
meals	Dinner £32.
closed	January.
directions	From St Austell, A390 west. Left on B3287, signed St Mawes, then left at Tregony on A3078 for about 7 miles. Signed left down lane.

Paul & Fiona Robinson

tel	01872 580644
fax	01872 580801
e-mail	info@driftwoodhotel.co.uk
web	www.driftwoodhotel.co.uk

Hotel

Trevalsa Court Country House Hotel

School Hill Road, Mevagissey, Cornwall PL26 6TH

Oh, the stylishness of the place! A slate bar, a leather sofa, a splash of red rug on a parquet floor. Matthew is from east Germany, Klaus is from the west, and Trevalsa Court is their business and hobby rolled into one. It is immaculate, polished, spotless, but not minimalist-modern – there's an irresistible whiff of 1930s Berlin. Bedrooms are luxurious, comfortable and varied – a shapely bed, a Deco lamp, a black and white photograph on an ochre wall. And binoculars in some rooms: the views of sea and coast demand them. Other rooms look to the garden, from which you may wend your way down to the coves and sands of Polstreath Beach. Back to food worth coming home for: two starters, two mains – tomato tartlets, pasta with scallops and sugar snap peas – fresh, caught-that-day, delicious. The dining room has dark wood on wall and floor, starched linen, discreet candles and comfy chairs… and windows through which the sun sets and the moon rises. Klaus and Matthew take an interest in every guest and fill the place with flowers. They have fulfilled their dream; yours is to sit back and enjoy it.

rooms	14: 8 doubles, 2 twins, 2 singles, 2 suites.
price	£98-£138. Singles £49-£80. Suites £165.
meals	Dinner £25. Restaurant closed Sunday & Monday.
closed	December-February.
directions	From St Austell, B3273, signed Mevagissey, for about 5.5 miles past beach caravan park, then left at top of hill. Over mini-r'bout. Hotel on left, signed.

Klaus Wagner & Matthew Mainka

tel	01726 842468
fax	01726 844482
e-mail	stay@cornwall-hotel.net
web	www.cornwall-hotel.net

Hotel

map 1   entry 30

The Old Quay House Hotel
28 Fore Street, Fowey, Cornwall PL23 1AQ

The Old Quay House has everything going for it: a gorgeous waterside setting, owners passionate about good service, and staff determined to deliver. Fowey is an enchanting place – recently voted by *Country Life* as "the third best place to live in Britain" – bustling with local life, passing sailors and the August regatta. Chef Henry, recently returned from his sabbatical at the Tresanton in St Mawes, is a blessing, too. He walked off the street one day and has been cooking brilliantly ever since: try his sauté potatoes with rosemary for breakfast. The hotel, with a colourful history dating back to 1889, has a characterful old building at its core, extended in recent years to create new bedrooms and a restaurant with estuary views. Bedrooms are blessed with the latest technology and are stylish too, with chic wrought-iron beds, pure white linen, angled balconies and patios that look out to sea. Older bedrooms are more traditional, but equally luxurious. Come to combine the best of old Cornwall – narrow cobbled streets, beach, quaint harbour – with a contemporary, laid-back and friendly place to stay.

rooms	12 twins/doubles.
price	£120-£180. Singles £110.
meals	Lunch about £14. Dinner about £22.
closed	Rarely.
directions	Entering Fowey, follow one-way system past church. Hotel on right where road at narrowest point, opp. Old House of Foye.

Jane & Roy Carson
tel	01726 833302
e-mail	info@theoldquayhouse.com
web	www.theoldquayhouse.com

Restaurant with Rooms

Cormorant on the River

Golant, Nr Fowey, Cornwall PL23 1LL

Golant is well-hidden from Cornwall's tourist trail and the Cormorant is well-hidden from Golant. You drive along the quay, then climb a short, steep hill. The reward is a breathtaking view of the Fowey estuary (pronounced 'Foy'), flowing through a wooded landscape. Boats tug on their moorings and birds glide lazily over the water – this is a very English paradise. The view is so good the architect made sure it leapt into every room; 10 of the 11 bedrooms have French windows, so they're fabulous to wake up in. Not bad to sleep in either, with comfy beds, pastel colours and spotless bathrooms. From the entrance, steps lead to a huge light-filled sitting room with log fire, colourful pictures and a big map of the estuary to help plan adventures – walks start from the door. There's a small bar with a good smattering of whiskies and a pretty dining room themed on the legend of Tristan, Isolde and jilted King Mark (the love story was made into an opera by Wagner; a nearby 13th-century church once belonged in the king's domain). In summer, have tea under parasols on the terraced lawn and watch the boats zip by.

rooms	11 twins/doubles.
price	£110–£180. Singles from £65 (winter only).
meals	Dinner, 4 courses, from £24.50.
closed	Rarely.
directions	A390 west for St Austell, then B3269 to Fowey. After 4 miles, left to Golant. Into village, along quay, hotel signed right, up very steep hill.

Carrie & Colin King

tel	01726 833426
e-mail	relax@cormoranthotels.co.uk
web	www.cormoranthotels.co.uk

Hotel

map 1   entry 32

Talland Bay Hotel

Talland, Porthallow, Cornwall PL13 2JB

The air is clear and fresh, the sea sparkles through the pines... there's a Mediterranean feel here, with French windows opening from the oak-panelled dining room, sitting room, library and bar onto a paved terrace and heated pool. It's a glorious spot, with two acres of subtropical gardens and a perfectly mown lawn ending in a ha-ha and a 150-foot drop down to the bay. Long views stretch to the sea. Lie by the pool with a good book (from the library, perhaps) as the seagulls wheel overhead, or, if you want to be alone, drift down to the end of the garden. Play croquet or badminton, or practise your putting. The bedrooms are traditional and stylish, impeccable and bathed in light, many with sea views. Some of them have a self-contained feel and their own piece of garden – this would be a super place for a small wedding or house party. The house is surprisingly ancient, mentioned in the Domesday book and once owned by the famous Trelawney family. The walking is all you'd hope for – link up with the glorious Coastal Path – as is the food; there are fresh fish and seafood from Looe, including lobster, crab and scallops.

rooms	23: 21 twins/doubles, 2 singles.
price	£90-£180. Singles £45-£90.
meals	Light lunch £5-£15. Packed lunch from £5. Dinner £27.50.
closed	Rarely.
directions	From Looe, A387 for Polperro. Ignore 1st sign to Talland. After a mile, left at sign. Follow lane for a mile.

George & Mary Granville

tel	01503 272667
fax	01503 272940
e-mail	reception@tallandbayhotel.co.uk
web	www.tallandbayhotel.co.uk

Hotel

Crosby Lodge

High Crosby, Carlisle, Cumbria CA6 4QZ

Restful, grandly comfortable, blissfully detached from the outside world, Crosby Lodge is almost like walking into a gentleman's club – only it welcomes all. Come to elope – Gretna is close – or just to escape. Patricia is everywhere, always impeccably dressed, never seeming to stop, but never seeming to hurry, either. She used to be a banker – the considerate kind, what else! – and this original 'country-house hotel' remains a laid-back family affair. Michael and Patricia came here 30-odd years ago, son James has a bistro in Low Crosby village and their daughter, Pippa, owns a wine company that… you guessed, supplies their wine. There could be grandchildren around as well – not that you'd mind. Inside is warm and cosy, with open fires, the odd *chaise-longue*, oak furniture and lots of rugs. Bedrooms are fun. They're big and bright, with good fabrics, and maybe arrow slits, or a lovely gnarled half-tester. Pat won't have "square corners" – you get arches and alcoves instead. Outside, you might find the local blacksmith, or an artist sketching a gorgeous pastoral view. Hadrian's Wall is only 10 miles away.

rooms	11: 2 doubles, 5 twins/doubles, 1 single, 3 family.
price	£120–£160. Singles £85–£90.
meals	Lunch from £5. Dinner, 4 courses, £30; à la carte, £13–£30.
closed	Christmas–mid-January.
directions	M6, junc. 44, A689 east for 3.5 miles, then right to Low Crosby. Through village. House on right.

Michael & Patricia Sedgwick

tel	01228 573618
fax	01228 573428
e-mail	enquiries@crosbylodge.co.uk
web	www.crosbylodge.co.uk

Hotel

map 10   entry 34

Lovelady Shield

Nenthead Road, Nr Alston, Cumbria CA9 3LF

From the front door of Lovelady, walk straight into an area of the High Pennines that is remote and utterly unspoilt. The River Nent runs through the garden and at the bridge, four footpaths meet. The house, hidden down a long and suitably bumpy drive, was rebuilt in 1832. The cellars date from 1690, the foundations from the 14th century when it is thought a religious order stood here. No noise, save for sheep in the fields and a burbling river that you can hear if you sleep with your window open. Peter and Marie have been here five years and run the place with a hint of eccentricity and a lot of good-natured charm. A small rag-rolled bar and pretty sitting rooms give a low-key, country-house feel. Long windows in all rooms bring the views inside and French windows open up in summer for Pimms on the lawn. The food is wonderful, Barry is a Master Chef – you eat in the pretty dining room surrounded by gilt mirrors, sash windows and fresh flowers. Upstairs, dark hallways lead through old pine doors to bright bedrooms with window seats, maybe a sofa, good furniture and Scrabble; most have gorgeous views.

rooms	12: 9 doubles, 2 twins, 1 four-poster.
price	Half-board only £60-£120 p.p.
meals	Dinner, 4 courses, included; non-residents £33.50. Lunch by arrangement.
closed	Rarely.
directions	From Alston, A689 east for 2 miles. House on left at junction of B6294, signed.

Peter & Marie Haynes

tel	01434 381203
fax	01434 381515
e-mail	enquiries@lovelady.co.uk
web	www.lovelady.co.uk

Hotel

Augill Castle

Brough, Kirkby Stephen, Cumbria CA17 4DE

In our fair quest to find places for you to stay, fate led us to a castle in the garden of Eden... well, almost. Augill Castle is an early Victorian folly in Cumbria's beautiful Eden Valley. It was completed in 1841 for John Bagot Pearson, the eldest of two brothers; he was determined to build a bigger and better house overlooking the family pile at Park House after a sibling row. The result is wonderfully over the top, with turrets, arched fairytale windows, a castellated tower and monstrously large rooms – how green with envy his brother must have been! Simon and Wendy rescued the building after years of neglect in 1997 and lavishly decorated the whole caboodle; there's no stinting on anything here, be it fabric, colour, food or welcome. The bedrooms ooze baronial style: four-posters, roll-top baths, swagged curtains, maybe a turret wardrobe. Downstairs, relax in the elegant library bar, and banquet around a huge table in the grand dining room beneath a panelled ceiling of stunning blues. Perfect for weddings or house-parties with seating for up to forty or roaming feasts for 60 and the food will be perfect.

rooms	10: 4 doubles, 3 twins/doubles, 3 four-posters.
price	£140-£250. Singles £100.
meals	Dinner, £30; most Fridays & Saturdays, or by arrangement.
closed	Christmas & mid-week in January.
directions	M6, junc. 38, A685 through Kirkby Stephen, then right 2 miles out of town, signed to hotel. On left.

Simon & Wendy Bennett

tel	01768 341937
fax	01768 341936
e-mail	enquiries@augillcastle.co.uk
web	www.augillcastle.co.uk

Other Place

map 6   entry 36

The Pheasant

Bassenthwaite Lake, Nr Cockermouth, Cumbria CA13 9YE

The snug at The Pheasant is wonderful, a treasured relic of times past as a busy coaching inn. A barman guards 40 malts at a low-slung wooden bar and walls shine from a combination of 300 years of tobacco smoke and polish. The inn has since turned into a hotel, and drinks are now usually served in sitting rooms of understated elegance: gilt mirrors, sprays of garden flowers, trim carpets, fresh, yellow walls and fine furniture – all immaculate, yet immediately relaxing. The bedrooms have been beautifully remodelled, too, revealing the odd hidden beam; mellow lighting has been added, warm colours put on the walls and a rug or two thrown in for good measure. Most are in the main part of the inn; three are in a nearby garden lodge… and though pristine throughout, you'll still come across Housekeeping armed with feather dusters! There's a kennel for visiting dogs, Skiddaw to be scaled and Bassenthwaite Lake to be paddled. A perfect place to take your time. *Children over 8 welcome.*

rooms	13: 10 twins/doubles, 1 single, 2 suites.
price	£110–£160. Half-board (min. 2 nights) from £71 p.p. Singles £65–£80.
meals	Light lunch from £5. Dinner, à la carte, about £30.
closed	Christmas Day.
directions	From Keswick, A66 north-west for 7 miles. Hotel on left, signed.

Matthew Wylie

tel	01768 776234
fax	01768 776002
e-mail	info@the-pheasant.co.uk
web	www.the-pheasant.co.uk

Inn

The Mill Hotel

Mungrisdale, Nr Penrith, Cumbria CA11 0XR

A small, eclectic bolt hole, this 1651 mill house on the northern border of the lakes has a stream racing past that is fed by fells that rise behind. Richard and Eleanor belong to that band of innkeepers who do their own thing instinctively and immaculately — this is the antithesis of a big, impersonal hotel. Richard comes out to greet you at the car, to help with the bags, to show you up to your room, and finally, invites you down for drinks "whenever you're ready". Downstairs you'll find a tiny library and a homely sitting room with rocking chair, ancient stone fireplace, wood carvings and piles of reference books on every subject under the sun. Meanwhile Eleanor has been cooking up five courses of heaven for your supper, all home-made and organic where possible, from the olive bread to the watercress soup; breakfasts, too, are first class. Bedrooms vary in size and style. The old mill, wrapped in *Clematis montana*, has its own sitting room where you can fall asleep to the sound of the river. In the main house, beams, bowls of fruit, African art, fresh flowers and good linen induce perfect slumber.

rooms	9: 4 doubles, 3 twins; 1 double, 1 twin, sharing bath.
price	Half-board only, £59-£79 p.p.
meals	Dinner, 5 courses, included.
closed	November-February.
directions	M6, junc. 40 (Penrith), A66 west for Keswick for 7 miles, then right, for Mungrisdale. Hotel next door to Mill Inn.

Richard & Eleanor Quinlan

tel	01768 779659
fax	01768 779155
e-mail	themill@quinlan.evesham.net
web	www.themillhotel.com

Hotel

map 6   entry 38

Swinside Lodge

Grange Road, Keswick, Cumbria CA12 5UE

A short stroll takes you to the edge of Derwentwater – the Queen of the Lakes. Immediately behind, fells rise and spirits soar. At Swinside – a small-scale model of English country-house elegance – reception rooms are crisp and fresh, with fine period furniture offset by pastel blues and yellows. In the bold dining room, deep reds combine with oil-burning lamps... formal, yet relaxed. There are lots of books in the sitting rooms, maps for walkers, bowls of fruit, fresh flowers and no clutter. Every tiny detail has been well thought out, not least in the bedrooms where flair and forethought have pulled off a maestro's touch – the rooms have been furnished with cream furniture to make them feel bigger than they are, and it works a treat. The bedrooms are all good and two are huge. You'll find drapes, more crisp materials and uplifting views – you can watch the weather change. Food is honest and delicious; perhaps try asparagus and herb risotto, celery and apple soup, lamb, or warm chocolate mousse. *Children over five welcome.*

rooms	7: 5 doubles, 2 twins.
price	Half-board omly, £67-£95 p.p.
meals	Dinner, 4 courses, included; non-residents £29.50.
closed	Rarely.
directions	M6, junc. 40. A66 west past Keswick, over r'bout, then 2nd left, for Portiscale & Grange. Follow signs to Grange for 2 miles. House signed on right.

	Kevin & Susan Kniveton
tel	01768 772948
fax	01768 772948
e-mail	info@swinsidelodge-hotel.co.uk
web	www.swinsidelodge-hotel.co.uk

Hotel

Old Dungeon Ghyll
Great Langdale, Ambleside, Cumbria LA22 9JY

This is an old favourite of hardy mountaineers and it comes as no surprise to learn that Tenzing and Hilary stayed here. The hotel is at the head of the valley, surrounded by spectacular peaks, heaven for hikers and climbers, a place to escape to. The scenery is breathtaking, and this is a solid and genuine base from which to plan your ascent. Eclectic bedrooms are decorated with the odd brass bed, patchwork quilts, floral wallpaper and patterned carpets. All are blissfully free of phones and TVs — you wouldn't want them here, not when there's so much going on downstairs. In winter, a fire crackles in the sitting room, all the food is home-cooked — fresh bread, teacakes and flapjacks every day — and there's a small snug resident's bar. Best of all is the famous hiker's bar — hotel wedding parties always seem to end up here. Guitars and fiddles appear — do they carry them over the mountain? — ceilidhs break out and laughter fills the rafters, all overseen by Neil, Jane and great staff. Come to walk and to leave the city far behind.

rooms	14: 4 doubles, 4 twins/doubles, 1 twin, 2 family, 3 singles, all sharing 4 baths & 1 shower.
price	£73–£82. Singles from £35.
meals	Packed lunch £3.95. Bar meals from £6. Dinner £18.50.
closed	Christmas.
directions	From Ambleside, A593 for Coniston, right on B5343. On right after 5 miles, signed, past Great Langdale campsite.

Neil & Jane Walmsley

tel	01539 437272
fax	01539 437272
e-mail	neil.odg@lineone.net
web	www.odg.co.uk

Inn

map 6   entry 40

White Moss House

Rydal Water, Grasmere, Cumbria LA22 9SE

This is the epicentre of Wordsworth country; walk north a mile to his home at Dove Cottage or south to his somewhat more salubrious house at Rydal Mount. The paths are old and you can follow his footsteps up fell and through wood. He knew White Moss, too – he bought it for his son and came here to escape. The Dixons have lived here for 23 years and they have kept the feel of a home: flowers everywhere, a woodburning stove, pretty floral fabrics and lots of comfy sofas and chairs. There's a small bar in an old linen cupboard, and after-dinner coffee in the sitting room brings out the house-party feel. Bedrooms range in size, but not comfort. All are different and have good views: a glazed pine-panelled bay window maybe, an old wooden bed, a sprinkling of books and magazines, and a bathroom, with Radox to soothe fell-worn feet. The cottage is in a quiet, beautiful spot further up the hill, with the best view of all right out across Rydal Water – perfect for longer stays. Then there's the small matter of food, all cooked by Peter – five courses of famed indulgence await. *Children over 5 welcome.*

rooms	5 + 1: 2 doubles, 3 twins/doubles. Also 1 cottage for 4.
price	Half-board only, £65-£95 p.p.
meals	Dinner, 5 courses, included; non-residents £30. Restaurant closed Sunday night.
closed	December-mid-February.
directions	From Ambleside, north on A591. House signed on right at far end of Rydal Water.

	Susan & Peter Dixon
tel	01539 435295
fax	01539 435516
e-mail	sue@whitemoss.com
web	www.whitemoss.com

Restaurant with Rooms

The Samling
Ambleside Road, Windermere, Cumbria LA23 1LR

Possibly the best hotel in Britain? It's hard not to reach this conclusion after you've been to The Samling. The brochure for once is telling the truth: "it's like no other place you've stayed" – especially in the Lakes, which has been gasping for an alternative to chintz and rhododendron for years. There's not a swirly carpet in sight, just lots of good taste in 67 acres overlooking Lake Windermere – Wordsworth came here to pay his rent. The Maxfields are great patrons of the arts so you'll find beautiful paintings inside and sculptures to contemplate on garden wanderings. Nothing's showy or grand, it's about relaxing in style – hotel policy encourages breakfast in bed! Designer Amanda Rosa did the interiors – in the autumnal sitting room there are checked sofas, fresh lilies, a bowl of apricots and a big, open fire. Fabulous bedrooms named after the Cumbrian counting system are full of texture, colour and surprises: stucco walls of orange ochre, slate floors, candles in every bathroom and most have lake views; suites in the "bothy" are superb... so are the food and the service. Worth every penny.

rooms	10: 7 doubles, 1 twin/double, 2 suites.
price	£175-£375. Half-board from £245 p.p. Singles from £175. Suite £375.
meals	Dinner, à la carte, £40; menu gourmand, 8 courses, £60.
closed	Rarely.
directions	From Windermere, A59 towards Ambleside for 3 miles. Hotel on right up steep drive, signed.

	Tom Maxfield
tel	01539 431922
fax	01539 430400
e-mail	info@thesamling.com
web	www.thesamling.com

Hotel

map 6   entry 42

Miller Howe Hotel & Restaurant

Rayrigg Road, Bowness-on-Windermere, Cumbria LA23 1EY

Looking over Lake Windermere to majestic peaks in the distance, Miller Howe can justly claim to have one of the best views in England. The cottage containing the luxurious suites uses it to amazing effect: huge windows on three walls suck in fell, lake, hill and mountain. The cottage can be used individually, or by groups wanting extra privacy; you get the best of both worlds as the hotel is just a short walk through a fragrant herb garden. Charles, a former national newspaper editor, has taken the whole place "up a notch" since he arrived in 1997, improving an already enviable reputation for good food and service. Staff are trained to be "brilliant today, better tomorrow". He's hands-on, too, welcoming guests with a friendly arm round the shoulder. Gail does the design side. Handsome rooms use the best of everything: Beaumont & Fletcher wallpaper, handmade fabrics, the odd chesterfield. In the evening, you'll be served the view with your meal in a dining room of wrought-iron verdigris, gilded ceilings and honey limestone tiles; menus point out landmarks. Perfect whatever the weather.

rooms	15: 7 twins/doubles, 5 doubles, 3 suites.
price	Half-board only, £75–£135 p.p. Suite £135–£175 p.p.
meals	Light lunch from £7. Picnic £14. Tea £4.50–£9.99. Dinner, 5 courses, included; non-residents £39.50.
closed	Rarely.
directions	From Kendal, A591 to Windermere. Left at mini-r'bout onto A592 for Bowness; 0.25 miles on right.

Charles & Gail Garside

tel	01539 442536
fax	01539 445664
e-mail	lakeview@millerhowe.com
web	www.millerhowe.com

Hotel

Aynsome Manor Hotel

Cartmel, Nr Grange-over-Sands, Cumbria LA11 6HH

Stand at the front door of Aynsome and look across ancient meadows to Cartmel Priory, still magnificent after 800 years, still the heart of a small, thriving community: the view is almost medieval. Strike out across the fields to the village – a walk of about three-quarters of a mile – and discover its gentle secrets. The house, too, echoes with history: it was home to the descendants of the Earl of Pembroke; in 1930, it gave up a long-held secret when a suit of chain armour dating back to 1335 was found behind a wall in an attic bedroom. The panelled dining room has a remarkable tongue-and-ball ceiling, the hall a melodious grandfather clock, a wood and coal fire and carved oak panels – the gift of an 1839 storm. A cantilevered spiral staircase with a cupola-domed window leads up to the sitting room where newspapers hang from poles and a welcoming fire burns in a marble Adams-style fireplace. Bedrooms are simple and comfortable, some with gently sloping floors. Race-goers will love the National Hunt racecourse – the August Bank Holiday meet is one of the oldest in Britain. *No under fives in restaurant.*

rooms	12: 5 doubles, 4 twins, 2 family, 1 four-poster.
price	£75–£90. Singles from £45. Half-board £52–£73 p.p.
meals	Dinner, 4 courses, £22.
closed	January.
directions	From M6 junc. 36 take A590 for Barrow. At top of Lindale Hill, follow signs left to Cartmel. Hotel on right 3 miles from A590.

Christopher & Andrea Varley

tel	01539 536653
fax	01539 536016
e-mail	info@aynsomemanorhotel.co.uk
web	www.aynsomemanorhotel.co.uk

Hotel

map 6   entry 44

Hipping Hall

Cowan Bridge, Kirkby Lonsdale, Cumbria LA6 2JJ

One of Lancashire's best kept secrets, Hipping Hall is the surviving remnant of a 15th-century hamlet. The only other clues are an old stone wash-house, a stream and spring-fed pond, and an ancient well that's now part of a flagstoned conservatory. The Skeltons have kept the feel much as it always was: informal, stylish and relaxed, adding a treasure trove of antiques, paintings, prints and numerous teddy bears and dolls for good measure. Jean's father used to be an antique dealer but she prefers to consider her passion a hobby. Groups can dine in true house-party style in the Great Hall – once the hamlet's town hall – with old oak floors, rugs, candles and beams. Smaller groups eat in the old morning room, now an intimate dining room. Richard grows organic vegetables for the table – beans, spinach and carrots – and home-made truffles round off your meal. Bedrooms are warm and homely, stacked with books, and bathrooms are spotless. Wander in three acres of garden, or majestic countryside – a path leads over Leck Fell to Barbondale. Ingleton waterfalls are also close. *Pets welcome in cottage suites.*

rooms	6: 3 doubles, 1 twin, 2 cottage suites.
price	From £96. Singles from £75.
meals	Lunch £12.95. Dinner £29.
closed	23 December-9 January; Mondays & Tuesdays, September-February. Groups all year by arrangement.
directions	M6, junc. 36, then A65 east. House on left, 2.5 miles after Kirkby Lonsdale.

	Richard, Jean & Tamara Skelton
tel	01524 271187
fax	01524 272452
e-mail	hipping-hall@kirkby-lonsdale.com
web	www.dedicate.co.uk/hipping-hall

Hotel

Biggin Hall

Biggin-by-Hartington, Buxton, Derbyshire SK17 0DH

Biggin Hall, a 17th-century Grade II*-listed farmhouse, lies knee-deep in lovely countryside. A path from the house leads out past the geese hut and stables to fields, hills, woods, rivers and waterfalls. Not far away is the 1831 Cromford and High Peak Railway, one of the first in the world — now the preserve of cyclists and walkers. James knows his patch of England well and will guide you to its many secrets. He came here decades ago and started his labour of love, the restoration of Biggin Hall, keeping its fine old character — stone-flagged floors, old beams, the original fireplace, mullioned windows and leaded lights — while adding contemporary comforts. Ask for bedrooms in the old house — they have bags of character — and there's also a pretty dining room for wholesome, home-cooked English food. The view through its big window is a seamless transition from garden to paddock, then country beyond. Close to Kedleston Hall, Chatsworth House and Haddon Hall, there's plenty to do by car or on foot. *Children over 11 welcome. Pets by arrangement.*

rooms	20: 16 twins/doubles, 1 single, 3 suites.
price	£88–£112. Singles £57. Suite £106–£132. In annexe £64–£94.
meals	Continental breakfast included; full English £3.80. Dinner, 4 courses, £15.50. Tea & packed lunch available.
closed	Rarely.
directions	From Ashbourne, A515 for Buxton, then left, signed to Biggin. Entrance on right in village just after Waterloo pub.

	James Moffett
tel	01298 84451
fax	01298 84681
e-mail	enquiries@bigginhall.co.uk
web	www.bigginhall.co.uk

Hotel

map 6   entry 46

Riber Hall

Matlock, Derbyshire DE4 5JU

Alex is wonderfully 'old school', very much his own man, and has run this 14th-century Elizabethan manor house for 30 years with one foot firmly in the past. Fires gently smoulder all year in the sitting room and dining room, giving the grandeur of Riber a warm intimacy. Bedrooms are great fun; most have antique four-posters, timber-framed walls, beams, mullioned windows, thick fabrics, good furniture. And you're pampered rotten: beds turned down discreetly, super bathrooms with Royal Spa toiletries, umbrellas, fresh fruit and home-made shortbread. There's a secret conservatory full of colour and scent, and a walled orchard garden with long views – pure tranquillity – look out for the grafted 180-year-old weeping copper beech that lets you walk under its stunning canopy. The food has won many awards and the cellar is stocked with some of the best wine in Britain. Alex is a gentle, engaging host, who speaks with passion about Spain, wine and the 37 species of bird that live in the garden. Darley Dale, for one of the best views in Derbyshire, is five minutes on foot. *Children over 10 welcome.*

rooms	14: 3 doubles, 2 twins, 9 four-posters.
price	£136–£182. Singles £101–£116.
meals	Continental breakfast included; full English £8. Lunch from £13. Dinner, 2 courses, £29.75; 3 courses £35.75.
closed	Rarely.
directions	From Matlock, A615 to Tansley, turn at Royal Oak into Alders Lane. Wind up hill for 1 mile to hotel.

Alex Biggin

tel	01629 582795
fax	01629 580475
e-mail	info@riber-hall.co.uk
web	www.riber-hall.co.uk

Hotel

Tor Cottage
Chillaton, Lifton, Devon PL16 0JE

Maureen is delightful and spiritual and understanding. She will give you space and yet pamper you in her lovely old Devon longhouse with its wild woodland walks and themed rooms. One room is simple and rustic, one filled with Art Deco, one straight out of *House and Garden* and there's a cottage wing in the main house. Wander through the gardens to the heated outdoor pool edged on three sides by a tall, immaculately groomed Leylandii. Choose to eat with others in the pretty conservatory or hole up in your own space with the trug of goodies that waits on your bed. Everything you might need is in your room: log-burning stove, fridge, trays of smoked salmon sandwiches that appear as if by magic when you get peckish. Each room has its own private little garden with birdsong and tinkling water. Breakfast is the best: home-made muesli, local sausages and bacon and the dreamiest orange-yolked eggs. You will be lulled into simply wanting to stay put, but beaches are a short drive away, there are miles of superb walking and the market town of Tavistock is a good find for book lovers or antique-seekers. *Special deals available.*

rooms	3: 2 doubles, 1 twin/double.
price	£130. Singles £89.
meals	Breakfast until 9.30am. 3 miles to nearest pubs/restaurants.
closed	Christmas & New Year.
directions	In Chillaton keep pub & post office on your left, up hill for Tavistock. After 300 yds, right (bridlepath sign). Cottage at end of lane.

	Mrs Maureen Rowlatt
tel	01822 860248
fax	01822 860126
e-mail	info@torcottage.co.uk
web	www.torcottage.co.uk

Other place

map 2   entry 48

The Arundell Arms

Lifton, Devon PL16 0AA

A tiny interest in fishing would not go amiss – though the people here are so kind, they welcome anyone. Anne has been at the helm for 40 years – an MBE for services to tourism is richly deserved – while chef Philip Burgess has been here for half that time. This is a *very* settled hotel, with Mrs VB, as staff call her fondly, quietly presiding over all: during a superb lunch – St Enodoc asparagus, scallops and home-made chocs – she asked after an 80th birthday party, ensuring their day was memorable. Over the years, the hotel has resuscitated buildings at the heart of the village: the old police station and magistrates court is a pub, the old school a conference centre. Pride of place is the funnel-roofed cock-fighting pit, one of only two left in England and now the rod room where novice and hardy fisherfolk alike begin salmon and trout fishing courses; spy otter and kingfisher on 20 miles of their own water on the Tamar and five tributaries. No surprise it's the best fishing hotel in England – Anne's late husband wrote about fly-fishing for *The Times*; Ambrosia rice started life just down the road.

rooms	27: 8 doubles, 11 twins, 7 singles, 1 suite.
price	£104–£136. Singles from £52.
meals	Bar meals £7–£15. Dinner from £34; à la carte from £39.
closed	Christmas.
directions	A30 south-west from Exeter, past Okehampton. Lifton 0.5 miles off A30, 3 miles east of Launceston & signed. Hotel in centre of village.

	Anne Voss-Bark
tel	01566 784666
fax	01566 784494
e-mail	reservations@arundellarms.com
web	www.arundellarms.com

Inn

Lewtrenchard Manor

Lewdown, Nr Okehampton, Devon EX20 4PN

A thrilling, historical pastiche set in a Tudor mansion, outstanding in every way; only Edwardian radiators belie the fact you're not in 16th-century England. Entering the hall, your senses explode with the magnificence of it all... you almost expect to be set upon by hounds. Nothing so ill is in store, however. New manager Sarah has shot up the ranks to take over the helm and is coping magnificently. Most of what you see was put together in the late 1800s by the Reverend Sabine Baring-Gould, author of *Onward Christian Soldiers*. He was an avid collector of ornamental wooden friezes – the ones in the dining room are extraordinary – but he left no record of where they came from. One fabulous room follows another until you reach the 1602 gallery, with the salvaged, honeycombed, plaster-moulded ceiling, grand piano and 1725 Bible – one of the most beautiful rooms you will see in this book. Bedrooms are exemplary, too, and tremendous value for money; one has Queen Henrietta Maria's four-poster. The gardens are outstanding, as is sixth century St Petroc's church next door.

rooms	9: 5 doubles, 2 four-posters, 2 suites.
price	£135-£185. Singles from £100. Suites £200.
meals	Lunch from £12-£18, Tues to Sun. Dinner from £35.
closed	Rarely.
directions	From Exeter, exit A30 for A386. At T-junc., right, then 1st left, for Lewdown. After 6 miles, left for Lewtrenchard. House signed left after 0.75 miles.

	Sarah Harvey
tel	01566 783222
fax	01566 783332
e-mail	info@lewtrenchard.co.uk
web	www.lewtrenchard.co.uk

Restaurant with Rooms

map 2   entry 50

The Hoops Country Inn & Hotel

Horns Cross, Bideford, Devon EX39 5DL

Blissfully out of kilter with the outside world, entering Hoops Inn is like stepping into a timewarp. It's changed little in 800 years – there are just fewer smugglers rubbing shoulders with the local gentry at the bar these days. The lack of road signs to say you've arrived in this tiny hamlet – Hoops comes from 'hoopspink', the Devon word for bullfinch – adds to the splendid sense of disorientation. The signs were taken down to confuse an enemy invasion during the Second World War and never put back. The bar has a mellow tick-tock atmosphere, with lots of irregular beams, uneven floors, snug corners, low-hung doorways and blazing fires in winter; newspapers are there to browse over a pint. Above the bar, baroque-style bedrooms are magnificent; the four-poster beds were made from one massive oak bed that originally slept up to 20 people (sic). Pass a pretty courtyard – lovely for afternoon tea – to bedrooms in an old coach house. They're smaller, but have the same luxurious period feel. Fresh fish, an ample vegetarian menu and the friendliest welcome makes this special indeed.

rooms	12: 7 doubles, 2 twins/doubles, 1 twin, 1 family, 1 suite.
price	£90–£140. Singles £50–£85. Suite £170.
meals	Bar lunch from £8.50. Dinner £12–£24.
closed	Christmas Day.
directions	From Bideford, A39 towards Bude (North Devon coastal road) for 6 miles. Just past Horns Cross, road dips. Inn on right.

	Gay Marriott
tel	01237 451222
fax	01237 451247
e-mail	sales@hoopsinn.co.uk
web	www.hoopsinn.co.uk

Inn

The Red Lion Hotel

The Quay, Clovelly, Bideford, Devon EX39 5TF

Clovelly has been spared time's march, partly because of its position – and partly because it is a tenanted estate. It is completely car-free. The houses perch like seagulls' nests on ledges cut into the cliff and many still have original cob walls of red earth and straw. A steep cobbled path snakes down to a small harbour. The Red Lion is right on the quayside, looking out across the Atlantic – you'll hear the sound of the sea from every room. It's an eccentric place, but pleasantly so, with laid-back staff and friendly management. Smart bedrooms are up-to-date, thanks to a recent makeover; all have sea or harbour views. Wonderful seafood is delivered straight from the fishing boat to the kitchen. Travel out to Lundy Island, a wildlife sanctuary, or walk along Hobby Drive, a beautiful coastal walk laid out in the early 1800s. The late Christine Hamlyn, anointed 'Queen of Clovelly', restored many of the cottages and is still loved by villagers. There's nowhere quite like it.

rooms	11: 7 doubles, 2 twins, 2 family.
price	£87.50–£108. Half–board (for 2 nights) £113.50–£149 p.p. Singles from £43.75.
meals	Bar lunch from £3.25. Dinner £25.
closed	Rarely.
directions	From Bideford, A39 for Bude for 12 miles, right at r'bout, for Clovelly. Left fork before Visitor Centre, left at white rails down steep hill.

	John Rous
tel	01237 431237
fax	01237 431044
e-mail	redlion@clovelly.co.uk
web	www.clovelly.co.uk

Hotel

map 2   entry 52

Northcote Manor

Burrington, Umberleigh, Devon EX37 9LZ

As it was for the monks who came here to spend their last days in the 15th century, Northcote remains a haven from the bedlam of life. The setting is magical, reached by a long driveway that climbs lazily through woodland. The hotel is surrounded by 20 acres of lawn and garden and dreamy views that stretch across the soft, yielding countryside of the Taw River Valley. All is deliriously peaceful: beautiful specimen trees, sweet birdsong and the faint smell of wood smoke on the breeze. The older half of the building was completed in 1716, the rest was added in the Victorian era – you enter via the later part through a studded oak door to an open hallway with lilies, newspapers and an open fire which welcomes all year. Stairs lead to bedrooms in matching fabrics; no surprises but all is smart. Cheryl manages with genuine care, while Christophe stars in the kitchen. The formal dining room is in the oldest part, down carpeted steps; hand-painted murals on the wall bathe one corner in a warm, pinky glow. We can but look forward to the advent of flying monks shown in one; in the meantime, let your spirits soar.

rooms	11: 4 doubles, 1 twin/double, 1 twin, 1 four-poster, 4 suites.
price	£140–£235. Half-board (min. 2 nights) from £95 p.p. Singles from £80.
meals	Dinner £35.
closed	Rarely.
directions	M5, junc. 27, A361 to South Molton. Fork left onto B3227, then right on A377 for Barnstaple. Entrance 6 miles on left, signed (ignore signs to Burrington).

	Jean-Pierre Mifsud
tel	01769 560501
fax	01769 560770
e-mail	rest@northcotemanor.co.uk
web	www.northcotemanor.co.uk

Hotel

Halmpstone Manor

Bishop's Tawton, Barnstaple, Devon EX32 0EA

Charles and Jane are preserving a long tradition of true farmhouse hospitality at Halmpstone that's gently at odds with the rough and tumble of the 21st century – in 1630, John Westcote described his stay here as "delightful". The handsome Queen Anne manor you see today was completed in 1701, after fire destroyed much of the original house of 22 rooms in 1633; its proportions remain charming. Fresh flowers adorn every room, pink walls cheer, family photos beam from silver frames, china figures stand on parade… all is traditional. Bedrooms in pink and peach are immaculate, with floral coronets, draped four-posters, a decanter of sherry, fresh fruit and more flowers. Afternoon tea is included, as are the newspapers. Dine by candlelight in the lovely panelled dining room. Jane's cooking has won heaps of awards: try Clovelly scallops, local lamb, and maybe a selection of north Devon cheeses. Charles was born here and has run the farm for much of his life. Both are 'hands-on' and welcoming. Halmpstone means 'Holy Boundary Stone' and the building faces south to Dartmoor. Walk in the pretty garden, or stray further.

rooms	5: 3 twins/doubles, 2 four-posters.
price	£100–£140. Singles £70.
meals	Dinner, 5 courses, £25.
closed	Christmas & New Year; February.
directions	From Barnstaple, south on A377. Left opp. petrol station, after Bishop's Tawton, for Cobbaton & Chittlehampton. After 2 miles, right. House on left after 200 yds.

Jane & Charles Stanbury

tel	01271 830321
fax	01271 830826
e-mail	charles@halmpstonemanor.co.uk
web	www.halmpstonemanor.co.uk

Hotel

map 2   entry 54

Broomhill Art Hotel & Sculpture Gardens
Muddiford, Devon EX31 4EX

An important and inspiring gallery gently dominates the ground floor of this rambling Victorian house; eight international exhibitions a year haul in thousands of art lovers, and it doesn't stop there. The informal, terraced, 10-acre garden has a cool, tree-lined lake around which geese plod and 150 contemporary sculptures lurk. Some are huge and scary, some amusing, but all are for gasping at (and taking home if you're feeling flush). Rinus and Aniet run house, gallery, garden and energetic young children with kind, relaxed, enthusiasm and very few rules. Wander at will, ask questions if you want – you won't be bothered in any way. The bedrooms have one or two ugly hangovers from the 1970s but the beds are new, the lighting modern and the art original. Rinus cooks good, award-winning mediterranean food and can be generous with wine and hospitality! It's clear that he and Aniet are passionate about their subject: live jazz, a ceramics shop, be-bop, lectures and poetry... if it comes along they put it on. A unique experience.

rooms	5: 4 twins/doubles, 1 four-poster.
price	£55-£65. Singles £35-£45.
meals	Lunch from £5. Dinner, 2 courses, £16. Restaurant closed Sundays & Monday evenings.
closed	20 December-mid-January.
directions	From Barnstable, A39 north towards Lynton, then left onto B3230, following brown signs to Sculpture Gardens & hotel.

Rinus & Aniet Van de Sande

tel	01271 850262
fax	01271 850575
e-mail	info@broomhillart.co.uk
web	www.broomhillart.co.uk

Restaurant with Rooms

The Old Rectory Hotel

Martinhoe, Devon EX31 4QT

As you quietly succumb to the wonderful sense of spiritual calm, it's hard to conceive that one field away the land skids to a halt and spectacular cliffs drop 800 feet. The Exmoor plateau meets the sea abruptly at the village of Martinhoe – 'hoe' is Saxon for high ground – creating a breathtaking view as you approach. This lovely understated hotel stands next to an 11th-century church in three acres of mature garden. Nurtured by clergy past, the garden now occupies the affection of Christopher and Enid: birdsong, waterfalls, scented azaleas and the bizarre gunnera only hint at its allure. This is a gentle retreat, dedicated to food and marvellous hospitality. Enid has been cooking since she was a child and makes her own marmalade, bread and cakes, biscuits and ice cream. Meat is fresh, local and organic; even the water, filtered and purified, is from a local borehole. Traditional bedrooms have Laura Ashley wallpaper and the odd Waring & Gillow antique, and one has a balcony; bathrooms sparkle. Grapes from the 200 year old vine above your head fill fruit bowls in season.

rooms	9: 4 doubles, 2 twins, 3 twins/doubles.
price	£95–£115. Singles £65–£75. Half-board plus afternoon tea £69–£85 p.p.
meals	Dinner, 5 courses, £29.
closed	November–February.
directions	A39 for Lynton, by-passing Parracombe, then left after about 3 miles, signed Martinhoe. Across common, left into village, entrance 1st on right by church.

Christopher & Enid Richmond

tel	01598 763368
fax	01598 763567
e-mail	reception@oldrectoryhotel.co.uk
web	www.oldrectoryhotel.co.uk

Hotel

map 2 entry 56

Bark House Hotel

Oakfordbridge, Nr Bampton, Devon EX16 9HZ

Alastair describes this small hotel as "a little haven where you can unwind and enjoy good cooking for a few days." He nips smartly across the main, but not busy, road to help you with your luggage; Justine is waiting inside to offer tea and home-made cake. The low-ceilinged sitting and dining rooms are comfortable and warm with patterned carpets and curtains. Bedrooms are cottagey with good beds upon which lie teddies and one has a fine bay window; all have rural, pretty views. Apart from being incredibly spoilt you will be bowled over by the food. Alastair makes almost everything himself and is a true enthusiast – ask him! Meat, fish and vegetables are local and seasonal; canapes, ice creams, sorbets and little sweets are home-made. Wine is taken seriously and the list evolves regularly, so if you are sybaritic by nature and adore a bit of attention you will love it here. A garden to explore or sit in, the gorgeous wooded valley surrounding the River Exe to wander through and birds, lots of birds, will keep nature-lovers happy.

rooms	5: 2 doubles, 2 twins/doubles; 1 double with separate bath.
price	£79–£110. Half-board from £66 p.p. Singles £45–£55.
meals	Dinner £26.50.
closed	Mondays & Tuesdays in summer.
directions	From Tiverton, A396 north towards Minehead. Hotel on right, 1 mile north of junction with B3227.

	Alastair Kameen & Justine Hill
tel	01398 351236
web	www.barkhouse.co.uk

Restaurant with Rooms

Kings Arms
Stockland, Nr Honiton, Devon EX14 9BS

Stay for a week and you'll almost be a fully-fledged local – this is a cross between a pub and a community centre with a vast overflowing notice board to fill you in on the gossip you didn't catch at the bar. You'll also be a stone or two heavier with seemingly endless menus, masses of fish, locally-reared game and even ostrich. Ramble at will past crackling fires, beams, gilt-framed mirrors, stone walls, cosy low ceilings and, eventually, the stone-flagged Farmer's Bar where you meet the "fair-minded, fun-loving locals". One comes from as far as Birmingham to take his place at the bar; they'll have you playing darts in no time. As for Paul, "he's a tyrant to work for," said one of his staff with an enormous smile on his face. Bedrooms are not grand but perfectly traditional, with maybe a walnut bed or a cushioned window seat. It is a working pub and won't be quiet until about 11pm so don't try to sleep earlier, just join in. Lose yourself in the Blackdown Hills or simply laze around inside with Princess Ida, the cat. If you like inns, stay here.

rooms	3: 2 doubles, 1 twin.
price	£60. Singles £40.
meals	Lunch from £4. Dinner, 3 courses, from £15.50.
closed	Christmas Day.
directions	From centre of Honiton, head north-east out of town. Stockland signed right just before junction with A30. Straight ahead for 6 miles to village.

	Paul Diviani, John O'Leary & Heinz Kiefer
tel	01404 881361
fax	01404 881732
e-mail	reserve@kingsarms.net
web	www.kingsarms.net

Inn

map 2   entry 58

Combe House Hotel & Restaurant

Honiton, Nr Exeter, Devon EX14 3AD

If the spirit of Combe House could be bottled and sprinkled over the world, good would surely come of it. As it is, Ruth and Ken have distilled their own worldly experience to create a sublime place to stay. Globe-trotting careers have seen them put Australia's Hunter Valley on the map and Ken cook in the Antarctic for three years. But what makes here so special is the modest way they apply themselves to each task, big or small. Their latest project has been the faithful restoration of a Georgian kitchen – a deliciously romantic spot for a private party. By the light of the Tilly lamp you are treated to the best Devon produce, local as can be, with the chef finishing your main course on the huge wood-burning range. The rest of the house is just as fabulous – meet history at every turn as Elizabethan and Restoration eras meld into one: cavernous fireplace, mullioned windows, oak panelling, ancestral portraits – not theirs! – comfortable bedrooms, *trompe l'œil* murals. All this on 3,500 acres with a "lost" arboretum. The long, wooded drive that brings you here will unravel all.

rooms	15: 11 twins/doubles, 1 four-poster, 3 suites.
price	£138–£198. Half-board from £96 p.p. Singles from £99. Suites £265.
meals	Lunch £16.50; 3 courses, £21. Dinner £34. Parties in Georgian kitchen £38 p.p. plus room hire.
closed	Rarely.
directions	A30 south from Honiton for 2 miles; A375 for Sidmouth & Branscombe. Signed through woods.

	Ruth & Ken Hunt
tel	01404 540400
fax	01404 46004
e-mail	stay@thishotel.com
web	www.thishotel.com

Hotel

Alias Hotel Barcelona

Magdalen Street, Exeter, Devon EX2 4HY

This extraordinary place reinvents the British hotel experience. Hotel Barcelona belongs to an exciting new breed which uses fresh design and classic memorabilia to put folk up in affordable style – without losing its sense of humour in the process. Barcelona is the brainchild of hotel visionary Nigel Chapman. Here, he has taken a former Victorian eye infirmary and turned it into a psychedelic ark of shape and colour that heals all the senses, even the most jaded. Nothing says 'Barcelona' directly, except the odd Jujol-inspired handrail and bedroom doors taken from Gaudi's Casa Mila. More, it's the vibrant buzz of the Catalan capital that's arrived in this terribly English city. There is so much to see that it is hard even to scratch the surface. The stunning collection of 50s and 60s furniture in the lobby, Café Paradiso with its rainbow-coloured mural and authentic Naples pizza oven, the Kino cabaret club performing every weekend and elegant bedrooms that curve, angle and slope. Go see for yourself. ¡Arriva! ¡Arriva!

rooms	46: 20 twins/doubles, 19 doubles, 7 singles.
price	£85–£105. Singles £75.
meals	Continental breakfast included; full English £10.50. Lunch £12. Dinner £22.25.
closed	Rarely.
directions	M5, junc. 30, A379 for Exeter, 3rd exit Countess Wear r'bout, signed City Centre, for 2 miles to main traffic junction. Keep in right lane into Magdalen St. Hotel on right.

Fiona Dollan

tel	01392 281000
fax	01392 281001
e-mail	info@aliasbarcelona.com
web	www.aliashotels.com

Hotel

map 2   entry 60

Kingston House

Staverton, Nr Totnes, Devon TQ9 6AR

It's hard to know where to begin describing this stupendous house – the history in one bathroom alone would fill a small book. "It's like visiting a National Trust home where you can get into bed," offers Elizabeth, your gentle and erudite host. Set in a flawless Devon valley, Kingston is one of the finest surviving examples of early-18th-century architecture in England. Arrive down a long country lane that rises and falls, increasing your expectations; at the brow of the last hill, the house comes into view... utterly majestic, demanding your attention – as do the Great Danes that come to greet you. Completed in 1735 for a wealthy wool merchant, many original features remain, including the 24 chimneys. The craftsman who carved the marble hallway later worked on the White House in Washington DC, the marquetry staircase is the best example in Europe, and the magnificent bed in the Green Room has stood there since 1830. There's a thunder-box loo, an Angel tester bed, a painted china closet, ancient wall paintings... The cooking is historic, too – devilled kidneys, syllabub and proper trifle. A genuine one-off and so welcoming.

rooms	3 doubles.
price	£130–£150. Singles £85–£95.
meals	Dinner £32.50, 4 courses £34.50.
closed	Christmas & New Year.
directions	From A38, A384 to Staverton. At Sea Trout Inn, left fork for Kingston; halfway up hill right fork; at top of hill, straight ahead at x-roads. Road goes up, then down to house; right to front of house.

	Michael & Elizabeth Corfield
tel	01803 762235
fax	01803 762444
e-mail	info@kingston-estate.co.uk
web	www.kingston-estate.co.uk

Other Place

Fingals

Dittisham, Dartmouth, Devon TQ6 0JA

Richard miraculously combines a rare *laissez-faire* management style with a passionate commitment to doing things well. He is ever-present without intruding, fun without being challenging, spontaneous without being demanding. This is his place, his style, his gesture of defiance to the rest of the hotel world. He does things his way, and most people love it. And he is backed by Sheila, whose kindness and perennial good nature are a constant source of wonder. The food is good, with a Gallic appeal, and the meals around the big table memorable. This is a place to mingle with kindred spirits into the early hours; though the accent is on conviviality, you can eat at separate tables if you prefer. You find children wandering freely, happy adults – certainly, mooching dogs, and Sheila's ducks being marshalled home in the evening. Ask for rooms in the main house – they're bigger. The indoor pool beckons, and sauna and jacuzzi, ping-pong and croquet for all, perhaps tennis on the lawn and cosy conversation in the bar. But don't be misled, you can do peace and quiet here, too. Perfect for the open-hearted.

rooms	10: 8 doubles, 1 twin, 1 family. Also self-catering barn for 4.
price	£70-£140.
meals	Dinner £27.50.
closed	2 January-26 March.
directions	From Totnes, A381 south up hill; left for Cornworthy & Ashprington. Right at x-roads, for Cornworthy; right at ruined gatehouse for Dittisham. Down steep hill, over bridge. Hotel signed on right.

Richard Johnston

tel	01803 722398
fax	01803 722401
e-mail	richard@fingals.co.uk
web	www.fingals.co.uk

Restaurant with Rooms

map 2　entry 62

Hazelwood House

Loddiswell, Nr Kingsbridge, Devon TQ7 4EB

Set in 67 acres of woodland, meadows and orchards in an untamed river valley, Hazelwood House is no ordinary hotel. It is a place of exceptional peace and natural beauty, created more as a relaxed, unpretentious country house. It might not be for everyone, but those who like it, love it. Through the front door, past rows of books and paintings, and enter a world to revive the spirit. Chances are Daisy the dog will be there to roll over and greet you. Lectures and courses and evenings of music from classical to jazz play a big part – they have a knack of attracting the best – and all is carried off with a friendly approach. Anabel and Gillian, who are involved with 'Through the Heart to Peace', a peace initiative started in 1993, came here some years ago and the place has evolved ever since. The atmosphere outweighs any decorative shortfalls, the food is delicious and fully organic and they produce their own spring water. Cream tea on the veranda is wonderful, or roam past rhododendrons and huge camellias to fields of wild flowers and grazing sheep.

rooms	15: 1 twin, 1 twin/double; 2 singles, 8 twins/doubles, 3 family, sharing 4 baths.
price	£50–£95. Singles £35.25.
meals	Lunch from £8. Packed lunch £5–£8. Dinner £15–£18.
closed	Rarely.
directions	From Exeter, A38 south then A3121 south. Left onto B3196 south. At California Cross, 1st left after petrol station. After 0.75 miles, left for Hazelwood. Gates on right.

Janie Bowman, Gillian Kean & Anabel Watson

tel	01548 821232
fax	01548 821318

Other Place

The Henley

Folly Hill, Bigbury-on-Sea, Devon TQ7 4AR

The view from this Edwardian summer house is truly uplifting, a glorious vision of sand, sea and lush patchwork of fields. The garden falls away gently, disappearing over a shallow cliff to an inviting expanse of golden sand and white surf – nothing jars the eye and a private footpath leads the way down. The hotel entrance creates the second good impression: bold red walls lead to two sitting areas and a conservatory, all decorated with homely elegance. A dining room of Lloyd Loom chairs, pot plants, seagrass and candles pulls in the view to maximum effect; every table has its own special portion. Martyn conjures up flavoursome, fresh, beautiful looking food: one reviewer said the view and dinner combined were enough to make her feel at peace with the world. Bedrooms are small and adequate; all have the view. The beaches are popular with surfers and sun-seekers, and you can reach Burgh Island by a sandy causeway at low tide, by sea tractor at high tide – great fun. A special setting, lovely people... and visiting pets are made welcome, too. *Children over 12 welcome.*

rooms	6 doubles.
price	£78-£88. Singles £49-£54.
meals	Dinner £20.
closed	November-March.
directions	From A38, A3121 to Modbury, then B3392 to Bigbury-on-Sea. Hotel on left as road slopes down to sea.

Martyn Scarterfield & Petra Lampe

tel	01548 810240
fax	01548 810240
e-mail	enquiries@thehenleyhotel.co.uk

Hotel

map 2   entry 64

Bridge House Hotel

3 Prout Bridge, Beaminster, Dorset DT8 3AY

There is much here to make one happy – good food, award-winning hospitality and the inestimable beauty of Hardy country. At the heart of Bridge House is the food – traditional and as local as possible, and probably not for slimmers. You eat in the panelled, Georgian dining room, with a fine Adam fireplace and the palest of pink linen. The bedrooms, too, are solidly traditional, with padded headboards, floral duvet covers and curtains – no surprises but stacks of space. Peter is very much the convivial host; his good-natured professionalism has won him accolades and rightly so. The Pinksters have a gift for inspiring loyalty: their staff enjoy their work and they stay. The history of this ancient building gives it a sense of dignity and solidity; an ancient monument first, probably a 13th-century priest's house next, a dwelling house in the Tudor period which explains the variety of mullioned windows… later eras saw the creation of a priest's hole. Beaminster is a pretty town not far from the south coast, there's llama trekking nearby if you crave a little adventure.

rooms	14: 3 doubles, 9 twins/doubles, 1 single, 1 family.
price	£102–£134. Half-board (min. 2 nights) from £75 p.p. Singles £54–£96.
meals	Lunch £11. Dinner, 5 courses, £28.50.
closed	Rarely.
directions	From Yeovil, A30 west, then A3066, signed Bridport, for 10 miles to Beaminster. Hotel at far end of town, as road bends to right.

Peter Pinkster

tel	01308 862200
fax	01308 863700
e-mail	enquiries@bridge-house.co.uk
web	www.bridge-house.co.uk

Hotel

Innsacre Farmhouse

Shipton Gorge, Nr Bridport, Dorset DT6 4LJ

This is a perfect place in 10 acres of orchard, valley and wooded hills, elegant without pretension and wrapped up in peace and quiet. Inside, 17th-century stone walls, low-beamed ceilings and warm French flair. Behind it all are Sydney and Jayne, two easy going francophiles who share a gift for unwinding city-stressed souls. Come to relax – bedrooms with antique French beds, bold colours and crisp linen sheets will help unravel the tightest knot. There's a bar in the sitting room – Sydney is keen on his wines, knowledgeable too – piled high with books, with an open fire and soft, deep chairs to sink into. In summer, spill out onto the large terrace with your pre-dinner drink and watch the setting sun. The orchard is heavy, in season, with plums, apples and figs that Jayne turns into compotes – have them at breakfast along with cured ham sausages and American-style pancakes. Walk the fields and you may bump into the Jacob sheep – you can buy their undyed wool – or keep going and head for cliff walks, beaches and the Dorset Coastal Path. Rejuvenating.

rooms	4: 3 doubles, 1 twin.
price	£70-£85. Singles from £50.
meals	Dinner £18.50. Late arrival supper £15.50.
closed	24 December-2 January.
directions	From Dorchester, A35 for Bridport for 13 miles, then left on 2nd road for Shipton Gorge & Burton Bradstock. Follow 1st driveway on left up to farmhouse.

Sydney & Jayne Davies

tel	01308 456137
e-mail	innsacre.farmhouse@btinternet.com
web	www.innsacre.com

Other Place

 map 2 entry 66

The Fox Inn

Corscombe, Nr Dorchester, Dorset DT2 0NS

Clive, an ex-accountant, has been here for 18 months and is keen to keep this 17th-century thatched inn as one of the most sought-after places to stay and eat in the south of England. Hospitality is first rate, food excellent and the setting is Hardy's Wessex at its most peaceful and beautiful. In days of yore, drovers on the way to market would wash their sheep in the stream opposite and stop for a pint of cider; the inn only received a full licence 40 years ago. The old feel of the inn is intact with clever additions like a slate-topped bar, a flower-filled conservatory with benches and a long table made from a single oak blown down during the storms of 1987. You're surrounded by eye-pleasing detail: stuffed owls in glass cases, blue gingham tablecloths, paintings, flowers, antlers, flagstones and fires in winter. Bedrooms have simple country charm with floral and mahogany touches; one in a converted loft is reached by stone steps. Special, indeed, and the sea isn't far, either.

rooms	4: 3 doubles, 1 twin.
price	£80–£100. Singles £55–£75.
meals	Dinner, à la carte, about £20.
closed	Christmas Day.
directions	From Yeovil, A37 for Dorchester for 1 mile, then right, for Corscombe, for 5.5 miles. Inn on left on outskirts of village. Use kitchen door to left of main entrance if arriving before 7pm.

	Clive Webb
tel	01935 891330
fax	01935 891330
e-mail	dine@fox-inn.co.uk
web	www.fox-inn.co.uk

Inn

The Acorn Inn

Evershot, Dorchester, Dorset DT2 0JW

Thomas Hardy called this 400-year-old inn The Sow and Acorn and let Tess rest a night here; had he visited today he might have let her stay longer. New owners, Todd and Louise, are keen to improve upon the already high ideals of The Acorn but this is very much a traditional inn: as much a place for locals to sup their ale as for foodies to sample some of the best food in Dorset – you're free to mix. The locals' bar still represents the heart of village life; black and white photographs of villagers cover the walls as stories are swapped by an open fire. Walk through to the dining room and the atmosphere suddenly changes to rural country house, with smartly-laid tables, terracotta tiles, soft lighting and elegant hamstone fireplaces – it's here the food is taken seriously, especially fresh local fish. Bedrooms creak with age *and* style: painted shutters, a bay window, a glimpse of the pub sign, uneven floors and beautiful drapes that soften dark oak four-posters – all work well together. Unspoilt Evershot, ancient woodland and rolling countryside provide ample walks. Hardy would approve.

rooms	9: 3 doubles, 3 twins, 3 four-posters.
price	£90-£130. Singles from £75.
meals	Lunch from £3.75. Dinner, à la carte, about £25.
closed	Rarely.
directions	Evershot 1 mile off A37 midway between Yeovil & Dorchester.

	Todd & Louise Moffat
tel	01935 83228
fax	01935 83707
e-mail	stay@acorn-inn.co.uk
web	www.acorn-inn.co.uk

Inn

map 2   entry 68

Plumber Manor

Sturminster Newton, Dorset DT10 2AF

Best of all at Plumber is the family triumvirate of Brian in the kitchen, Richard behind the bar cracking jokes and Alison, who is simply everywhere. They know exactly how to make you feel at home. This has been *their* family home for 300 years, though ancestors have lived "in the area" since they arrived with William the Conquerer. Outside, a large, sloping lawn, a white bridge over the river and deckchairs scattered about the well-groomed garden. Inside, the house remains more home than hotel with huge family portraits crammed on the walls; everything in this house seems to be *big*. The atmosphere is relaxed without a trace of pomposity. Stay in the main house if you can; bedrooms have had a recent makeover with fresh colours and fabrics, similar to those in the converted stables which are bigger but have less character. The stone path between the two came from a local river bed, and kept one guest amused for hours looking for dinosaur fossils... The enormous old sofa on the landing may be the most uncomfortable ever made – but this is the *only* discomfort you'll find. The rest is irresistible. *Pets by arrangement.*

rooms	16: 2 doubles, 13 twins/doubles; 1 twin/double with separate bath.
price	£100–£160. Singles from £90.
meals	Dinner £19–£25.
closed	February.
directions	From Sturminster Newton, follow signs to hotel & Hazlebury Bryan for 2 miles. Entrance on left, signed.

Richard, Alison & Brian Prideaux-Brune

tel	01258 472507
fax	01258 473370
e-mail	book@plumbermanor.com
web	www.plumbermanor.com

Restaurant with Rooms

The Museum Inn

Farnham, Nr Blandford Forum, Dorset DT11 8DE

This delightful, part-thatched 17th-century inn owes its name to General Augustus Lane Fox Pitt Rivers, the 'father of archaeology'; it fed and bed folk who came to see his museum in the 1800s. He opened three museums in all to house his fabulous collection; only the Pitt Rivers Museum in Oxford survives today. No sign either of the yaks and zebu that the General once released into a nearby pleasure park. What you will discover is one of the best inns in the south of England. Vicky and Mark work well together to create a wonderfully warm and friendly place to stay: she does bubbly, he does laid-back. The smart refit has a lovely period feel, with flagstones, inglenook, fresh flowers and a mismatch of wooden tables and chairs. Leading from the restaurant is a gorgeous drawing room, with lots of books. Bright, comfortable bedrooms upstairs have antique beds and many prints; all are impeccably done. Chef Mark Treasure is as good as his name suggests, and sure to win more accolades for his imaginative cooking. Farnham is a pretty thatched idyll in the middle of Cranborne Chase, ideal for walks and horses.

rooms	8 doubles.
price	£75–£120. Singles £65.
meals	Light lunch from £3.95. Dinner, à la carte, about £24.
closed	Christmas Day & New Year's Eve.
directions	From Blandford, A354 for Salisbury for 6.5 miles, then left, signed Farnham. Inn on left in village.

Vicky Elliot & Mark Stephenson

tel	01725 516261
fax	01725 516988
e-mail	enquiries@museuminn.co.uk
web	www.museuminn.co.uk

Inn

map 3   entry 70

Mortons House Hotel

Corfe Castle, Wareham, Dorset BH20 5EE

One day, the old railway will reach Wareham and collect you from your London train. Meanwhile, just enjoy the passing steam from the terrace of this wonderful 1590 manor house – the station is below. Mortons was built from Purbeck stone in the shape of an 'E' to honour Queen Elizabeth I and overlooks the ruins of Corfe Castle. Bit by bit, these hugely enthusiastic owners are uplifting the whole hotel after rescuing it from dereliction. They've initiated a complete overhaul, signed up an award-winning chef, and the garden is under review. Traditional bedrooms make good use of four-posters, one suite has its own private staircase and the finest views, another a fine four-poster and stone fireplace. What makes this place special is the unwavering friendliness of mostly local staff. Spend a wintry evening before a log fire among the oak panelling, or strike out along the coast in summer – the headlands and beaches are so clearly formed they're used to teach coastal erosion to children. The village is protected and perfect, the old 'capital' of the Isle of Purbeck… you've even a sunny micro-climate here.

rooms	17: 11 doubles, 3 twins, 3 suites.
price	Half-board, 2 nights, £134–£158 p.p. Singles £75–£130.
meals	Lunch, 3 courses, £20. Dinner, 5 courses, £34.50. Bar meals from £7.50.
closed	Rarely.
directions	From Wareham, A351 to Corfe Castle. Hotel on left 50 yds from market square.

Andy & Ally Hageman,
Ted & Beverly Clayton

tel	01929 480988
fax	01929 480820
e-mail	stay@mortonshouse.co.uk
web	www.mortonshouse.co.uk

Restaurant with Rooms

entry 71   map 3

Lord Bute Hotel

Lymington Road, Christchurch, Highcliffe, Dorset BH23 4JS

Tucked away behind the original entrance lodges to Highcliffe Castle, Lord Bute Hotel & Restaurant is causing a big stir, and not only among locals; you need to book well in advance now to eat their fresh, locally sourced food: a daily changing menu of modern English with a continental twist. The restaurant is glamorous and elegant with black carpets and crisp white and gold linen – Raffles with a dramatic spin. Light spills in from the gorgeous wooden-floored orangery and the conservatory which overlook the garden. Here, Thai-style pots stuffed with bamboo and colourful acers sit on terracotta-block paving terraced down to a pretty grassed area. Air-conditioned, double-glazed bedrooms come smart with mahogany furniture and muted wall colours, fully tiled bathrooms are spotless and all mod cons are handy. Gary and Simon are fun and they work hard to give you a good time – all this and monthly cabaret evenings with famous names, or live music on most weekends. Take the path down to the beach behind the castle, or drive into the New Forest. Bournemouth is nearby for shopping or clubbing.

rooms	12: 11 twins/doubles, 1 suite.
price	From £85. Singles from £65. Suite from £140.
meals	Lunch £11.95. Dinner £26.95; à la carte also available.
closed	Rarely. Restaurant closed Mondays.
directions	From Christchurch, A337 for Lymington to Highcliffe. Hotel 200 yds past castle.

Gary Payne & Simon Box

tel	01425 278884
fax	01425 279258
e-mail	mail@lordbute.co.uk
web	www.lordbute.co.uk

Hotel

map 3   entry 72

Rose and Crown

Romaldkirk, Barnard Castle, Durham DL12 9EB

Few country inns match one's expectations as well as the Rose and Crown. Built in the 1750s when Captain Bligh, Romaldkirk's famous son, was still a young sprite, this dreamy inn is superbly comfortable, gently informal and utterly unpretentious. In the small locals' bar, sit at settles and read the *Stockton Times*, or the *Teesdale Mercury*, warmed by an open fire, while a few trophies peer down. A shiny brass door latch reveals more: an elegant lounge where a grandfather clock sets a restful pace, and a bright, panelled dining room for more formal fare and breakfast. Food is excellent and fantastic value. Bedrooms are vibrant, with slanting eaves, window seats, fun colours and the reassuring smell of proper furniture polish. Rooms in a nearby annexe suit walkers and pet owners. Outside, a village green, with church and unblemished stone cottages, opens onto countryside as good as any in Britain. Alison and Christopher are easy-going perfectionists — their hard work has made this the place to stay, the place to eat… a perfect antidote to England's fickle clime.

rooms	12: 5 doubles, 5 twins, 2 suites.
price	£96–£110. Singles £70.
meals	Bar meals £6–£13.95. Dinner, 4 courses, £26.
closed	Christmas.
directions	From Barnard Castle, B6277 north for 6 miles. Right in village towards green. Inn on left.

Christopher & Alison Davy

tel	01833 650213
fax	01833 650828
e-mail	hotel@rose-and-crown.co.uk
web	www.rose-and-crown.co.uk

Inn

Seaham Hall Hotel

Lord Byron's Walk, Seaham, Durham SR7 7AG

Seaham Hall is designed to make you feel *you* own the place – and we bet you never feel so spoiled. Perhaps the most remarkable thing about this ever so modern hotel is there are so few rooms for such a large building. Texture, shape and electronic gadgets knit together to create a stunning series of set-piece designs; every bedroom is separated from the world by two thick oak doors, and every bath fits two. The building was once a heart hospital; it was also where Lord Byron was married. You feel enormously good here. Get lost and cosy with a newspaper in the huge drawing room – the ceiling feels several double decker buses high. Tall French windows open onto a wide and formal garden terrace with stone steps leading to the bleak and beautiful north-east coast. The owner is a great patron of the arts, sculptures and paintings are added all the time. Pride of place goes to Charybdis, a water sculpture by William Pye, outside the front entrance. The cone-shaped spa is arguably the best in the country, the food is exceptional – and why bother to get dressed when breakfast in bed is all part of the service... just relax.

rooms	19: 13 doubles, 5 suites, 1 penthouse for 4.
price	£175–£295. Singles from £165. Suites £255–£325. Penthouse £500.
meals	Breakfast £7.50. Dinner £34; à la carte £30–£40.
closed	Rarely.
directions	A1(M), junc. 62, A690 through Houghton le Spring, A19 south on to Seaham. At seafront, left on B1287 for 2 miles. On left.

	Tom & Jocelyn Maxfield
tel	0191 516 1400
fax	0191 516 1410
e-mail	reservations@seaham-hall.com
web	www.seaham-hall.com

Hotel

map 10   entry 74

The Bell Inn & Hill House

High Road, Horndon-on-the-Hill, Essex SS17 8LD

Christine is an original fixture in this Great Inn of England – her parents ran the Bell for years and she was born here. John is also a key figure, much admired in the trade, as is Joanne, their loyal manager of 17 years – a recent industry award for hospitality proved what folk had known a long time. Christine's beautifully decorated suites upstairs are by far the best places to stay – they're named after famous mistresses: Lady Hamilton, Madame du Barry and Anne Boleyn, who's said to be buried in the local church. The other bedrooms are next door in Hill House; all are comfortable. Dining areas suit the mood of the day. The breakfast room is light and airy, with elegant white table and chair coverings; the flagstoned bar, with oak panelled walls and French wood carvings – part of a huge collection built up by Christine's father – bustles with working folk at lunchtime; and the smart restaurant is busy in the evening. Waiters serve in white aprons and black ties under the close eye of the Master Sommelier, Joanne. The food rightly picks up awards, too, as should Christine's flower arangements. Great value and so close to London.

rooms	15: 7 doubles, 3 twins, 5 suites.
price	£50-£60. Suites £75-£85.
meals	Breakfast £4.50-£7.50. Bar meals from £5.50. Dinner, à la carte, about £23. No food on Bank Holidays.
closed	Christmas.
directions	M25, junc. 30/31. A13 towards Southend for 3 miles, then B1007 to Horndon. On left in village.

	Christine & John Vereker
tel	01375 642463
fax	01375 361611
e-mail	info@bell-inn.co.uk
web	www.bell-inn.co.uk

Restaurant with Rooms

The Pier at Harwich

The Quay, Harwich, Essex CO12 3HH

The Pier stands smartly on the quayside in the historic port of Harwich. Owners the Milsoms took over the next-door pub in 2000 to carve out a handsome lounge: loads of space, seagrass matting, simple bold colours and deep sofas around an open fire. The Harbourside Restaurant upstairs takes the pick of the views over the harbour and the Stour and Orwell estuaries and fresh fish is, of course, what you should eat. Chris and Vreni Oakley – he's the seafood expert, she's front of house and his absolutely charming Swiss-born wife – have been here nearly 25 years; they clearly love the place and go out of their way to see that guests do too. Informal eating takes place in the H'apenny Bistro and on the buzzing quayside. Bedrooms are beautifully done: more seagrass, painted tongue and groove panelling, great colour, good quality fabrics – splash out on the Mayflower suite for the best views. The hall and bar have a modern feel and a maritime sprinkling of ship's wheels and brass portholes. Book a mooring.

rooms	14 doubles.
price	£90–£160. Half-board (min. 2 nights) from £100 p.p. Singles £67.50–£90.
meals	Lunch £16. Dinner, à la carte, £25–£28.
closed	Rarely.
directions	M25, junc. 28, A12 to Colchester bypass, then A120 to Harwich. Head for quay. Hotel opposite pier.

Chris & Vreni Oakley
tel	01255 241212
fax	01255 551922
e-mail	info@pieratharwich.co.uk
web	www.pieratharwich.com

Hotel

map 4   entry 76

Three Choirs Vineyards

Newent, Gloucestershire GL18 1LS

A fondness for cooking and the wine-making process will thoroughly equip you for the full-bodied and very English experience of Three Choirs. Thomas has run the vineyard with thoughtful and gentle reserve for almost a decade. There are 100 acres of grounds, of which 75 grow 16 varieties of grape; the rest have been left to encourage wildlife, including birds of prey that live around five ponds in the valley. The wine from here went to the wedding of Charles and Diana and still lubricates British embassies. The hotel and restaurant evolved more recently as an addition to the winery. The bedrooms are in a modern building and are crisply clean and functional, nothing quirky, but that's not what you're here for; each has French windows, a small patio and cast iron furniture: relax with a glass of wine and drink in the peaceful views that produced it. At breakfast, don't be embarrassed to ask for more wine with your smoked salmon and scrambled eggs – it's a house special. Chef Darren has won many accolades and runs monthly cookery courses. Dick Wittington was born up the road – you may wonder why he ever left.

rooms	8 twins/doubles.
price	From £85. Half-board, 2 nights, £125 p.p. Singles £65.
meals	Lunch about 12.50. Dinner, à la carte, about £28.
closed	Christmas & New Year.
directions	From Newent, north on B4215 for about 1.5 miles, following brown signs to vineyard.

	Thomas Shaw
tel	01531 890223
fax	01531 890877
e-mail	info@threechoirs.com
web	www.threechoirs.com

Other Place

Corse Lawn House Hotel

Corse Lawn, Gloucestershire GL19 4LZ

It would be much more fun to arrive here by carriage – preferably a mud-streaked one. The last circular 'wash' for cleaning your wheels and horses sits serenely outside this Queen Anne house – like a large pond with a little track going into it. Ducks, pheasants, doves and squirrels potter about it now in this quietest part of Gloucestershire. The Hine family (of Cognac fame) run the hotel – also their home – like clockwork. Baba is in the kitchen making everything from scratch: bread, sausages, jams, marmalades, ice creams, sorbets, and even smoking her own salmon and chicken. A vegetable and herb garden provides greens and the fields and hedgerows around are trawled for mushrooms, elderflowers and other goodies. The lovely flowers, arranged with flair, are all grown in the cutting bed here. Denis and Giles operate front of house and a superb wine cellar. Comfortable rooms downstairs are stuffed with good antiques and pictures, old-fashioned and elegant, the colours mainly greens and pinks. Bedrooms are large, immaculate and traditional – "we don't follow trends particularly'" says Giles.

rooms	19: 14 twins/doubles, 2 four-posters, 2 suites, 1 single.
price	£105-£165. Singles from £85.
meals	Dinner £29.50, a la carte from £32.50.
closed	24-26 December.
directions	From Tewkesbury A438 to Ledbury. After 3 miles left onto B4211. Hotel on right after nearly 2 miles.

	Giles Hine
tel	01452 780771
fax	01452 780840
e-mail	enquiries@corselawn.com
web	www.corselawn.com

Hotel

map 3   entry 78

Hotel on the Park

Evesham Road, Cheltenham, Gloucestershire GL52 2AH

Symmetry and style to please the eye in the centre of the spa town of Cheltenham. The attention to detail is staggering – everything has a place and is just where it should be. The style is crisp and dramatic, a homage to the Regency period in which the house was built, but there's plenty of good humour floating around, not least in Darryl himself, who's brilliant at making you feel at home. He's the first to encourage people to dive in and enjoy it all. There are lovely touches too: piles of fresh hand towels in the gents' cloakroom, where there's a sink with no plug hole – you'll work it out; newspapers hang on poles, so grab one and head into the drawing room where drapes swirl across big windows. Lose yourself in a book from the library, dine on poached salmon with lemon noodles, chocolate marquise with mint ice cream... the restaurant is sumptuous, with Doric columns and Greek and Roman busts, fun too. Upstairs, bedrooms are fabulous, crisp and artistic, all furnished to fit the period, one blessed with a jacuzzi and an adjustable massaging bed. The whole house is classically dramatic – a huge treat.

rooms	12: 5 doubles, 4 twins, 3 suites.
price	£108–£133. Singles £84.50. Suite £138–£158.
meals	Breakfast £7–£9.25. Dinner, à la carte, from £23.50.
closed	Rarely.
directions	From town centre, join one-way system, & exit signed Evesham. On down Evesham Road. Hotel on left opposite park, signed.

	Darryl Gregory
tel	01242 518898
fax	01242 511526
e-mail	stay@hotelonthepark.co.uk
web	www.hotelonthepark.com

Hotel

Alias Hotel Kandinsky

Bayshill Road, Montpellier, Cheltenham, Gloucestershire GL50 3AS

Kandinsky, Russian painter, theorist and pioneer of the abstract – a fitting name for a hotel pushing back the boundaries of British hospitality. The first hotel to come from the Alias stable has hotel innovator Nigel Chapman's signature written all over it. Like its sister hotel in Exeter, Kandinsky gives free rein to Nigel's design-obsession with sitting down in the right chair in the right surroundings. Religious lithographs from Blake's *Marriage of Heaven and Hell* in the entrance hall suggest that what you're about to receive will prepare you for what you'll have to endure when you leave this vibrant port of call. Bedrooms are compact, stylish, with all mod cons. Puppets from Bali hang above reception. The bar and lounge with painted wooden floors and rugs is in the Raffles colonial style, as are bamboo plants in the conservatory. Gates from a French monastery lead to the restaurant with its trademark Italian pizza oven. The private club downstairs feels like a New York lounge, with soft lighting, black leather couches and 50s party dresses in the ladies loo that are there to be worn by all, and are! Welcome to the party.

rooms	48: 14 doubles, 26 twins/doubles, 8 singles.	
price	£89–£115. Singles £79. B&B 2 nights + 1 dinner from £105 p.p.	
meals	Breakfast £7.75–£10.95. Lunch £14–£25. Dinner, à la carte, £20–£30.	
closed	Rarely.	
directions	M5, junc. 11, A40 to centre; left at r'bout end of Lansdown Road for Montpellier. Road veers to left, hotel ahead.	

	Lorraine Jarvie
tel	01242 527788
fax	01242 226412
e-mail	info@aliaskandinsky.com
web	www.aliashotels.com

Hotel

map 3   entry 80

Heavens Above at The Mad Hatters Restaurant

3 Cossack Square, Nailsworth, Gloucestershire GL6 0DB

In Carolyn's words, you "never know what's coming next" at this exceptional, fully organic restaurant with rooms. Arrive to a bowl of cherries one day, some fragrant sweet peas picked from the garden the next. She and Mike were smallholders once. They lived at the top of the hill, worked the land, kept livestock, made bellows and earned next to nothing. In the early Nineties, they came down the hill to open a restaurant. Locals flocked in, and still do. The food is delicious, consistently so, some still grown back up the hill: try fabulous fish soup, lamb with garlic and rosemary, and a mouth-puckering lemon tart. It's a place with heart, not designed to impress, which is probably why it does, and full of warm, rustic charm: cookery books squashed into a pretty pine dresser, mellow stone walls, big bay windows, stripped wooden floors, simple ash and elm tables and exceptional art. Two bedrooms share a bathroom but that's soon to change. All are delightful – huge, like an artist's studio, with wooden floors, whitewashed walls and rag-rolled beams. Fabulous.

rooms	3: 1 double; 1 double, 1 twin, sharing bath.
price	£60. Singles £35.
meals	Lunch £15. Dinner, à la carte, £25. Restaurant closed Sunday evenings, Mondays & Tuesdays.
closed	Rarely.
directions	M5, junc. 13, A419 east to Stroud, then A46 south to Nailsworth. Right at r'bout, then immediate left. On right, opposite Britannia pub.

Carolyn & Mike Findlay

tel	01453 832615
fax	01453 832615
e-mail	mafindlay@waitrose.com

Restaurant with Rooms

The Priory

Priory Fields, Horsley, Stroud, Gloucestershire GL6 0PT

Suzie does good company and long, lazy meals with the odd glass or two so well that one guest even recommends the Priory hangover! A definite 'other place', this 1880s Cotswold stone house defies an obvious label. Suzie is someone you immediately warm to: she's such an exuberant hostess that you want to feel a part of the fun and energy here. There's a well-stocked bar and deep feather-filled sofas to sink into for chats by the log fire. Take your time over traditional English meals around a walnut table in the splendid terracotta dining room with sparkling chandelier, big mirrors, gold sconces and cut glass. Fresh flowers and plants are everywhere. Suzie has laboured heroically to transform a dilapidated home into a sophisticated country house. Her eclectic style and quirky sense of humour have brought together an elegant hotchpotch of treasures collected over the years. The comfortable, smallish bedrooms come with impeccable bathrooms; some have tree-top views, all have the dawn chorus. The garden is being restored and the local pub is a pleasant stroll away. A great place for that special house party, too.

rooms	10: 4 doubles, 3 twins, 3 singles.
price	£75. Singles £45. House party rates on application.
meals	Dinner by arrangement. Restaurants nearby.
closed	24-26 December.
directions	M4, junc. 18, towards A46 north for Stroud. Enter Nailsworth on B4058, signed Horsley. Left at Bell & Castle pub. Entrance 200 yds on right.

Suzie Lamplough
tel	01453 834282
fax	01453 833750
e-mail	theprioryhorsley@onetel.net.uk
web	www.theprioryhorsley.com

Other Place

map 3   entry 82

No. 12

Park Street, Cirencester, Gloucestershire GL7 2BW

No. 12 is that rare phenomenon in Britain, not a hotel but a small 'other place' run with enormous thought and care. Sarah wanted to create a welcome alternative to the diet of faceless, corporate hotels that she endured herself for many years as a senior marketing manager. She has succeeded admirably, lavishly converting this splendid, listed Georgian townhouse right down to the last detail; some beams date back to the early 1600s. Bedrooms mix antique and contemporary furniture, while feather pillows, merino wool blankets and fine bed linen spoil further... extra-long beds include a *bateau lit* and an antique brass. Ultra-modern bathrooms, almost minimalist in style, come with dressing gowns and Molton Brown goodies. Cranberry-red walls and white china make a striking contrast in the dining room at breakfast, while checked sofas, fresh flowers and *Condé Nast Traveller* and *Vogue* in the sitting room encourage you to linger. Old Cirencester, 'capital of the Cotswolds', is equally splendid, a favourite destination for travellers since Roman times – civilised in every way. *Children over 12 welcome.*

rooms	3 doubles.
price	£70. Singles £50.
meals	Restaurants in Cirencester.
closed	Rarely.
directions	M4, junc. 15, A419 to Cirencester. Follow signs into town centre. House on right opp. museum.

Sarah Beckerlegge
tel	01285 640232
e-mail	no12cirencester@ukgateway.net
web	www.no12cirencester.co.uk

Other Place

The New Inn At Coln

Coln St-Aldwyns, Nr Cirencester, Gloucestershire GL7 5AN

Built by decree of Elizabeth I, this lovely coaching inn of roaring fires, low beams and oil paintings by Angela Kimmett provides old-fashioned hospitality at its best. The New Inn At Coln is a real way of life for the Kimmett family and their general manager Paul Swain. They and their staff take the time to talk you through a local walk, the ales on tap, the wonderful menu – chef Pascal Clavauds' food is exceptional – traditional with a continental twist. The bedrooms have everything – Jacobean-style four-posters or half-testers with a romantic floral theme; those in the converted dovecote have views across meadows to where the River Coln splashes along. In summer, sip drinks outside under the generous shade of parasols. Brown-trout-fishing on the river at the bottom of the meadow can be arranged and golf, biking and horse riding are all nearby. Walk from the front door through this sleepy Cotswold village, past grazing cows and gliding swans, into some of England's loveliest countryside; nothing too dramatic, just a classic of its type, inspiration to the artist, the poet… and maybe you.

rooms	14: 10 doubles, 3 twins/doubles, 1 single.
price	£115–£148. Singles £85–£99.
meals	Bar lunch from £8.50. Dinner, 2 courses £28. 3 courses £33.
closed	Rarely.
directions	From Oxford, A40 past Burford, B4425 for Bibury. Left after Aldsworth to Coln St-Aldwyns.

	Paul Swain
tel	01285 750651
fax	01285 750657
e-mail	stay@new-inn.co.uk
web	www.new-inn.co.uk

Inn

map 3   entry 84

The Swan Hotel at Bibury
Bibury, Gloucestershire GL7 5NW

The Swan must be the most photographed hotel in Britain; its setting by a bridge over a gentle river in a pretty village is pure Cotswold bliss. Inside is no less enchanting. Everywhere you look, something wonderful appears: Mackintosh chairs, a baby grand piano in the lobby; the sky-blue panelling in the entrance hall is so impressive, it's been listed. Further on, the dining room is a spectacular monument to the decadent Twenties – high ceilings, claret wallpaper, oils and chandeliers make it a fabulous place to eat. Bedrooms are equally indulgent, with a mix of old and contemporary: maybe an Art Deco mirror or a ceramic bedside light the size of a barrel. Old Roberts radios, thick bathrobes in Italian-tiled bathrooms and the hotel's own spring water are nice touches. Every room has something delightfully extravagant; the best face the front. Retire at night to find the bed turned down, wake in the morning to find a newspaper waiting to be read. Walk in perfect countryside, or fish the hotel's beat – the trout farm opposite is an artistic triumph.

rooms	18: 9 doubles, 3 twins, 2 twins/doubles, 1 family, 3 four-posters.
price	£116–£260.
meals	Lunch from £5. Dinner £28.50; à la carte also available.
closed	Rarely.
directions	From Oxford, A40 west, past Burford, then left on B4425 to Bibury. Hotel in village by bridge.

	John Stevens
tel	01285 740695
fax	01285 740473
e-mail	info@swanhotel.co.uk
web	www.swanhotel.co.uk

Hotel

Dial House

The Chestnuts, Bourton-on-the-Water, Gloucestershire GL54 2AN

The 'Venice of the Cotswolds' and such a peaceful setting, with distinctive sandstone Georgian houses and the slow, meandering River Windrush drifting by. Bourton is popular with the Cotswolds' traveller, drawn to the genteel buzz of village life. There's lots going on, and right in its midst stands The Dial House, built in 1698 by architect Andrew Paxford – his and his wife's initials are carved on the front. Originally The Vinehouse, it was renamed after the large sundial above the front door. Inside, Jane and Adrian have created an oasis of old world charm, with Jacobean-style furniture, wonderful four-posters, old portrait paintings and impressive stone fireplaces lit in winter. Elegant, relaxed and friendly, it epitomises the traditional country-house hotel. The best bedrooms are in the main house, with lovely antiques, a refreshing lack of chintz, Penhaligon smellies and views of the village and river through leaded window panes. Rooms in an extension look out onto the walled garden, a lovely spot to keep the world at arm's length for a while, and the classic English menu takes a lot of beating.

rooms	13: 9 doubles, 1 suite, 3 four-posters.
price	£110–£120. Family suite from £171. Half-board (min. 2 nights) £75 p.p.
meals	Packed lunch available. Dinner £14.95; à la carte also available.
closed	Rarely.
directions	From Oxford, A40 to Northleach, right on A429 to Bourton. Hotel set back from High St. opp. main bridge in village.

	Jane & Adrian Campbell-Howard
tel	01451 822244
fax	01451 810126
e-mail	info@dialhousehotel.com
web	www.dialhousehotel.com

Hotel

map 3   entry 86

Wesley House

High Street, Winchcombe, Gloucestershire GL54 5LJ

Wesley House, a 15th-century half-timbered townhouse, entices you off the street and seduces you once inside. Old timber-framed white walls, a terracotta-tiled floor, a big, open fire and a cosy bar were made for lazy afternoons flicking through the papers. Downstairs is open-plan; the split-level dining area stretches back in search of countryside – and finds it. French windows lead out to a small terrace where breakfast and lunch, or evening drinks, are enjoyed against a backdrop of the gentle Cotswold hills. Winchcombe was once the sixth-century capital of Mercia. Bedrooms, each with its own shower room, have more of those ancient whitewashed, timber-framed walls that need little decoration. They are warm, smart, well-lit and compact, with good wooden beds, crisp cotton sheets, new carpets and the occasional head-cracking bathroom door; one room has a lovely balcony. Find fresh milk and coffee in every room, and indulge in breakfast in bed, with home-baked bread, croissants, pains au chocolat… even kumquat, orange and whisky marmalade. *Children over seven and babies welcome.*

rooms	5 doubles.
price	£75–£85. Singles £55.
meals	Lunch from £6.95. Dinner, à la carte, £21.50–£31.
closed	Christmas.
directions	From Cheltenham, B4632 to Winchcombe. Restaurant on right. Leave luggage, parking nearby.

Matthew Brown

tel	01242 602366
fax	01242 609046
e-mail	reservations@wesleyhouse.co.uk
web	www.wesleyhouse.co.uk

Restaurant with Rooms

The White Hart Inn & Restaurant

High Street, Winchcombe, Gloucestershire GL54 5LJ

The Swedes have arrived in Gloucestershire but there's nothing to fear – they come in peace, bearing a *smörgåsbord* of vibrant chic and warm hospitality. It's a far cry from the sixth century when this Cotswold village was the Saxon capital of Mercia; any mention of Scandinavians on the loose would have resulted in a call to arms! Not anymore. Locals have welcomed their arrival at this 16th-century coaching inn. Thanks to the discerning interior design of Nicole's mother Ursula, it feels more like a stylish rural hotel in Sweden: scrubbed wooden floors, sisal matting, big windows and Gustavian style blue-grey furniture in the restaurant. Bedrooms smell inviting; the best have views of the high street. One named after Swedish painter Carl Larsson has a stunning four-poster in the middle of the room, just as the artist did, with green checked fabric and fresh flowers. Nicole, who's half Swedish, employs solely Swedish staff on six-month stints to improve their English; all take it in turns to serve, clean, or cook authentic food: *sil*, marinated herring, is superb. They've even introduced Santa Lucia, a winter festival of song and candles.

rooms	8: 2 doubles, 4 twins/doubles, 2 four-posters.
price	£65–£125. Half-board (min. 2 nights) £75 p.p. Singles £55–£115.
meals	Lunch about £10. Dinner, à la carte, about £25.
closed	Christmas Day.
directions	From Cheltenham, B4632 to Winchcombe. Inn on right.

	Nicole Burr
tel	01242 602359
fax	01242 602703
e-mail	enquiries@the-white-hart-inn.com
web	www.the-white-hart-inn.com

Restaurant with Rooms

map 3   entry 88

The Malt House

Broad Campden, Chipping Campden, Gloucestershire GL55 6UU

You could imagine that one of the Famous Five lived in this substantial English house in the middle of an untouched Cotswold village, with climbing roses, magnolia trees and deckchairs on the lawn. A place that so echoes to the past, you almost expect the vicar to call for tea, or a post boy to bring a telegram to say the London train is running late. Still much in evidence is that very English ritual of sipping gin in a lovely setting: the manicured garden has its own 'gin and tonic' bench! A thatched summer house for afternoon tea, a walled kitchen garden that grows figs and a small brook complete the idyllic scene. The house itself has a mellow grandeur: polished wooden floors, ancient oak panelling, walls of shimmering gold and a 17th-century fireplace beneath a mantelpiece that rises to within a foot of the ceiling. Bedrooms vary, with mullioned windows, sloping floors, gilt mirrors, and muralled bathrooms; some have painted floorboards. Judi is very English, too. Friendly staff and good food, locally sourced and cooked by an American chef, will keep you smiling for days.

rooms	7: 1 four-poster, 1 double, 4 twins/doubles, 1 suite.
price	£118.50-£139.50. Singles from £91. Suite from £139.
meals	Dinner, à la carte, £34.50.
closed	Christmas.
directions	From Oxford, A44, through Moreton-in-Marsh; left B4081 north to Chipping Campden. Entering village, 1st right, for Broad Campden. Hotel 1 mile on left.

	Judi Wilkes
tel	01386 840295
fax	01386 841334
e-mail	info@the-malt-house.freeserve.co.uk

Hotel

The Churchill Arms

Paxford, Chipping Campden, Gloucestershire GL55 6XH

Above all, The Churchill is fun, an engaging mixture of the old and new that creates a relaxed, informal atmosphere. Walk into the bar, with stone floors and wooden tables, and find a hub of happy chatter. Leo and Sonya are proud of their creation – one guest described it as "Fulham in the country", and the locals seem to like it that way. Many were reluctantly starting to leave when our inspector arrived just after lunch. Bedrooms right above the bar are equally fun and stylish; two are small but good use of space won't leave you feeling hemmed in. "Frills and drapes are not us," says Sonya. Beams, old radiators and uneven floors obviously are. Add good fabrics, pastel colours and country views from the heart of this picture-perfect village and this is a place worth getting away for. The food is quite superb, too. One usually cantankerous Sunday critic conceded that the sticky toffee pudding was perfect. Such perfection might explain the prayer stool in one corner.

rooms	4 doubles.
price	£70. Singles £40.
meals	Lunch from £10.50. Dinner from £14.50.
closed	Rarely.
directions	From Moreton-in-Marsh, A44 for Worcester & Evesham. Through Bourton-on-the-Hill, right at end to Paxford. Through Blockley, over railway & tiny bridge into Paxford. In village on right.

Leo Brooke-Little & Sonya Kidney

tel	01386 594000
fax	01386 594005
e-mail	info@thechurchillarms.com
web	www.thechurchillarms.com

Inn

map 3   entry 90

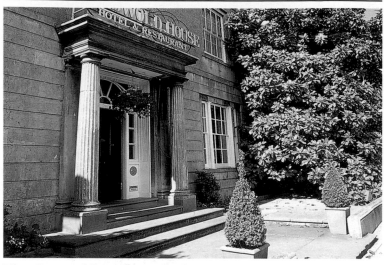

The Cotswold House Hotel

The Square, Chipping Campden, Gloucestershire GL55 6AN

Few brochures quite capture the spirit of a place, often losing their way in hackneyed cliché – Cotswold House's is one exception. It pulls out like a concertina, revealing a tantalising glimpse of what to expect behind the impressive colonnaded entrance of this 19th-century wool merchant's house. Ian and Christa's philosophy was to create a hotel where the bedrooms felt better than your own room at home – they've succeeded. National Trust colours, cashmere underblankets and Frette linen sheets on luxurious beds, French colognes and lotions in stylish bathrooms, fresh coffee percolators, Bang & Olufsen film and stereo systems, remote controls to fine-tune your viewing and listening pleasure... even a Pillow Menu. Downstairs, relax in red and terracotta drawing rooms, with antiques, fresh flowers and paintings, or stroll in two acres of walled garden, with meandering paths and secluded spots; the vegetable garden supports a well-regarded menu in season. Wine, music and celebrity events are held through the year; the village has chichi shops to browse – and you can park free. Go on, spoil yourself.

rooms	20: 2 doubles, 16 twins/doubles, 2 four-posters.
price	£175–£395.
meals	Brasserie meals from £9. Dinner £40.
closed	Rarely.
directions	From Oxford, A44 north for Evesham. 5 miles after Moreton-in-Marsh, right on B4081 to Chipping Campden. Hotel in square by town hall.

Ian & Christa Taylor

tel	01386 840330
fax	01386 840310
e-mail	reception@cotswoldhouse.com
web	www.cotswoldhouse.com

Hotel

Hotel du Vin & Bistro

Southgate Street, Winchester, Hampshire SO23 9EF

Flair, high standards and exquisite attention to detail in an easy atmosphere… and all very French. There's a bistro with old wooden floors and tables, big windows that draw in light, a garden for *al fresco* dining in summer and a mirrored champagne bar in gold and blue, with *bergère* sofas to loll on like kings and queens for the night. Elsewhere, sweeping expanses of cream walls covered in prints and oils and handsome furniture. Bedrooms use strikingly simple colours, fine fabrics and Egyptian linen, beds are big and tempting and bathrooms have deep baths and 'smellies' specially made on a Scottish isle. Rooms are split between the bustling main house and the quieter Garden rooms; light sleepers should go for the latter. Food and wine are the hotel's raison d'être and staff are excellent – artisans who speak with passion about their work. Go completely *français* and play boules in the garden, or explore England's ancient capital. Winchester Castle is home to 'The Round Table of King Arthur'; Merlin crowned the 15 year old Arthur at nearby Silchester, or so it's claimed.

rooms	23: 22 doubles, 1 suite.
price	From £105. Suites £185.
meals	Breakfast £9.50-£13.50. Lunch & dinner £25-£30.
closed	Rarely.
directions	M3, junc. 11, signed Winchester South. At 1st r'bout, follow signs to St Cross & Winchester. Hotel on left after 2 miles.

Mark Huntley

tel	01962 841414
fax	01962 842458
e-mail	info@winchester.hotelduvin.com
web	www.hotelduvin.com

Hotel

map 3   entry 92

Master Builder's House Hotel

Bucklers Hard, Beaulieu, Hampshire SO42 7XB

By the River Beaulieu in a timeless end-of-the-road idyll, Master Builder's has the feel of a well-heeled yacht club. The hotel shares this blissful spot with two rows of cottages still lived in by workers of the nearby Montague Estate. Yachts and sailing boats glide past on their way to the Solent following the same route taken by Nelson's fleet two centuries before. It was here that the great shipwright Henry Adams built many of the warships which would go on to fight in the Battle of Trafalgar; ancient slipways that launched the ships still survive at the river's edge. Bedrooms in a wing named after Adams are uniformly done to a high standard, each with a king-size bed. More expensive bedrooms in the main part of the hotel have darker colour schemes and superb river views. There's a traditional pub, full of sailors in summer, a hall that seems to tumble down to the water, a restaurant with a view, and a terrace for *al fresco* meals. Beaulieu is a one-hour walk upstream past marshland teeming with birdlife and the New Forest stretches to the west. Also charter a boat to their other hotel on the Isle of Wight.

rooms	25 twins/doubles.
price	£170–£225. Singles £125.
meals	Bar lunch from £4.95. Lunch from £16.95. Dinner from £29.50.
closed	Rarely.
directions	From Lyndhurst, B3056 south past Beaulieu turn-off, then 1st left, signed Bucklers Hard. Hotel signed left after 1 mile.

Samanatha Brinkman

tel	01590 616253
fax	01590 616297
e-mail	res@themasterbuilders.co.uk
web	www.themasterbuilders.co.uk

Hotel

Westover Hall

Park Lane, Lymington, Hampshire SO41 0PT

A hotel, but family-run and without the slightest hint of stuffiness. It was built for the German industrialist Siemens in 1897 to be the most luxurious house on the south coast; a fortune was lavished on wood alone. It is still vibrant with gleaming oak and exquisite stained glass and it's hard to stifle a gasp when you enter the hall – it's a controlled explosion of wood. The Mechems are generous and open-minded, keen that people should come to unwind and treat the place as home. Private parties can take over completely and throw the rule book towards the window. Bedrooms are exemplary: some have sea views, all are furnished with a mix of the old and the contemporary; bathrooms are spotless. The whole place indulges you. Romantics can take to the bar or restaurant and gaze out to sea. The more active can dive outside and walk up the beach to Hurst Castle. Alternatively, sink into a sofa on the sunny balcony for great views of the Needles, or visit their nearby mediterranean beach hut.

rooms	12: 8 doubles, 2 twins, 1 family, 1 single.
price	£145–£200. Half-board £102.50–£135 p.p.
meals	Light lunch £10–£15. Dinner £32.50.
closed	Rarely.
directions	From Lymington, B3058 to Milford-on-Sea. On through village. House on left up hill.

Nicola & Stewart Mechem

tel	01590 643044
fax	01590 644490
e-mail	info@westoverhallhotel.com
web	www.westoverhallhotel.com

Hotel

map 3　entry 94

Glewstone Court Country House Hotel & Restaurant

Glewstone, Ross-on-Wye, Herefordshire HR9 6AW

Glewstone is grand, yet relaxed enough to have no rule book to throw out the window. Bill does front of house, Christine cooks – brilliantly; they are charming and fun. There's faded glamour and an easy conviviality in the drawing room bar, full of squashy sofas, interesting things and an open log fire in front of which resident dogs lounge. The centre of the house is early Georgian, with a stunning stair that spirals up to a galleried landing. Big bedrooms have patchwork quilts, period pieces, Christine's pretty stencil work, *more* sofas and chairs. The Rose Room is wonderful and the Victoria Room enormous. All look over fruit orchards to the Wye Valley and the Forest of Dean beyond. Dominating the croquet lawn at the front is the largest cedar of Lebanon in the west; there's a modest helipad, too. Dine in the lovely restaurant, the bistro at the back, or outside in good weather. The relaxed dress code welcomes all styles, except baseball caps and mobile phones. Some food is organic – the Hereford beef is exceptional – and much comes straight from Christine's potager. Heaven for those in search of the small and friendly.

rooms	8: 5 doubles, 1 single, 2 suites.
price	£95–£110. Singles £47–£63.
meals	Lunch & dinner in bistro about £19. Dinner in restaurant £27. Sunday lunch £16.
closed	25–27 December.
directions	From Ross-on-Wye, A40 towards Monmouth, then right 1 mile south of Wilton r'bout, for Glewstone. Hotel on left after 0.5 miles.

	Christine & Bill Reeve-Tucker
tel	01989 770367
fax	01989 770282
e-mail	glewstone@aol.com

Hotel

The Wee Stable

Wall of Thel, Bit Gallop, Herefordshire HO R5E

Herefordshire is famous for its gloriously lovely buildings. This is not one of them. However, it has its charms – in a scruffy sort of way. We have included it for its authenticity, always a useful excuse when one wonders if one has done the right thing. The steeply sloping roof has the original tiles, the door has its original paint – well, some of it – and the brickwork was the inspiration of Irish navvies. The annexe is useful if there are two of you, though we regret the obscure lack of windows. Is this the new minimalism? Indeed, there is little to say about the interior, other than that it is cosy, dark and in need of a visit from Hercules. It is a place to stay in only if the rest of the country is full, but the 'specialness' might be seen to lie with the one inhabitant, here seen grazing in the nearby field. He's a handsome little fellow, used to making do with the most meagre of pasture and will therefore make few, if any, demands. The door is always half open, a welcoming sign.

rooms	1 + annexe.
price	Bring a bale.
meals	Permanently available.
closed	See open door for details.
directions	Follow your nose.

Mr C Heval

tel	+99 (-0)467128 986756
e-mail	equine@clippetyclop.com
web	www.neeciigh.net

Other place

map   entry 96

Kilverts Hotel

The Bullring, Hay-on-Wye, Herefordshire HR3 5AG

Those wanting to stay in the thick of this literary outpost bang on the Welsh border could do no better than check into Kilverts. The hotel sits in narrow streets teeming with bookshops, art galleries and antique shops… they wind round the town's crumbling castle which peers over all. Hay is the second-hand bookshop capital of Britain, and holds an internationally famous literary festival every May. If you've been searching for that elusive tome, this is the place to come. The front terrace of the hotel is also the place to people-watch with a drink or a meal; the bar is a cosy retreat if the weather drives you inside – stone floor, wooden tables, local ales and home-made pizzas. The more formal restaurant has a mural on the wall of a ballroom in chaos! The menu is the same wherever you eat and has daily specials. There's also the quieter garden out back – the biggest undeveloped plot in the town. Upstairs, go for one of two lovely beamed attic rooms at the top; one has an 18th-century oak tester. The rest have few surprises but all are comfortable. Colin is a likeable chap, as is Tired Ted the hotel cat. And the countryside seduces.

rooms	11: 6 doubles, 3 twins/doubles, 2 twins.
price	£70–£90. Singles £50.
meals	Bar meals from £3.25. Lunch & dinner, à la carte, about £19.
closed	Christmas Day.
directions	On entering Hay pass Nat West Bank, take next right turn & continue downhill for 40 yds. Kilverts on right. Car park at rear.

	Colin Thomson
tel	01497 821042
fax	01497 821580
e-mail	info@kilverts.co.uk
web	www.kilverts.co.uk

Hotel

Penrhos Hotel

Kington, Herefordshire HR5 3LH

The great medieval cruck hall, a stone-flagged masterpiece, seems just the right place to eat organic food of such high quality. Superb home-baked bread, local cheeses and vegetables grown in the most natural possible way – anything else would seem a travesty among the rough-hewn slabs of oak, candlelight and tapestries. Daphne's interest in nutrition and her resulting passion for organic food are the backdrop to the meals. They are unpretentious and delicious, and Daphne becomes animated when discussing them, as Martin does when chatting about environmental issues. There is a snug, fire-blazing sitting room from the 14th century and a deep sense of authenticity. The bedrooms are comfortable and modern, with views across fields. The star of Penrhos, perhaps, is the serenely lovely setting: on one side of the grassy courtyard, the magnificent house; along another, the bedrooms; and along another, the wooden-planked cow-byre. In the middle is a puddleduck pond, where – in summer – swallows swoop and fish glide, both in pursuit of the insects that belong to balmy evenings.

rooms	15: 9 doubles, 4 twins, 2 four-posters.
price	£95–£120. Singles from £65.
meals	Dinner, 4 courses, £31.50.
closed	January.
directions	From Leominster, A44 for Kington. Hotel 1 mile before Kington on left, 200 yds up drive, signed.

Martin Griffiths & Daphne Lambert

tel	01544 230720
fax	01544 230754
e-mail	martin@penrhos.co.uk
web	www.penrhos.co.uk

Hotel

map 2   entry 98

The George Hotel

Quay Street, Yarmouth, Isle of Wight PO41 0PE

The position is fabulous, with the old castle on one side, the sea at the end of a sunny garden, and the centre of Yarmouth, the island's oldest town, just beyond the front door – handy if you're a corrupt governor intent on sacking ships that pass. Admiral Sir Robert Holmes moved here for that very reason in 1668, demolishing a bit of the castle to improve his view. The house has been rebuilt since Sir Robert's day but a grand feel still lingers: the entrance is large, light and stone-flagged; a drawing room next door panelled, with kilim-covered sofas. Six newly refurbished bedrooms were done in Colefax and Jane Churchill, while the bigger, more expensive bedrooms are also beautifully panelled; one has a huge four-poster, and two have timber balconies with views out to sea. Meals can be taken outside in the garden bar; or else eat in the buzzy, cheerful, yellow-and-wood brasserie, or the sumptuous, burgundy dining room. Dig even deeper into your pocket and charter a private boat to take you to lunch at their other hotel on the mainland.

rooms	17: 15 twins/doubles, 2 singles.
price	£175–£223. Singles from £125.
meals	Lunch & dinner in brasserie from £25. Dinner in restaurant, 4 courses, £45. Restaurant closed Sundays & Mondays.
closed	Rarely.
directions	Lymington ferry to Yarmouth, then follow signs to town centre.

	Jacki Everest
tel	01983 760331
fax	01983 760425
e-mail	res@thegeorge.co.uk
web	www.thegeorge.co.uk

Hotel

Priory Bay Hotel

Priory Drive, Nettlestone, Isle of Wight PO34 5BU

Medieval monks thought Priory Bay special, so did Tudor farmers and Georgian gentry; all helped to mould this tranquil landscape. Parkland rolls down from the main house and tithe barns to a ridge of trees. The land then drops down to a long, clean sandy beach and a shallow sea; it's as mediterranean as Britain gets. Fishermen land their catch here for the freshest grilled seafood. Huge rooms in the house mix classical French and contemporary English styles. The sun-filled drawing room has tall windows – exquisite rococo-style chairs obligingly face out to sea, and afternoon cream teas by the winter log fire are a treat. The dining room has a mural of the bay on the wall, and elaborate flower decorations at each table. Bedrooms in the main house are luxurious; some have a fresh and modern feel, others oak panelling, maybe a crow's nest balcony and telescope. Bedrooms in nearby outbuildings are less enticing but much cheaper. Andrew is a humorous host, and a supporter of the organic movement – they grow as much as they can. The grounds also support falcon and red squirrel, and the odd golfer.

rooms	26: 16 twins/doubles, 10 family.
price	£90–£270. Singles from £65. Half-board £65–£125 p.p.
meals	Lunch & dinner £25. Picnic hampers available.
closed	Rarely.
directions	From Ryde, B3330 south through Nettlestone, then left up road, signed to Nodes Holiday Camp. Entrance on left, signed.

Andrew Palmer

tel	01983 613146
fax	01983 616539
e-mail	reception@priorybay.co.uk
web	www.priorybay.co.uk

Hotel

map 3   entry 100

The Walpole Bay Hotel
Fifth Avenue, Cliftonville, Kent CT9 2JJ

Edwardian through and through… and as much a museum as a hotel, The Walpole is just as it always was, if not more so, splendidly faded and run with true devotion. It's been Jane and Peter's long ambition to preserve that period between the wars when genteel English folk flocked to the seaside in their best attire. Step back in time as you walk up marble steps to a beautiful wrought iron veranda with wicker chairs and old sedans. Inside, swirly carpets, flowery wallpaper, huge palms, working gas lights, Lincrusta panelling and old photos of guests posing outside with their charabancs; many of the museum's artefacts were donated. The ballroom with its sprung maple floor ballroom is retro heaven – the 20s and 40s nights are recommended! The 1927 gated Otis lift travels three floors to bedrooms with sea views; the balconies are next to be restored. Jane and Peter live in the butler's quarters and are as fun as the hotel is authentic – everything fits so well, you can't help falling for its nostalgic charm. There's lots to do as well. Visit the extraordinary shell grotto, or stroll along the Thanet coastline and find an 80-million-old fossil.

rooms	42: 34 doubles, 3 four-posters, 5 suites.
price	£60–£105. Singles £40–£75.
meals	Lunch from £3.50. Dinner, à la carte, from £15. Afternoon tea from £3.50.
closed	Rarely.
directions	From Margate, to Cliftonville along coast road with beach on left, past Winter Gardens and Lido. Fifth Ave. on left after Butlins Hotel. Hotel on right opp. indoor bowls centre.

Jane & Peter Bishop

tel	01843 221703
fax	01843 297399
e-mail	info@walpolebayhotel.co.uk
web	www.walpolebayhotel.co.uk

Hotel

The Ringlestone Inn

Ringlestone Hamlet, Nr Harrietsham, Kent ME17 1NX

Two old sisters once ran The Ringlestone; if they liked the look of you, they'd lock you in; if they didn't, they'd shoot at you. Michael and his daughter Michelle have let that tradition slip, preferring to run their 1635 ale house with a breezy conviviality. Glass tankards dangle above the bar, a woodburner throws out heat from the inglenook and old *Punch* cartoons hang on the original brick and flint walls between oak beams and stripped wooden floors. They stock 30 fruit wines and liqueurs as well as excellent local ales to sup in settles or on quirky, tiny, yet very comfy chairs. Across the lane in the farmhouse, bedrooms are perfect: oak furniture, sublime beds, crisp linen and big, luxurious bathrooms. The food is delicious – try a Ringlestone pie – and in the garden you can play *pétanque*. The inn has a children's licence, they sometimes host vintage car rallies, there's good walking and Leeds Castle is close. As for the breakfasts, they'll keep your strength up for a week.

rooms	3: 2 twins/doubles, 1 four-poster.
price	£99–£110. Singles £89.
meals	Breakfast £12–£15. Lunch from £5.50. Dinner £8–£25.
closed	Christmas Day.
directions	M20, junc. 8. Left after 0.25 miles at 2nd r'bout to Hollingbourne. Through Hollingbourne, up hill, then right at brown 'Knife and Fork' sign. Pub on right after 1.5 miles.

Michelle Stanley
tel	01622 859900
fax	01622 859966
e-mail	bookings@ringlestone.com
web	www.ringlestone.com

Inn

map 4 entry 102

Wallett's Court Country House Hotel

Westcliffe, St Margaret's at Cliffe, Dover, Kent CT15 6EW

Wallett's Court is *old*. Odo, half-brother of William the Conqueror, lived on the land in Norman times, then Jacobeans left their mark in 1627. When Chris and Lea renovated in 1975, the house gave up long-held secrets: tobacco pipes fell from a ceiling and 17th-century paintings were found in a blocked-off passageway, still hanging on the wall. Gavin, their son, now runs the business with the same passion and commitment – all feels warm and genuine... even the ghost is impeccably well-behaved. Old features catch the eye: ancient red-brick walls in the drawing room, an oak staircase with worn, shallow steps in the hall. Bedrooms in the main house are big, with heaps of character; those in the barn and cottages are good and quiet; above the spa complex – indoor pool, sauna, steam room and massage, aromatherapy and treatment suite – four excellent, contemporary rooms have been recently added. There's tennis, a terrace with views towards a distant sea and white cliffs within a mile for breezy walks, rolling mists and wheeling gulls. Great food, too; puddings to diet for. Popular with golfers.

rooms	16: 13 doubles, 2 twins, 1 family.
price	£90–£150. Singles £75–£110.
meals	Lunch £17.50. Dinner £27.50.
closed	Christmas.
directions	From Dover, A2/A20, then A258 towards Deal, then right, signed St Margaret's at Cliffe. Hotel 1 mile on right, signed.

	Chris, Lea & Gavin Oakley
tel	01304 852424
fax	01304 853430
e-mail	stay@wallettscourt.com
web	www.wallettscourt.com

Hotel

Romney Bay House Hotel

Coast Road, New Romney, Kent TN28 8QY

The library look-out upstairs has a telescope so you can spy on France on a clear day. Designed by Clough Williams-Ellis – creator of Portmeirion – for Hedda Hopper, the famous American columnist, this atmospheric dreamscape is as stunning as the photograph suggests. Inside, the whole place has a lingering 1920s house-party feel. There's an honesty bar full of colour, a drawing room with sofas to sink into, a conservatory for cream teas, a dining room where Clinton serves up great things. He and Lisa swapped jobs in top London hotels for the Good Life in Kent; they have impeccable pedigrees both, and know what works... whether you're here for a conference, a wedding or a great escape, you'll love their relaxed perfectionism. Curl up by the fire with a book or a game – there are plenty to borrow; go for a bracing beachside walk; whack a few balls on the tennis court, drive the fairways on the neighbouring green. Bedrooms are elegant and full of everything you'd hope for: pretty furniture, half-testers, sleigh beds, beautiful bathrooms and views – some to the links, some to the sea. A fabulously romantic place.

rooms	10: 6 doubles, 2 twins, 2 four-posters.
price	£85–£140. Singles £60–£95.
meals	Dinner, 4 courses, £35. Cream teas from £5.50.
closed	One week at Christmas.
directions	M20, junc. 10, A2070 south, then A259 east through New Romney. Right to Littlestone; left at sea & on for 1 mile.

Lisa Lovell

tel	01797 364747
fax	01797 367156

Hotel

map 4　entry 104

Cloth Hall Oast

Coursehorn Lane, Cranbrook, Kent TN17 3NR

Sweep up the rhododendron-lined drive to this immaculate Kentish oast house and barn. For 40 years Mrs Morgan lived in the 15th-century manor next door, where she tended both guests and garden; now she has turned her perfectionist's eye upon these five acres. There are well-groomed lawns, a carp-filled pond, pergola, summer house, pool and flowers – two beds of orange and yellow, four all-white. Light shimmers through swathes of glass in the dining room; off-white walls and pale beams that soar from floor to rafter. Mrs Morgan is a courteous hostess and an excellent cook; discuss in the morning what you'd like for dinner – duck with cherries, sole Veronique… later you dine at an antique table gleaming with crystal and candelabra. There are two bedrooms for guests: a four-poster on the ground floor, a triple on the first. Colours are soft, fabrics are frilled but nothing is busy or overdone; you are spoiled with good bathrooms and fine mattresses, crisp linen and flowered chintz. And there's a sitting room for guests, made snug by a log fire on winter nights.

rooms	2: 1 double, 1 triple.
price	£110–£120.
meals	Dinner, £20–£22.
closed	Rarely.
directions	1 mile SE of Cranbrook off Golford Road to Tenterden. Private road to right alongside the cemetery.

Mrs Katherine Morgan
| tel | 01580 712220 |
| fax | 01580 712220 |

Other Place

Hotel du Vin & Bistro

Crescent Road, Royal Tunbridge Wells, Kent TN1 2LY

A modern masterpiece in a Grade II-listed building, one of Tunbridge's landmarks. You enter immediately, and literally, into the spirit of the place – chatter spills from the bars and bistro into an ocean of wood below a faraway ceiling; the enormous hall is the hub of the place, and though magnificent bedrooms will tempt a linger, you'll be irresistibly drawn back to join the fun downstairs. The Burgundy bar buzzes with local life; open fires and facing sofas lead inevitably to 'later' dinners. The yellow-walled, picture-crammed bistro is distinctly French, with more wooden floors, while hops that tumble from the windows pay tribute to Kent. Afterwards, wander into the Havana room – relax, the bullet holes are fake for a game of billiards and a cigar, or take coffee in the Dom Perignon room where huge hand-painted copies of the Impressionists hang boldly. Bedrooms come in different sizes – the biggest is *huge* – and all have fantastic bathrooms with the finest lotions and potions; you'll sleep well on Egyptian linen.

rooms	36 doubles.
price	From £89.
meals	Breakfast £9.50–£13.50. Lunch & dinner £25–£30.
closed	Rarely.
directions	M25, A21 south for 13 miles, then A264, signed Tunbridge Wells, into town. Right at lights into Calverley Rd, then left at mini-r'bout, into Crescent Road.

	Matthew Callard
tel	01892 526455
fax	01892 512044
e-mail	info@tunbridgewells.hotelduvin.com
web	www.hotelduvin.com

Hotel

map 4   entry 106

The Inn at Whitewell

Whitewell, Clitheroe, Lancashire BB7 3AT

Richard was advised not to touch this inn with a bargepole, which must qualify as among the worst advice ever given, because you'll be hard-pressed to find anywhere better than this. The inn sits just above the River Hodder with views across parkland to rising fells in the distance. Merchants used to stop at this old deerkeeper's lodge and fill up with wine, food and song before heading north through notorious bandit country; superb hospitality is still assured but the most that will hold you up today is a stubborn sheep. Back at the inn, Richard, officially the Bowman of Bowland, wears an MCC tie and peers over half-moon glasses with a soft, slightly mischievous smile on his face, master of all this informal pleasure. The bedrooms are a triumph of style, warm and fun, some with fabulous Victorian showers, others with deep cast-iron baths and Benesson fabrics; all have great art and Bose music systems, and ones that look onto the river are bigger. The long restaurant and an outside terrace drink in the view, too. There are also seven miles of private fishing, even their own well-priced Vintner's. Book early – it's popular.

rooms	17: 11 twins/doubles, 5 four-posters, 1 suite.
price	£89–£114. Singles £66–£83. Suite £133.
meals	Bar meals from £5.50. Dinner, à la carte, from £23.50.
closed	Rarely.
directions	M6, junc. 31a, then B6243 east through Longridge, then follow signs to Whitewell for 9 miles.

	Richard Bowman
tel	01200 448222
fax	01200 448298

Restaurant with Rooms

The Austwick Traddock

Austwick, via Lancaster, Lancashire LA2 8BY

Friendly, unpretentious and full of traditional comfort, this family-run hotel is a terrific base for walkers – the Three Peaks of Whernside, Pen-y-Ghent and Ingleborough are at the door. The house is Georgian, with Victorian additions and its unusual name originates from the trading paddock – horse trading market – once held next door. Logs crackle in sitting room grates on winter days; deckchairs dot the garden in summer. Bruce and Jane are full of friendly enthusiasm and know how to look after you well. Bedrooms invite with soft carpets, antique dressing tables, quilted beds and Dales views; there are tins of shortbread, decanters of sherry, upmarket bathroom goodies and vases of flowers. Rooms vary in size, and those on the second floor have a cosy, attic feel. You eat well at the Traddock. Good British food combines the traditional and the contemporary and is generous – Aberdeen Angus fillet with Madeira sauce, lamb shank with puy lentils, Spotted Dick. Breakfast, too, is a hearty affair, with a big-choice buffet. There's a cheerful, William Morris feel to it all, and the village, with two clapper bridges, is a gem.

rooms	11: 6 doubles, 1 twin/double, 1 family, 3 singles.
price	£100–£110. Singles £45–£50.
meals	Dinner £18–£23.
closed	Rarely.
directions	0.75 miles off the A65, midway between Kirkby Londsdale & Skipton.

	Bruce & Jane Reynolds
tel	01524 251224
fax	01524 251796
e-mail	info@austwicktraddock.co.uk
web	www.austwicktraddock.co.uk

Hotel

map 6   entry 108

The Priory Hotel

149 Eastgate, Louth, Lincolnshire LN11 9AJ

Paul and Shelley are young, energetic and full of enthusiasm for their latest project. They fell in love with The Priory on sight, in spite of the amount of work that needed – and still needs – doing. Don't be put off by the rather ugly portico as you drive in – the parts they have reached so far are gorgeous: the hall has had its original tiles restored, colours are fun and the dining room is wooden floored with elegant sea-grass chairs. Louth still has proper shops, with a solid philosophy of keeping the supermarkets out and stocking Lincolnshire food – Paul shares that passion and takes enormous pride in his adopted county and what he can do with the best that is local and seasonal. All is fresh and tasty, bread is home-baked and soft fruits and herbs are home-grown. Bedrooms and bathrooms still have some fairly ugly hangovers from the 70s but they are good value and spotlessly clean. Come then for the food and the great view of the house from the garden which leads down to parkland, a little folly, a natural spring and a lake. Ask about Thomas Espin who built the house – Shelley is brimming with interesting anecdotes.

rooms	11: 3 doubles, 1 triple, 2 twins, 4 singles, 1 four-poster.
price	From £60.
meals	Dinner, 2 courses from £18.50, 3 courses from £22.50.
closed	Occasionally.
directions	From A16 or A157 follow Louth town centre signs. After 1st lights, left into Eastgate for 1 mile, over 2 r'bouts. Hotel on left after 100 yds.

Paul & Shelley Hugill

tel	01507 602930
fax	01507 609767
e-mail	info@theprioryhotel.com
web	www.theprioryhotel.com

Hotel

The Victoria

10 West Temple Sheen, London SW14 7RT

Mark, ex-Conran, now proprietor extraordinaire, meticulously scans his empire to make sure everything is just so. Which it is: not a teaspoon is out of place. This is the result of much hard work; three years ago Mark and Clare transformed the place into a cool, contemporary gastro-pub, with airy rooms, wooden floorboards, tongue and groove panelling and purple cushions on the sofas. It's got local tongues wagging, the good folk of Sheen keen to come and try the food. Their efforts will be well-rewarded, the menu appearing as apples did to Eve. Treat yourself to saffron and tomato quiche, Toulouse sausage and mash with onion gravy, and poached pear in red wine. After which you can retire to stylish bedrooms: white walls, Egyptian cotton, halogen lighting, beechwood beds, goosedown pillows, multi-coloured blankets and high-pressure showers. Great value for money, and with the Sheen Gate entrance to Richmond Park close by, you can walk off your indulgence lost to the world. A great little place.

rooms	7: 5 doubles, 2 twins/doubles.
price	£92.50. Singles £82.50.
meals	Lunch & dinner £7.50–£30.00.
closed	Rarely.
directions	Train: Waterloo to Mortlake. Buses: 33 & 337.

Mark & Clare Chester

tel	020 8876 4238
fax	020 8878 3464
e-mail	reservations@thevictoria.net
web	www.thevictoria.net

Restaurant with Rooms

map 4   entry 110

Twenty Nevern Square

Earl's Court, London SW5 9PD

A smart red-brick exterior with terracotta urns guarding the steps and an arched porch at the front door... This is a great little place, a fusion of classical and minimalist styles, with a clean, cool interior and beautiful things all around: Victorian birdcages, gilt mirrors, porcelain vases, a bowl full of dried rose petals. There's a real flow to the downstairs, all the way though to the conservatory-restaurant, with its stained glass, ceiling fans, hanging ferns, wicker chairs and glass tables. Bedrooms are equally stylish, with natural colours on the walls, cedar-wood blinds and rich fabrics throughout: silks, cottons and linens. Nothing here is synthetic, CD players and TVs have been hidden away in pretty wooden cabinets and there's no clutter. Rooms come in different shapes and sizes, each with something to elate: an Indonesian hand-carved wooden headboard, an Egyptian sleigh bed, a colonial four-poster, some sweeping blue and gold silk curtains. There are marble bathrooms, too. Great value for money, friendly staff, and close to the tube.

rooms	20: 13 doubles, 3 twins, 3 four-posters, 1 suite.
price	£110–£140. Four-posters from £150. Suite from £190. Singles £80–£110.
meals	Continental breakfast included, full English £5–£9. Dinner, 2 courses, from £10. Room service.
closed	Rarely.
directions	5-minute walk from Earl's Court tube station. Parking £17 a day, off-street.

	Sadik Saloojee
tel	020 7565 9555
fax	020 7565 9444
e-mail	hotel@twentynevernsquare.co.uk
web	www.twentynevernsquare.co.uk

Hotel

The Mayflower Hotel
26-28 Trebovir Road, London SW5 9NJ

Harry's Bar in New York was the inspiration for the interior of the juice bar on the ground floor: dark American walnut, creamy stone floors, original art (all by Vicky White) and colonial-style furniture in the wide and serene space that is two Edwardian London houses. Rooms are not huge but are beautifully designed, filled with unusual antiques from India and the Far East and gorgeous Andrew Martin fabrics. Mushroom and wine striped bedspreads, heavy curtains, Egyptian cotton sheets and Merino wool blankets soften the state-of-the-art technology; the use of space is clever and rooms are light. Bathrooms are hugely modern and sparkling, there is seating space in all but the very smallest rooms and the family rooms are super-funky with bunk beds. Don't imagine it is all design with no substance though – every room has something old and ethnic in it; maybe a finely carved headboard or a perfect vase, all chosen by the owner. The Mayflower is a great base for exploring London. The tube is a two-minute walk away and Earl's Court seems to have had a retail rejuvenation – good shops and restaurants abound.

rooms	47: 28 doubles, 11 twins, 3 singles, 5 family.
price	£89. Singles £59. Family room £120.
meals	Continental breakfast included; English breakfast £10.
closed	Rarely.
directions	Tube: Earl's Court. Bus: 74, 328, C1, C3. Parking: Tesco car park (5-minute walk), £25 for 24 hours.

Faisal Saloojee

tel	020 7370 3839
fax	020 7370 0994
e-mail	info@mayflower-group.co.uk

Hotel

map 4   entry 112

The Cranley Hotel
10 Bina Gardens, South Kensington, London SW5 0LA

In a charming, quiet London street of brightly painted Georgian houses, The Cranley has a neat front garden with wooden tables and chairs, clipped bay trees and wide steps to the front door. The hall leads straight in to a calm drawing room with deep Wedgewood-blue walls, original fireplaces, good antiques, coir carpets and the odd lively rug. Bedrooms are extremely comfortable: pale carpets, lilac walls, embroidered headboards over huge beds, plain cream curtains with bedspreads to match, pretty windows and cream-tiled, snazzy bathrooms. Robes and slippers, state-of-the-art technology, air-conditioning, prettily-laid tables for continental breakfast if you don't want it in bed and lovely Penhaligon smellies as a link back to the family that once owned the house. A cream tea with warm scones and clotted cream in the afternoon comes with the package, along with champagne and canapés at 7pm before you go off to an excellent local restaurant booked by the friendly staff. Hyde Park, Knightsbridge, the King's Road and Kensington High Street are all within an easy walk. A little gem.

rooms	39: 5 four-posters, 19 doubles, 9 twins, 4 singles, 2 suites.
price	From £147. Singles from £117.50.
meals	Plenty of restaurants close by.
closed	Rarely.
directions	4-minute walk from Gloucester Road tube station. Car parking 2 minutes away, £26 for 24 hours.

	Lina Stahl
tel	020 7373 0123
fax	020 7373 9497
e-mail	info@thecranley.com
web	www.thecranley.com

Hotel

L'Hotel

28 Basil Street, London SW3 1AS

L'Hotel is well-named – it has the feel of a small Parisian hotel, but chief among its many bounties is Isabel who, in her reign (long live the Queen), has proved it is not only what you do, but how you do it that matters. Her way is infectious; she is kind and open and nothing is too much trouble. The hotel's not bad either. Downstairs there's a great little restaurant/bar for breakfast, lunch and dinner – the social hub of the place – where the odd note of jazz rings out. You can have breakfast down here – excellent coffee in big bowls, pains au chocolat, croissants – or they'll happily deliver it to your room where you can laze about on vast beds that are covered in Egyptian cotton, with Nina Campbell fabric on the walls, little box trees on the mantlepiece, original art on the walls and an occasional open fireplace. Turn left on your way out and Harvey Nics is a hundred paces; turn right and Harrods is closer. If you want to eat somewhere fancy, try the Capital next door. It has a big reputation, is owned by the same family, and Isabel will book you in. A very friendly, very pretty place.

rooms	12: 11 twins/doubles, 1 suite.
price	£165–£175. Suite from £190.
meals	Continental breakfast included; full English from £6. Lunch & dinner £6–£15.
closed	Rarely.
directions	Tube: Knightsbridge. Bus: 14, 19, 22, 52, 74, 137, C1. Parking: £25 a day off-street.

	Isabel Murphy
tel	020 7589 6286
fax	020 7823 7826
e-mail	reservations@lhotel.co.uk
web	www.lhotel.co.uk

Hotel

map 4   entry 114

Miller's

111a Westbourne Grove, London W2 4UW

This is Miller's, as in the antique guides, and the collectables on show in the first-floor drawing room make it one of the great spots in London for undemanding hedonists. The week I visited, guests included Marianne Faithful, the top brass of a Milan fashion house, a professional gambler and an opera singer who was giving guests lessons. Breakfast is taken communally around a 1920s walnut table in a drawing room where, at ten o'clock on the morning I visited, a fire was smouldering in a huge carved-wood fireplace. You get an idea of what to expect when you step in off the street and pass an 18th-century sedan chair stuffed under the stairs, as if discarded, but in the drawing room, to give you a taster: a gilt-framed Sony Trinitron, a Tibetan deity (well, his statue), a 1750s old master's chair, a couple of hundred candles, flower pots embedded with oranges, a samurai sword, busts and sculptures, oils by the score, globes, chandeliers, plinths, rugs, sofas... Aladdin was a pauper if you compare his cave to this one. Bedrooms upstairs are equally embellished, just a little less cluttered. Affordable perfection.

rooms	8: 6 doubles, 2 suites.
price	£177–£260.
meals	Continental breakfast only & open bar.
closed	Rarely.
directions	Tube: Bayswater, Queensway, Notting Hill Gate. Bus: 7, 23, 28, 31, 70. Nearest car park, £25 for 24 hrs.

Martin Miller
tel	020 7243 1024
fax	020 7243 1064
e-mail	enquiries@millersuk.com
web	www.millersuk.com

Hotel

Portobello Gold

95-97 Portobello Road, Notting Hill, London W11 2QB

Portobello Gold is a cool little place smack in the middle of Ladbroke Grove, one of London's trendier districts for musicians. It's a bar, a restaurant, an internet café and a place to stay. Bedrooms are basic, with small shower rooms and good beds; the backpacker room is amazingly cheap. Ideal if the hippy in you is still active, or you're after a quirky place to stay in London – not for those who want luxury! Sit out on the pavement in wicker chairs and watch Portobello life amble by, or hole up at the bar for a beer with the locals, just as Bill Clinton did on his last visit to Britain as US president. Tiled floors, an open fire and monthly exhibitions of photography and modern art fill the walls. At the back, the conservatory restaurant with its retractable glass roof feels comfortably jungle – dine on Irish rock oysters, sashimi or Thai Moules to the sweet song of four canaries. Linda writes about wine, so expect to drink well. Michael is a cyber-visionary, hence the fold-away computers in the bar – internet use is free to guests. Ideal for the Notting Hill Carnival in August and Portobello antique market every Saturday.

rooms	6 + 1: 1 twin, 4 doubles, all with shower, 3 sharing wc; 1 twin, use of laundry room shower. Apart. for 4.
price	£35–£85. Singles £26–£75. Apartment £120–£180.
meals	Continental breakfast included; full English £5.50. Bar meals from £6. Dinner £20–£25.
closed	Rarely.
directions	Tube: Notting Hill. Bus: 12, 27, 28, 31, 52, 328. Parking meters outside (no charge Sat. pm/Sunday).

Michael Bell & Linda Johnson-Bell
tel   020 7460 4910
fax   020 7460 4911
e-mail   mike@portobellogold.com
web   www.portobellogold.com

Restaurant with Rooms

map 4   entry 116

La Gaffe

107-111 Heath Street, Hampstead, London NW3 6SS

Genuine Italian hospitality and great value mark out La Gaffe amid the wealth and Georgian splendour of leafy Hampstead. Bernardo and Androulla Stella opened the restaurant in 1962, adding rooms in 1976. Today it's run with the same ineffable charm by their sons, Lorenzo and Salvatore. The list of celebrities who've eaten here is too long to mention and many well-known actors are regulars. The hotel is made up of five former shepherd's cottages built in 1734, well before Hampstead became a desirable address. It's the highest point in London; views from the Heath just across the road are wonderful. The village is full of terraced cafés, boutiques and charming backstreets, including Church Row – said to be the most beautiful in London. Compact bedrooms have pretty floral fabrics; those at the back look onto a quiet square and two have steam baths. The restaurant has murals and faux-Roman walls which suit its classic style of Italian cooking – the olive oil, cheese and hams come from an uncle's farm in Abruzzo and the meatballs are terrific. A family-run gem voted number one best value London hotel in 2003.

rooms	18: 6 doubles, 4 twins, 4 singles, 4 four-posters.
price	£90-£125. Singles £65.
meals	Lunch & dinner, à la carte, 2 courses, £15-£18.
closed	Rarely.
directions	Tube: Hampstead. Bus: 46, 268. Parking: £10 a day on-street.

Lorenzo Stella

tel	020 7435 8965
fax	020 7794 7592
e-mail	la-gaffe@msn.com
web	www.lagaffe.co.uk

Restaurant with Rooms

Didsbury House

Didsbury Park, Didsbury Village, Manchester M20 5JT

Stylish Eleven Didsbury Park made a name for itself on the 'boutique hotel' circuit; now along comes a bigger, more stylish version in a converted Victorian villa. Didsbury House seduces the moment you enter: beautiful inlaid parquet floors and an original carved wooden staircase that carries the eye upwards to a magnificent stained-glass window. Planners and building regulations may have thwarted Eamonn and Sally's wilder ambitions at their first hotel down the street but here in this 1810 merchant's house their ideas run rampant: the luxurious attic suite has separate his and her roll-top baths as well as his and her seats in a gigantic shower cubicle; in every gorgeous room, baths fit two. Two split level 'duplex' rooms add further intrigue, a walkway spans a central atrium above your head; a sitting room, with ostrich-egg-shaped lights and pewter bar, leads outside through French windows; a floor below, the gym and spa. But best of all should be the planned roof-top terrace, with hot tub and jungle ferns and bamboo in big clay pots. Contemporary interior design and down-to-earth Mancunian humour. Superb.

rooms	26: 20 twins/doubles, 6 suites.
price	£99.50–£150. Suites £175–£250.
meals	Breakfast £9.50–£11.50.
closed	Rarely.
directions	From Manchester city centre, A34 south for 4 miles, then right on A5145 Wimslow Rd. Didsbury Park 4th on right; hotel on corner.

	Eamonn & Sally O'Loughlin
tel	0161 448 2200
fax	0161 448 2525
e-mail	enquiries@didsburyhouse.co.uk
web	www.didsburyhouse.co.uk

Hotel

map 6   entry 118

Eleven Didsbury Park

Didsbury Village, Manchester M20 5LH

Welcome to a warm 21st-century hotel experience, a townhouse that celebrates the urban minimalist style without paring down your comfort in the process. Unlike more brand-conscious contemporaries hell-bent on creating a new hotel order, Eleven Didsbury Park does design without the attitude. Eamonn has blended modern design with the sparing beauty of Georgian influences from his homeland – he hails from Co. Kerry – to create a hotel full of relaxed, uncluttered style, where simplicity delights the eye and old luxuries balance new. Lovely big bedrooms mix the best Egyptian linen and rich, earthy, handmade fabrics with mirror de-misters and hi-fi gizmos. In summer, the pretty garden with its terrace of tables and chairs feels like a country estate: peaceful and full of birdsong, and the surrounding buildings are masked by exuberant growth. Didsbury is a lush, leafy suburb, just a short bus ride from Manchester's mini-revival – exciting modern architecture, regenerated docklands and the Lowry Museum await. There's a free lift to local restaurants and bars, too.

rooms	14: 2 doubles, 10 twins/doubles, 2 suites.
price	£79.50–£125.50 Suites £165.50.
meals	Breakfast £8.50–£10.50. Room service until 10.30pm, £2.95–£8.95. Restaurants in Manchester.
closed	Rarely.
directions	From Manchester city centre, A34 south for 4 miles, then right on A5145 Wimslow. Didsbury Park 4th on right, hotel 200 yds on left.

Eamonn & Sally O'Loughlin

tel	0161 448 7711
fax	0161 448 8282
e-mail	enquiries@elevendidsburypark.com
web	www.elevendidsburypark.com

Hotel

The Lifeboat Inn

Ship Lane, Thornham, Norfolk PE36 6LT

They want you to be comfortable, relaxed and well-fed and there's every reason you should be. The Lifeboat Inn is ideal for some away-from-it-all, traditional, unpretentious good cheer — there's not enough of it about. It's been an ale house since the 16th century, they know how to serve a decent pint — Adnams, Greene King, Woodfordes — and use locally-sourced food whenever possible to good effect in both the beamy bar and the more formal, richly coloured restaurant. Try the bar for its staples — steaming cauldrons of Norfolk mussels and chips and real ale-battered fish — and the restaurant for dishes with a more sophisticated air. The bedrooms are pine furnished, not huge but entirely functional and well-equipped; most have mind-clearing views over the marsh to the sea. North-west Norfolk is a great place for being outdoors. Come when the wind blows and the hall fire flickers around damp dogs, while the odd stuffed animal looks on. Bask in the sheltered courtyard when it's sunny and let the children run. Staff are kind and unfussy, the atmosphere easy. But book ahead — people do know about this place.

rooms	14: 1 double, 13 twins/doubles.
price	£76–£108. Half-board (min. 2 nights) from £84 p.p. Singles £58–£74.
meals	Lunch £8.95. Dinner £25.
closed	Rarely.
directions	From King's Lynn, A149 via Hunstanton to Thornham. In village, left into Staithe Road; follow road round to right. Inn on right.

	Angela Coker
tel	01485 512236
fax	01485 512323
e-mail	reception@lifeboatinn.co.uk
web	www.lifeboatinn.co.uk

Inn

map 8   entry 120

The Hoste Arms

The Green, Burnham Market, Norfolk PE31 8HD

The Burnhams comprise seven villages on the north Norfolk coast and Burnham Market is the loveliest. Paul Whittome reckons he and the Hoste Arms were made for each other. In its 300-year history the place has been a court house, a livestock market, an art gallery and a brothel. Paul has been a potato merchant, a politician and a bouncer in a Chinese shanty pub in Australia; he has not shrunk since then, merely transformed himself from ejector to welcomer. Brilliantly, too, for The Hoste has won almost every prize going – *The Times* voted it their second favourite hotel in England, their 27th in the world, and gave it a 'Golden Pillow' award. The place has a genius of its own – brave and successful mixtures of bold colour, chairs to sink deep into, panelled walls, its own art gallery – and food to be eaten in rapture, anywhere and anytime. Every bedroom is different: a tartan four-poster here, a swagged half-tester there, a leather TV console in the brand-new, state-of-the-art Zulu wing. There's no one to rush you, breakfast lasts as long as you like and the bar pulls in an intriguing array of regulars – spot the stars.

rooms	36: 12 doubles/twins, 5 singles, 1 family, 6 suites, 4 four-posters. Zulu wing: 5 doubles, 3 suites.
price	£102–£156. Singles £74–£156. Suites £128–£156.
meals	Lunch & dinner £3.50–£25.
closed	Rarely.
directions	From King's Lynn, A149 north, then A148. After 2 miles, left onto B1153. At Great Bircham, branch right onto B1155 to Burnham Market via Stanhoe. Inn in village.

Paul & Jeanne Whittome

tel	01328 738777
fax	01328 730103
e-mail	reception@hostearms.co.uk
web	www.hostearms.co.uk

Inn

Saracens Head

Wolterton, Erpingham, Norfolk NR11 7LZ

Food, real ale, good wines, a delightful sheltered courtyard and walled garden, Norfolk's bleakly lovely coast – this is why people come here. But the food is the deepest seduction. Robert and his team cook up "some of Norfolk's most delicious wild and tame treats". Typical starters are Morston mussels with cider and cream, or fricassée of wild mushrooms. Expect pigeon, Cromer crab, venison. Then Robert works his own magic on old favourites such as bread and butter pudding... vegetarians are pampered too; try baked avocado with sweet pear and mozzarella. The bar is as convivial as a bar could be, a welcome antidote to garish pub bars with their fruit machines – Robert will have none of them. There's a parlour room where residents can sit, with a big open-brick fireplace, deep red walls, colourful plastic tablecloths, candles in old wine bottles, a black leather banquette along two walls. Bedrooms are plain, modest and comfortable with pine beds, quilted bedspreads and courtyard views. The whole mood is of quirky, committed individuality – slightly arty, slightly unpredictable and in the middle of Norfolk's nowhere.

rooms	4: 3 doubles, 1 twin.
price	£70. Singles £45.
meals	Bar meals from £3.95. Dinner about £17.
closed	Christmas Day.
directions	From Norwich, A140 past Aylsham, then left, for Erpingham. Through village to Calthorpe. Over x-roads. On right after about 0.5 miles.

Robert Dawson-Smith

tel	01263 768909
fax	01263 768993

Restaurant with Rooms

map 8 entry 122

Beechwood Hotel

Cromer Road, North Walsham, Norfolk NR28 0HD

There's an old-fashioned perfectionism about the Beechwood – it is impeccable, professional and immensely well-mannered. Agatha Christie was a frequent guest when it was a private house and it is not difficult even now to imagine quiet conspiratorial conversations over dinner. The atmosphere is that of a traditional country-house hotel but with imaginative flourishes: bold black and white tiling in one bathroom, with a splendid, old roll-top bath painted black on the outside – the cistern is still, quite rightly, high on the wall, the down-pipe gleaming. Curtains in the dining room are richly pelmeted, the separate tables elegant and attractive. The food is British with a strong mediterranean influence: *fettucine* with a wild mushroom, stilton and tarragon sauce, roast Scottish salmon on a saffron risotto, haddock, prawn and chive cakes… all sound delicious. The bread is home-made and organic ingredients are used whenever possible. In the bedrooms, curtains match the bedspreads; in the smart sitting room, old leather sofas and armchairs demand to be wallowed in. Above all, there is space – and peace.

rooms	11: 8 doubles, 1 twin, 2 four-posters.
price	£90-£160. Half-board £60 p.p. Singles £68.
meals	Lunch £18. Dinner £30.
closed	Christmas.
directions	From Norwich, B1150 to North Walsham. Under railway bridge, then left at next traffic lights. Hotel 150 yds on left.

Don Birch & Lindsay Spalding

tel	01692 403231
fax	01692 407284
e-mail	enquiries@beechwood-hotel.co.uk
web	www.beechwood-hotel.co.uk

Hotel

The Norfolk Mead Hotel

Coltishall, Norwich, Norfolk NR12 7DN

You can paddle your canoe from the bottom of the garden all the way along the River Bure to the Broads, though it involves a few miles of exertion. A better idea is to stay closer to home and potter lazily about in one of the hotel's rowing boats. Norfolk Mead is in a great position, with 12 acres of lawns, mature trees, a walled garden and a swimming pool... there's even a one-acre fishing lake. Come for the owners, the food and the easy-going luxury of a lovely old Georgian country house – the sort you dream of. The bedrooms, all different, are super-comfortable, with the best quality linen and every tiny, frivolous need anticipated. The food is just as good, all fresh and local, maybe samphire from Blakeney, or home-made ice cream. A fine entrance hall with high-backed sofas and an open fire unwind you immediately. Big, gracious, beautifully proportioned, yet perfectly relaxing. And if that's not enough, Jill and Don's daughter, Nicky, will provide a massage or manicure. Expect to be pampered.

rooms	12: 7 doubles, 3 twins, 2 suites.
price	£85-£150. Half-board from £65 p.p. Singles £70-£95.
meals	Dinner £28.50. Sunday lunch £16.
closed	Rarely.
directions	From Norwich, B1150 north to Coltishall, over humpback bridge, then 1st right before church down drive, signed.

Jill & Don Fleming

tel	01603 737531
fax	01603 737521
e-mail	info@norfolkmead.co.uk
web	www.norfolkmead.co.uk

Hotel

map 8   entry 124

The Café at Brovey Lair

Carbrooke Road, Ovington, Thetford, Norfolk IP25 6SD

A large 1970s house in a south Norfolk village, Brovey Lair is creating quite a stir among foodies. An open-plan hall with a steel and glass staircase, striking modern art and a spherical sculpture fountain leads into an immaculate state-of-the-art stainless steel kitchen where Michael will give you a sparkly drink while you watch Tina cook 'live'. There's no menu and no choice, your likes and dislikes are carefully researched over the telephone: everything is freshly prepared. Most likely it will be fish or seafood – a popular starter is thinly sliced yellow fin tuna marinated with a sashimi sauce – fusing flavours and spices collected from Tina's travels around the world as a food critic. The wine list is informed and mainly French. All is served in the airy conservatory: colours are aqua-marines and lilacs, elegant tables overlook the garden and swimming pool. Large contemporary bedrooms come with cream wool carpets, acres of bed, pale beech wood, designer tub chairs and bathrooms with bamboo floors and cool turquoise walls. Breakfast is American 'brunch' style and you can enjoy it by the pool and as late as you like.

rooms	2 doubles.
price	£110.
meals	Dinner, 4 courses, £37.50.
closed	Rarely.
directions	From Watton, through Ovington past 40mph signs, 500 m on right.

Mr Michael Pemberton

tel	01953 882706
fax	01953 885365
e-mail	mike.pemberton@broveylair.co.uk
web	www.broveylair.co.uk

Other place

`entry 125   map 8`

Strattons

4 Ash Close, Swaffham, Norfolk PE37 7NH

It's not just the feel of rural France, nor the spectacular interiors that make Strattons so special – it is also one of the most eco-friendly hotels in Britain. "Everything is home-made, recycled, bought locally, restored, renewed and rethought," says Vanessa. Enter a peaceful courtyard where Silky bantams strut – a minute's stroll from the market square – to charmingly informal gardens dotted with urns. Les and Vanessa met at art school, and have covered every square inch of this Queen Anne villa with mosaics, murals, marble busts, plump pillows, piles of books, bunches of dried roses, rugs on wooden floors – it feels like a wildly original French château. Bedrooms are exquisite: a carved four-poster, a tented bathroom, Indian brocade, stained glass, trompe l'œil panelling and sofas by a log fire; two suites added in 2002 are heaven. Dine in the pure and simple lower-ground floor bistro, with white-painted brickwork, crisp linen, voile curtains and gilt-framed paintings. Vanessa's fresh and seasonal cooking style has won many awards. E M Forster dreamed of a "holy trinity of soil, soul and society" – they've got it pretty close here.

rooms	8: 3 doubles, 1 twin, 1 four-poster, 3 suites.
price	£100–£130. Singles from £75. Suites £180.
meals	Dinner, 4 courses, £35.
closed	Christmas.
directions	Ash Close runs off north end of market place between W H Brown estate agents & fish and chip restaurant.

	Vanessa & Les Scott
tel	01760 723845
fax	01760 720458
e-mail	strattonshotel@btinternet.com
web	www.strattonshotel.com

Hotel

map 8   entry 126

The Falcon Hotel

Castle Ashby, Nr Northampton, Northamptonshire NN7 1LF

Follow the example of Purdy, The Falcon's gorgeous black labrador, and live life at a contented plod when you stay here. Stone-built and originally a farmhouse dating back to 1594, the inn lies opposite the castle after which this pretty village is named. The Easticks came here after Michael decided he needed another change – he has already been a farmer and a racing driver, among other things. These days, he is quite happy being a hotelier, making sure the cellar bar is full of beer, the oils hang symmetrically, the fire crackles with huge logs and guests get well fed in the pretty stone-walled restaurant; much of the produce comes from their vegetable garden. In summer, eat outside and watch cows saunter up to the dairy as sheep graze beyond; the garden is full of flowers. Bedrooms are split between the inn and a cottage next-door-but-one – the octogenarian ex-postmistress lives in between. All received a makeover recently, with country cottage fabrics, bright yellows and blues, bathrobes, fresh flowers and gentle village views. Wander round the spectacular castle grounds or mooch in nearby craft shops... no need to hurry.

rooms	16: 13 twins/doubles, 3 singles.
price	£89.50–£129.50. Half-board from £69.50 p.p. Singles £69.50–£95.
meals	Lunch from £14.95. Dinner from £19.95 or à la carte.
closed	Rarely.
directions	From Northampton, A428 towards Bedford for about 6 miles, then left, for Castle Ashby. Inn in village.

Michael & Jennifer Eastick

tel	01604 696200
fax	01604 696673
e-mail	falcon.castleashby@oldenglishinns.co.uk

Inn

The Pheasant Inn

Stannersburn, Kielder Water, Northumberland NE48 1DD

A really super little inn, the kind you hope to chance upon: not grand, not scruffy, just right. The Kershaws run it with huge passion and an instinctive understanding of its traditions. The stone walls hold 100-year-old photos of the local community; from colliery to smithy, a vital record of their past heritage – special indeed. The bars are wonderful: brass beer taps glow, anything wooden – ceiling, beams, tables – has been polished to perfection and the clock above the fire keeps perfect time. The attention to detail is staggering. Robin and Irene cook with relish, again nothing fancy, but more than enough to keep a smile on your face – game pies, salmon and local lamb as well as wonderful Northumbrian cheeses. Bedrooms next door in the old hay barn are as you'd expect: simple and cosy, super value for money. You are in the Northumberland National Park; hire bikes and cycle round the lake, sail on it or go horse-riding. No traffic jams, no hurry and wonderful Northumbrian hospitality – they really are the nicest people.

rooms	8: 4 doubles, 3 twins, 1 family.
price	From £65. Half-board from £48 p.p. Singles from £40.
meals	Bar meals from £7.95. Dinner £16–£26.
closed	Rarely.
directions	From Bellingham, follow signs west to Kielder Water & Falstone for 7 miles. Hotel on left, 1 mile short of Kielder Water.

Walter, Irene & Robin Kershaw

tel	01434 240382
fax	01434 240382
e-mail	thepheasantinn@kielderwater.demon.co.uk
web	www.thepheasantinn.com

Inn

map 10 entry 128

The Hope & Anchor

44 Northumberland Street, Alnmouth, Northumberland NE66 2RA

Hard to believe little Alnmouth was once a bustling port: it used to export more corn than Newcastle. Then in 1806 its banks burst in a great storm, the river became a channel and the port went into rapid decline. Now it's the gentlest of seaside villages. The Hope & Anchor, three dwellings knitted into one, has been an inn for as long as anyone can remember. And Debbie has swept in with a squeaky-clean broom, replacing artex and swirly carpets with 21st-century fabric and colour. You step off the street and into the bar – a straightforward, no frills affair, with a fire for winter snuggery. Then up the stair to creamy-walled bedrooms with new pine, soft lights and comfy beds – spotless and cosy. Debbie's enthusiasm and warmth animates every room; she cooks well, too, and plans a dinner menu for the future. This is a great little place for families – there's Alnwick Castle round the corner (worth a look for Harry Potter fans: it's Hogwarts in the film), the fabulous new Alnwick garden, Newcastle and Edinburgh are a train ride away, and mile upon mile of unspoilt beaches await buckets and spades.

rooms	8: 4 doubles, 1 twin, 3 family.
price	£68.
meals	Lunch from £5.95. Dinner from £14.
closed	Rarely.
directions	A1 to Alnwick. At r'bout follow sign for Alnmouth. 1st pub on left in village.

Debbie Philipson

tel	01665 830363
fax	01665 603082
e-mail	debbiephilipson@hopeandanchorholidays.fsnet.co.uk
web	www.hopeandanchorholidays.co.uk

Pub with rooms

Lace Market Hotel

29-31 High Pavement, Nottingham, Nottinghamshire NG1 1HE

Once 20,000 women toiled away in these streets in the centre of Nottingham, making lace for an empire. Now trendy bars, restaurants, shops and clubs dominate the scene. Bang opposite the old court house is Lace Market Hotel, perfectly carved out of four Georgian houses, and with all its old world charm intact. Inside the feel is swish and contemporary but not minimalist, with wholesome British food in the brasserie and distinctly modern service from cheery staff that is not in the least forced. At the helm is Mark, he is deeply non-corporate in his approach, loathes UHT milk and tea bags in bedrooms and doesn't approve of calling guests 'Sir' or 'Madam'. It works, and all very comfortably too: bedrooms are richly coloured – burgundy and olive – but light and airy with modern furniture and space to work or flop, beds are all Sealy Posturepedic and huge, bathrooms have pretty tiles and designer basins. Guests also get to use Holmes Place Health Club down the road – a stunning conversion of a Victorian railway station – as well as the hotel's traditional Victorian alehouse next door. Occasional promotional rates on web site.

rooms	42: 33 doubles, 6 singles, 3 suites.
price	£109-£159. Singles from £89. Suites £185.
meals	Set lunch 2 courses £9.90, 3 courses £12.50 (Tues-Fri). Dinner, 3 courses, £19.95 & à la carte.
closed	Rarely.
directions	From city centre follow brown information signs for Lace Market, Galleries of Justice & St Marys Church.

Mark Cox

tel	0115 852 3232
fax	0115 852 3223
e-mail	reservations@lacemarkethotel.co.uk
web	www.lacemarkethotel.co.uk

Hotel

map 7   entry 130

Langar Hall

Langar, Nottinghamshire NG13 9HG

Langar Hall is one of the most engaging and delightful places in this book – reason enough to come to Nottinghamshire. Imogen's exquisite style and natural *joie de vivre* make this a mecca for those in search of a warm, country house atmosphere. The house sits at the top of a hardly noticeable hill in glorious parkland, bang next door to the church. Imo's family came here over 150 years ago. Much of what fills the house came here then and once inside it's easy to feel intoxicated by beautiful things; statues and busts, a pillared dining room, ancient tomes in overflowing bookshelves, a good collection of oil paintings. Bedrooms are spectacular, some resplendent with antiques, others with fabrics draped from beams or *trompe l'œil* panelling. Good food, simply prepared for healthy eating make this more like a restaurant with rooms so you'll need to book if you want to enjoy their own lamb, fish from Brixham, game from Belvoir Castle and garden grown vegetables. Once a year there's Shakespeare on the lawn too – a cultural paradise.

rooms	12: 7 doubles, 2 twins, 1 four-poster, 1 suite,1 chalet.
price	£90-£185. Singles £65-£100.
meals	Lunch £15. Dinner £30 and à la carte.
closed	Rarely.
directions	From Nottingham, A52 towards Grantham. Right, signed Cropwell Bishop, then straight on for 5 miles. House next to church on edge of village, signed.

	Imogen Skirving
tel	01949 860559
fax	01949 861045
e-mail	langarhall-hotel@ndirect.co.uk
web	www.langarhall.com

Hotel

Falkland Arms

Great Tew, Chipping Norton, Oxfordshire OX7 1DB

In a perfect Cotswold village, the perfect English pub. Five hundred years on and the fire still roars in the stone-flagged bar under a low-slung timbered ceiling that drips with jugs, mugs and tankards. Here, the hop is treated with reverence; ales are changed weekly and old pump clips hang from the bar. Tradition runs deep; they stock endless tins of snuff with great names like Irish High Toast and Crumbs of Comfort. In summer, Morris Men stumble on the lane outside and life spills out onto the terrace at the front, and into the big garden behind. This lively pub is utterly down-to-earth and in very good hands. The dining room is tiny and intimate with beams and stone walls; every traditional dish is home-cooked. The bedrooms are snug and cosy, not grand, but fun. Brass beds and four-posters, maybe a heavy bit of oak and an uneven floor – you'll sleep well. The house remains blissfully free of modern trappings, nowhere more so than in the bar, where mobile phones meet with swift and decisive action.

rooms	5 doubles.
price	£65–£80.
meals	Lunch from £4. Dinner from £8.
closed	Christmas & New Year. Inn open all year for food & drink.
directions	From Chipping Norton, A361, then right onto B4022, signed Great Tew. Inn by village green.

**Paul Barlow–Heal
& Sarah–Jane Courage**

tel	01608 683653
fax	01608 683656
e-mail	sjcourage@btconnect.com
web	www.falklandarms.org.uk

Inn

map 3   entry 132

The Kings Head Inn

The Green, Bledington, Oxfordshire OX7 6AQ

About as Doctor Dolittle-esque as it gets. Achingly pretty Cotswold stone cottages around a village green with quacking ducks, a pond and a perfect pub with a cobbled courtyard. Archie is young, affable and charming with locals and guests, but Nic is his greatest asset – a milliner, she has done up the bedrooms on a shoe string and they look fabulous. All are different, most have a stunning view, some family furniture mixed in with 'bits' she's picked up, painted wood, great colours and lush fabrics. The bar is lively – not with music but with talk – so choose rooms over the courtyard if you prefer a quiet evening. The flagstoned dining room with pale wood tables is elegant and food is cooked by a Swedish chef who is just as good with meat (local) as with fish (truly tasty mackerel and haddock fishcakes). Home-made puds, serious cheeses, lovely unpompous touches like jugs of cow parsley in the loo, tons of things to do (there's a music festival in June) could make this your favourite place to unwind and remember that life isn't all about work.

rooms	12: 10 doubles, 2 twins.
price	From £65. Singles £50.
meals	Lunch from £7.95. Dinner from £9.50.
closed	24-25 December.
directions	A429 from Stow-on-the-Wold, left on A424. On right in village.

Archie & Nic Orr-Ewing

tel	01608 658365
fax	01608 658902
e-mail	kingshead@orr-ewing.com
web	www.kingsheadinn.net

Inn

Burford House

99 High Street, Burford, Oxfordshire OX18 4QA

Burford House is a delight, intensely personal, full of elegant good taste, relaxing and small; small enough for Simon and Jane to influence every corner, which they do with ease and good cheer "If only all hoteliers were like them," said our inspector. Classical music and the scent of fresh flowers drift through beautiful rooms; oak beams, leaded windows, good fabrics, antiques, simple colours, log fires, immaculate beds, roll-top baths and a little garden for afternoon teas... all in this pretty Cotswold town. And there's an honesty bar, with home-made sloe gin and cranberry vodka, to be sipped from cut-glass tumblers. Hand-written menus promise ravishing breakfasts and tempting lunches, and they will recommend the best places for dinner. Both are happy in the kitchen: Simon cooks and Jane bakes, and Cotswold suppliers provide honey, jams, smoked salmon and farmhouse cheeses. Jumble the cat is 'paws on', too. Unwind, then unwind a little more. Enchanting river walks start in either direction through classic English countryside. Guests return time after time. A perfect little find.

rooms	8: 3 doubles, 2 twins, 3 four-posters.
price	£95–£130. Singles from £80.
meals	Light lunch & afternoon tea (restaurant closed Sundays & Mondays). Dinner available in Burford & nearby villages.
closed	Rarely.
directions	In centre of Burford.

	Jane & Simon Henty
tel	01993 823151
fax	01993 823240
e-mail	stay@burfordhouse.co.uk
web	www.burfordhouse.co.uk

Hotel

map 3   entry 134

The Lamb Inn

Sheep Street, Burford, Oxfordshire OX18 4LR

Old inn – new owners. Bruno and Rachel say they don't want to make big changes and in many ways there's no need; the inn proper dates back to 1420 when it used to be a dormy house. In the old bar, the footsteps of monks and thirsty locals have worn a gentle groove into the original stone floor and there's a glorious smell of wood smoke. Make a grand tour and you'll come across four fires, two sitting rooms, rambling corridors, lots of polished brass and silver, thick rugs, mullioned windows, old parchments and a settle with a back high enough "to keep the draught off a giant's neck". Bedrooms are just as good, with plump-cushioned armchairs, heavy oak beams, brass beds and gorgeous antiques. Exciting changes though have been made in the kitchen under new Head Chef Ashley James' direction – lunch and dinner menus make the best use of seasonal, local food and you can choose to eat in the bar, lounges, dining room or outside. The new wine list is simply huge with some real surprises for a country pub. The locals must be rubbing their tummies with glee!

rooms	15: 11 doubles, 3 twins, 1 four-poster.
price	£125-£185. Singles from £80.
meals	Dinner £29.50.
closed	Rarely.
directions	From Oxford, A40 west to Burford. Sheep Street is 1st left down High Street.

Bruno & Rachel Cappuccini

tel	01993 823155
fax	01993 822228
e-mail	info@lambinn-burford.co.uk

Inn

The Feathers Hotel

Market Street, Woodstock, Oxfordshire OX20 1SX

Once a draper's, then a butcher's, this serene English townhouse hotel has stayed true to its roots, with the finest fabrics and award-winning food its proud standard. Follow labyrinthine corridors under mind-your-head beams to the four original staircases that once led their separate ways before these four 17th-century houses became one: open fires, stone floors, oil paintings, beautiful antiques and an elegant upstairs sitting room point to a luxurious past. A pretty terraced bar, Johann the grey parrot and tumbling, colourful flowers at windows that frame the bustle of old Woodstock. The restaurant is part library, half-panelled with soft yellow walls and low ceilings. Bedrooms are beautiful; some are smaller than others, but all have period furniture, towelling bathrobes, purified water and home-made shortbread; most have marble bathrooms and one suite has a steam room. Relax with backgammon in the study while devouring sinful afternoon teas, take to the sky in a hot-air balloon, or drift down the Thames in a chauffeured punt – all can be arranged. Blenheim Palace is on your doorstep as well.

rooms	20: 8 doubles, 8 twins, 4 suites.
price	£135–£185. Singles from £99. Suite £235–£290.
meals	Lunch from £17.50. Dinner about £38; menu gourmand, 6 courses with champagne & port, £65.
closed	Rarely.
directions	From Oxford, A44 north to Woodstock. In town, left after traffic lights. Hotel on left.

	Gavin Tomson
tel	01993 812291
fax	01993 813158
e-mail	enquiries@feathers.co.uk
web	www.feathers.co.uk

Hotel

map 3   entry 136

Old Parsonage Hotel
1 Banbury Road, Oxford, Oxfordshire OX2 6NN

It must have been a good year for cooks. Edward Selwood, master chef of nearby St John's College, completed his grand house in 1660 and the vast oak front door still hangs. Inside, sympathetic design details and use of materials have kept the old-house feel and the intimacy of a private club. The hall has glorious stone flags, huge original fireplace – log-stocked in winter – and urns of dried flowers. Bedrooms have fine florals and checks, some in the old house have magnificent fireplaces and panelling; all have gorgeous bathrooms. There's a first-floor roof garden, lush with plants, for tea or sundowner, and a snug sitting room downstairs for those seeking quiet. All roads seem to lead to the Parsonage bar/restaurant, the hub of the hotel; newspapers hang on poles, walls are heavy with pictures and people float in all day long for coffee, drinks and good food. First-class service from real people too – they'll do just about anything they can to help. Much comfort, not a whiff of pretension, and within strolling distance of the dreaming spires. Oscar Wilde reputedly had digs here.

rooms	30: 25 twins/doubles, 4 suites, 1 single.
price	£135–£170. Singles £125. Suites £195.
meals	Breakfast from £9. Lunch & dinner from £15. Gee's restaurant nearby.
closed	24–27 December.
directions	From A40 ring road, south at Banbury Road roundabout to Summertown city centre. Hotel on right next to St Giles Church. Private parking, limited spaces.

	Steven Vannozzi
tel	01865 310210
fax	01865 311262
e-mail	info@oldparsonage-hotel.co.uk
web	www.oxford-hotels-restaurants.co.uk

Hotel

Apartments in Oxford

St Thomas' Mews, 58 St Thomas' Street, Oxford, Oxfordshire OX1 1JP

Bang in the middle of the city, these stylish apartments are an excellent – and discreet – alternative to staying in a hotel. And great value! In the largest of the modern, mewshouse blocks, flats surround a pretty, central courtyard; the smaller block has a teak-tabled roof terrace *and a garden*. Each apartment is beautifully decorated in neutral colours with comfortable beds, feather duvets, perfect pelmets, immaculate bathrooms. Business folk will be thrilled with the PCs, internet access, scanner, printer, fax and customised e-mail address in each apartment; cooks will be charmed by the quality of the kitchen equipment and the white bone china. Those who simply want to let their hair down will make a bee-line for the sofas and welcome hamper. Continental breakfast is delivered to your door each morning, with a newspaper. Best of all, there's free parking – a treat in Oxford; leave your car while you explore. Theatres and restaurants can be booked by the lovely and unsnooty reception staff, and children are welcome, too. There's even a duck for the bath.

rooms	34 apartments for 2, 4 and 8.
price	From £90 (two-person apartment, low season).
meals	Available locally. Shopping or dinner party service available.
closed	Rarely.
directions	200 yds from Oxford railway & coach stations.

Roger Watts

tel	01865 254072
fax	01865 254079
e-mail	roger@oxstay.co.uk
web	www.oxstay.co.uk

Other place

map 3   entry 138

The Old Bank

92-94 High Street, Oxford, Oxfordshire OX1 4BN

A grand building of mellow, golden stone, in old Oxford, flanked by colleges and cobbled streets. Its hub is the big old tellers' hall, now a dynamic bar and restaurant, with stone floors, a zinc-topped bar, big arched windows that look out onto the High Street and huge modern oils on the walls – part of a good collection of 20th-century British art hung throughout the hotel. In summer, eat on the deck at the back, beneath umbrellas in a pretty, private garden. Bedrooms are gorgeous and just as contemporary, stylishly clean-cut with natural pastel colours, the best linen, velvet and silk; some have big bay windows or views to the back, and they're full of 21st-century gadgetry with bathrooms that are large and sparkling. Rooms at the top have long views across the fabled skyline of spires, towers and domes. Museums, theatres, shops, restaurants and pubs are on the doorstep, there are excellent guided walks around the colleges and their lovely gardens – check their opening times – and a five-minute stroll that takes you through Merton College, the Meadows and down to the river. Perfect.

rooms	42: 36 twins/doubles, 4 singles, 2 suites.
price	£160-£235. Singles from £140. Suites £265-£320.
meals	Breakfast £9-£12. Lunch & dinner £8.75-£25.
closed	25-26 December.
directions	Cross Magdalen Bridge for city centre. Keep left through 1st set of lights; 1st left into Merton St. Follow road right, 1st right into Magpie Lane. Car park 2nd right.

Jackie Wallis-Jones

tel	01865 799599
fax	01865 799598
e-mail	info@oldbank-hotel.co.uk
web	www.oxford-hotels-restaurants.co.uk

Hotel

The Flying Pig at the Stonor Arms Hotel

Stonor, Oxfordshire RG9 6HE

Something special is happening at the old Stonor that could transform this restaurant with rooms into one of most upbeat places to stay in the Thames Valley. New owners have swept in with a luxurious broom – and a passion for food and wine. The award-winning chef promises French cooking with an exotic, modern twist, the sommelier, 1,000 of the best old and new world wines. Lying on the edge of the Chiltern Hills, the Flying Pig at the Stonor Arms has the feel of deep country yet is no distance from London. Relax in the Big Snug or the Blue Snug, the sitting room or the Crocodile bar... deep comfort with a contemporary touch. Downstairs is cool and swish, with gleaming wooden floors and a real fire to toast yourself by. Chic bedrooms are individually designed; baths are big, showers 'walk-in', some rooms lead to a pretty walled garden. In summer, dine outside by candlelight; in the morning, breakfast among the roses. Service is tiptop but not stuffy. A beautiful setting in which to spoil yourself: footpaths lead out to hills and forest, red kites circle above the deer park and lanes lead up to pretty villages.

rooms	11 doubles.
price	£145-£175. Singles £110.
meals	Dinner £25-£30.
closed	Rarely.
directions	M40, junc. 6, B4009 to Watlington, B480 for Nettlebed. Left after 2 miles for Stonor. Inn in village.

Sharyn Van der Goot

tel	01491 638866
fax	01491 638863
e-mail	info@theflyingpigrestaurant.co.uk
web	www.theflyingpigrestaurant.co.uk

Inn

map 3   entry 140

The White Hart Hotel
Nettlebed, Oxfordshire RG9 5DD

It's quite a shock to happen across the White Hart. Outside it looks like a typical old roadside coaching inn, but you'll find gorgeous cream floor tiles, modern lighting, a crackling real fire, pale colours and the lovely, friendly, Chris. Passionate about food that is local, wild and home grown he changes the menu daily: try Welsh rarebit or home cured gravadlax in the bistro, which is painted grey and hung with modern art by Catherine Ducker. The restaurant – classic and cool – has aubergine walls and chairs, white linen, flowers in jugs from Chris's garden and cheeky glass pot sculptures. Upstairs the wonky walls are painted in light mushroom and all the bedrooms are stylish, with big beds, leather headboards, proper linen, silk bedspreads, feather pillows, thick fabric blinds and small but perfectly formed bathrooms in muted colours. Free 24-hour room service does away with the unglamorous kettle-in-the-room syndrome. Chris has got it right: excellent food, great staff, unfussy décor and a charming, relaxed professionalism which looks effortless but is hard-earned. Even the main road behaves itself at night.

rooms	12: 3 large doubles, 8 doubles, 1 twin.
price	£105–£145.
meals	Bistro: 2 courses from £10. Restaurant: 3 courses £30.
closed	Rarely.
directions	On A4130 in Nettlebed.

	Chris Barber
tel	01491 641245
web	www.whitehartnettlebed.com

Phyllis Court Club Hotel

Marlow Road, Henley-on-Thames, Oxfordshire RG9 2HT

Classically English right down to the rose emblem, with the sort of protocol you'd expect from a private member's club, Phyllis Court is a class apart. Founded almost a century ago to create somewhere swish for bright young things from the city to zoom up to in their new motor cars, it still attracts the great and the good. It isn't hard to see why. Apart from the grandstand and its own Thames frontage with moorings – it's bang opposite the finishing line of the Royal Regatta – the house itself is a grandly self-effacing place: tweed, tennis and *The Telegraph* blend with a sense of fun. Members number some 3,000 today, and run the place with great pride – and grace. There *are* 'rules' but Muirfield it isn't! The club is named after the old English word for a red rose, 'fyllis'. Once moated, Phyllis Court was rebuilt in the 17th century, then again in the 18th and 19th. Bedrooms are easy on the eye and full of spoiling touches; the long drive sweeps past lawn and croquet 'courts'. There are river walks, and Henley buzzes with day-trippers just as it always has. *Teas & meals for residents only.*

rooms	17: 9 doubles, 8 twins/doubles.
price	£129–£158. Singles £110–£123.50.
meals	Lunch, 3 courses, £20.75. Dinner, 3 courses, £26.30.
closed	Rarely.
directions	From Henley-on-Thames, A4155 towards Marlow. Club on right.

	Sue Gill
tel	01491 570500
fax	01491 570528
e-mail	enquiries@phylliscourt.co.uk
web	www.phylliscourt.co.uk

Hotel

map 3   entry 142

Thamesmead House Hotel

Remenham Lane, Henley-on-Thames, Oxfordshire RG9 2LR

Patricia's eye for a news story has proved equally adept at creating a wonderful place to stay in the home of the Royal Regatta. The former arts correspondent has transformed a "seedy" 1960s Edwardian guest house into a chic getaway just a short amble from the centre of Henley-on-Thames; the walk over the famous three-arched bridge (1786) is easily the best introduction to this charming town. Soak up lazy, idyllic river views in both directions, then walk along towpaths or mess about in a rowing boat. Thamesmead is small but perfectly formed. Elegant bedrooms are decorated in a comfortably crisp Scandinavian style: mustard yellows, terracotta and soothing blues, big Oxford pillows to sink into, modern art on the walls, an extraordinary fossil fireplace in one, and painted wooden panelling in the bathrooms. The breakfast/tea room is relaxing, with Thompson furniture – spot the distinctive carved mouse motif – and French windows that let in lots of light, and maybe a gentle summer's breeze. Presiding over all is the erudite and fun-loving Patricia, a Dubliner to the core.

rooms	6: 4 doubles, 1 twin/double, 1 single.
price	£115–£140. Singles £95–£115.
meals	Afternoon tea. Restaurants in Henley.
closed	Rarely.
directions	From M4 junc. 8/9, A404 (M) to Burchett's Green, then left on A4130, signed Henley (5 miles). Before bridge, right just after Little Angel pub. House on left.

	Patricia Thorburn-Muirhead
tel	01491 574745
fax	01491 579944
e-mail	thamesmead@supanet.com
web	www.thamesmeadhousehotel.co.uk

Hotel

Mr Underhill's at Dinham Weir

Dinham Bridge, Ludlow, Shropshire SY8 1FH

Chris and Judy moved Mr Underhill's from its Suffolk home after 16 years, to the foot of Ludlow Castle in 1998 – they regained their Michelin star in the first year. The setting of this restaurant with rooms, right on the bank of the River Teme, is dreamy, particularly in summer when you can eat out in the lovely courtyard and watch the river drift by. The dining room, too – long, light and airy, modern, warm and fun – has river views and masses of glass to draw them in. Bedrooms are at the other end of the house and have been completely transformed: natural fabrics, locally-woven carpet, lots of cherry, maple and blond oak… big, comfy beds that appear to float and more watery views. Judy has cleverly designed the smaller rooms so they feel bigger; all are good and restful with stylish bathrooms. Back downstairs, you're bound to meet Mungo and Toby, two British blues and heirs to Frodo's empire after whose alias, as Tolkien fans will confirm, the restaurant is named. Good people with huge commitment – a special place.

rooms	6: 4 doubles, 2 twins/doubles.
price	£90–£140. Singles from £85.
meals	Dinner £34. Restaurant closed Tuesdays.
closed	Occasionally.
directions	Head to castle in Ludlow centre, then take 'Dinham' Road to left of castle; follow down short hill, right at bottom before crossing river. On left, signed.

Chris & Judy Bradley

tel	01584 874431
web	www.mr-underhills.co.uk

Restaurant with Rooms

map 6   entry 144

Cleobury Court

Cleobury North, Shropshire WV16 6RW

It's been quite a spending spree since Bill and Christina took over this former dower house. Francophiles both, they've collected furniture, tapestries and prints on their travels across the Channel. There's also a hint of the East as Christina ran a Balinese shop. The colour schemes are hers, such as the pale lemon sitting room carpet; fabrics, boldly floral, are dramatically swathed. She makes the curtains and upholsters, too. Bill's more in charge of the food – good, local – and the garden. There are two suites: Ludlow, with its open country views, has a smart sitting room, a huge specially-made four-poster and a big, luxurious bathroom. The more intimate Garden suite has twin beds, set together under a super king-size half-tester, a charming Regency-striped sitting room, and a roll-top bath. The cosy double is blue and white in a French style. Be pampered in the manner of a private home rather than a hotel – Bill, who's Canadian, and Christina, a Londoner, are both extremely hospitable. Play the grand piano, or billiards, or stretch yourself in the gym. Ludlow is a short drive, or walk up Brown Clee from the back door.

rooms	3: 1 double, 2 suites.
price	£75. Singles from £60. Suites £90–£99.
meals	Available locally.
closed	Occasionally.
directions	From Bridgnorth, B4364 to Cleobury North. On right 0.5 miles from Cleobury Court signpost.

	Bill & Christina Mills
tel	01746 787005
fax	01746 787005
e-mail	cleoburycourt@aol.com

Other Place

Pen-y-Dyffryn Country Hotel

Rhydycroesau, Nr Oswestry, Shropshire SY10 7JD

Staggeringly beautiful scenery surrounds this old rectory, commissioned in 1845 by its first rector, Robert Williams, who compiled the first Celtic dictionary. He was said to be a stuffy character... the very opposite of Miles and Audrey – and their staff – whose relaxed and easy-going manner suffuses the house with comfort and joy. The entrance hall doubles as a bar; the bar itself an old *chiffonier* – "a posh sideboard," says Miles – with menus tucked away in the drawers. The bedrooms are 'comfy old house', with good fabrics and some with hand-painted furniture. One little double has its own flight of stairs, while the four rooms in the old stable are big and contemporary, with private terraces. Nearly every room has spectacular views. There's a sitting room with log fire to curl up in, a restaurant for all tastes serving wonderful food (breakfasts, too, are spot on), organic beers and wines and a front terrace on which to sip long drinks. The five green acres of Pen-y-Dyffryn start at the top of the hill and roll down to Wales, the river at the foot of the beautiful valley marks the natural border.

rooms	12: 6 doubles, 4 twins, 1 single, 1 family.
price	£90–£120. Singles £73.
meals	Dinner £27.
closed	Christmas & 1–14 January.
directions	From A5, head to Oswestry. Leave town on B4580, signed Llansilin. Hotel 3 miles on left just before Rhydycroesau.

	Miles & Audrey Hunter
tel	01691 653700
fax	01691 650066
e-mail	stay@peny.co.uk
web	www.peny.co.uk

Hotel

map 6   entry 146

Little Barwick House

Barwick Village, Yeovil, Somerset BA22 9TD

Emma and Tim belong to a vanguard of British hoteliers blending depth of experience with a new-found freedom to experiment and do their own thing. Little Barwick is a delightful restaurant with rooms that produces superb food in a relaxed atmosphere: flair, lots of ability and a rare sense of vocation and commitment (there are regular wine-tasting evenings) are all in evidence. Step out of your car and the smell of something irresistible is likely to waft your way. They make whatever they can – marmalades, chutneys, sorbets, ice creams, breads, shortbreads, jams – even pasta. The house is full of variety as well. Emma has given the graceful Georgian interior a fresh, contemporary makeover: natural colours, stripped wooden floorboards and polished stone floors are the order of the day; anything stuffy or frilly has been banished. The bedrooms are all different, with pampering touches. In winter, a three-day stay is incredible value; indulge yourself at breakfast with house champagne by the glass… go on, spoil yourself.

rooms	6: 4 doubles, 2 twins.
price	£93–£103. Half-board from £78.50 p.p.
meals	Lunch from £15.50. Dinner £32.50. Restaurant closed Sunday & Monday evenings, & Tuesday lunchtimes.
closed	2 weeks in January.
directions	From Yeovil, A37 south for Dorchester; left at 1st r'bout by Red House pub. Down hill, past church, house on left after 200 yds.

	Emma & Tim Ford
tel	01935 423902
fax	01935 420908
e–mail	reservations@barwick7.fsnet.co.uk
web	www.littlebarwickhouse.co.uk

Restaurant with Rooms

Greyhound Inn

Staple Fitzpaine, Taunton, Somerset TA3 5SP

The Greyhound typifies the classic English country pub, walls bedecked with collages of pictures and fishing memorabilia that create an atmosphere of warmth and hospitality. Let the eye wander... while sitting at old, wooden tables, worn nicely from frequent use and decorated simply with vases of wild flowers. A roaring hearth in winter, a flagstoned bar busy with friendly locals – ask after Mr Flack and Mr Grabham – and a good meal, with fish delivered daily from Brixham and meat from within four miles. Then "retreat in good order", as one boxing print wisely suggests, to clean, comfortable bedrooms: more hotel than individual. Ivor and Lucy bought the inn after leaving careers in the pharmaceutical industry. "We still work long hours but we see each other now," says Ivor, a relaxed host, seemingly made for the job of community landlord. The Back Room restaurant serves a new fusion of fresh food. All this in deepest rural Somerset with walks through forestry to Castle Neroche and stunning views from the Blackdown Hills. Henry VIII's heart is said to be buried in the churchyard. *Children over 12 welcome.*

rooms	4: 2 doubles, 1 twin/double, 1 twin.
price	£75–£90. Singles £49.95.
meals	Lunch from £4. Dinner, à la carte, about £20.
closed	Rarely.
directions	M5, junc. 25, A358 towards Ilminster for 4 miles, then right, for Staple Fitzpaine. Left at T-junc. Village 1.5 miles further. Inn on right at x-roads.

	Ivor & Lucy Evans
tel	01823 480227
fax	01823 481117
e-mail	stay@the-greyhoundinn.com
web	www.thegreyhoundinn.fsbusiness.co.uk

Inn

map 2   entry 148

Orchards Restaurant at Wrexon Farmhouse

Dipford Road, Angersleigh, Taunton, Somerset TA3 7PA

The axiom that some people are made for each other surely applies to the immensely likeable owners of Orchards Restaurant. Norman and Julie have known each other since they were toddlers and this charming, established restaurant in an old Somerset crofter's cottage marks a lifetime of unswerving devotion. Relax with an aperitif by a wood stove in a cosy bar, or sit out in summer in a courtyard full of honeysuckle and rosemary. Herbs, salads, apples, damsons and plums grow on four acres for the table. Norman is a no-frills cook, preferring classic English methods to current trends: fish from Brixham, roast duckling, pavlovas, home-made ice creams and an excellent dessert trolley. In the restaurant, tables lit by candlelight fit snugly around gnarled beams and an elm trunk that seems to grow upstairs. You stay in huge comfort in a barn next door and breakfast arrives at the time of your choosing. As for the traffic, you'll be too busy enjoying yourself to notice the march of the nearby motorway. The cottage's thick walls insulate and the prevailing wind blows the sound in the other direction!

rooms	1 apartment for 2-3.
price	£69. Singles £55.
meals	Continental breakfast £6.75. Dinner, à la carte, about £25. Lunch for groups of 12 or more. Restaurant closed Sundays & Mondays.
closed	Rarely.
directions	From Taunton centre, follow signs to Trull; right after Queen's College, into Dipford Road, signed Angersleigh. 2 miles on right, just after bridge over M5.

Norman & Julie White
tel 01823 275440
e-mail mail@orchardsrestaurant.co.uk
web www.orchardsrestaurant.co.uk

Restaurant with Rooms

Bindon Country House Hotel

Langford Budville, Wellington, Somerset TA21 0RU

An extraordinary, beautiful building, Bindon hides on the edge of woodland where rare and colourful wild flowers flourish. Six years ago, it was a derelict mansion full of dust and cobwebs; now it's full of Mark and Lynn's enthusiasm. What strikes you most, entering through the large glass front door, is the crispness of it all: the tiled entrance hall, the stained glass, the wall tapestries, the plaster mouldings on the ceiling, the galleried staircase, the glass-domed roof... absolutely pristine. Keep going into the snug panelled bar, past the wrought-iron candlesticks, for coffee served with piping hot milk and delicious home-made biscuits. In summer, move outside through open hall doors and sit by a magnificent stone balustrade that looks over rose gardens down to an old dovecote. Bright bedrooms come in different sizes: two oval rooms at the front of the house are *huge*, with dusky pink furniture, patterned wallpaper depicting genteel garden scenes, a high brass bed and Victorian baths; the others are large and very comfortable. Add gorgeous food and a luxuriously heated pool for a hidden treasure.

rooms	12: 10 twins/doubles, 2 four-posters.
price	£115–£215. Half-board (min. 2 nights) from £67.50 p.p. Singles £95.
meals	Lunch £12.95. Dinner, 5 courses, £29.95.
closed	Rarely.
directions	From Wellington, B3187 for 1.5 miles, then left at sharp S-bend for Langford Budville. Right in village for Wiveliscombe, then 1st right. House on right after 1.5 miles.

	Lynn & Mark Jaffa
tel	01823 400070
fax	01823 400071
e-mail	stay@bindon.com
web	www.bindon.com

Hotel

map 2   entry 150

The Royal Oak Inn

Withypool, Somerset TA24 7QP

The drive to this oasis of luxury through twisting lanes shrouded in early morning mist leaves a magical impression of Exmoor which is impossible to shake. Look on any map and Withypool is the point at which all roads across the moor meet. A small, forgotten place made immune to outside cares by the barren embrace of stone and bog, and heather that blazes a resplendent purple in summer – there's no better place to flee. The 300-year-old Royal Oak will indulge you completely. Gail has a background in producing adverts for television but she isn't exaggerating when she says her bedrooms are "the nicest on the moor". Full of style and simple good taste, they are divided between the inn and two superb cottages across the courtyard, also let as holiday homes: *toile de Jouy* fabrics and wallpaper, panelled bathrooms, maybe an antique half-tester, or an old slipper bath, and dyed sheepskin rugs to cosset tired feet. The food is excellent, the welcome warm and the bar bustles with country brio. Walk to Tarr Steps, but heed Jake the barman's advice: an Exmoor mile is longer than an ordinary mile. Wildly invigorating.

rooms	8: 6 doubles, 2 twins/doubles.
price	£90–£110. Singles £60–£70.
meals	Lunch from £4.75. Dinner about £20.
closed	Christmas Day.
directions	M5, junc. 27. A4361 to Tiverton, then right on A396, for Bampton & Dulverton. At Exbridge, left on B3222 to Dulverton & onto Withypool.

	Gail Sloggett
tel	01643 831506/7
fax	01643 831659
e-mail	enquiries@royaloakwithypool.co.uk
web	www.royaloakwithypool.co.uk

Inn

The Crown Hotel

Exford, Somerset TA24 7PP

Entering Hugo and Pamela's mildly eccentric world in the middle of Exmoor is guaranteed to be entertaining – don't be surprised to find a horse propping up the bar! The Crown is their latest venture, following on from the success of the Rising Sun in Lynmouth. These generous hosts have an in-built knack of looking after you. "People work so hard these days, they deserve to be spoilt," says Pamela, a scientist by trade and big-hearted by nature. Hugo is a gentleman of the old school, impeccably dressed beneath a shock of white hair. He sharpens his wits playing bridge with seasoned oldies who "clout me over the head if I make a foolish bid". You're in unspoilt, horsey country where laid-back locals draw just comparison with the easy-going outlook of rural Ireland. The building itself is Exmoor's oldest coaching inn, set in front of the village green – its angled eaves and peaked roof look like a crown from the front. The Jeune way is gradually transforming floral bedrooms while good service and imaginative cooking is making a difference downstairs. Watch this place – it's destined to get better and better.

rooms	17: 8 doubles, 4 twins, 3 singles; 2 doubles, both with separate bath.
price	£95–£110. Half-board £70–£77.50. Singles £55.
meals	Lunch, 3 courses, £18.50. Dinner £29.50. Bar meals from £3.95.
closed	Rarely.
directions	M5, junc. 25, A38 to Taunton, A358 towards Minehead, then B3224 to Exford, via Wheddon Cross. Hotel by village green.

Hugo & Pamela Jeune

tel	01643 831554
fax	01643 831665
e-mail	info@crownhotelexmoor.co.uk
web	www.crownhotelexmoor.co.uk

Inn

map 2   entry 152

Porlock Vale House
Porlock Weir, Somerset TA24 8NY

Exmoor National Park runs into the sea here, tiny lanes ramble down into lush valleys while headlands rise to meet the waves. Saddle a horse from the hotel and ride off into the sunset. Well, maybe not, but this is an exceptional riding school – all levels welcome. But you don't have to ride – come to sit out under the wisteria on the terrace and watch the deer eat the garden, or walk down across fields and paddle in Porlock Bay. Whatever you do, you'll enjoy coming back to this splendid country house with its comforting smells of polish, woodsmoke and fresh flowers. Good 'imaginative English' food – most of it local – in the oak-panelled, burgundy dining room, crackling log fires and leather sofas in the hall, deep sofas in the pretty sitting room, books and games, prints and pictures galore. Bedrooms, many newly-dressed and styled, are enticing – big and bright with sofas if there's room; most have sea views and the biggest are huge. Make sure you see the beautiful Edwardian stables… you may find the blacksmith at work in the yard. The horses here couldn't be better looked after and you will be too – owners and staff are just great.

rooms	15: 9 doubles, 5 twins, 1 single.
price	£80–£130. Singles £45–£85. Half-board £55–£89 p.p.
meals	Lunch from £5. Dinner £23.50.
closed	Mid-week in January & early February.
directions	West past Minehead on A39, then right in Porlock, for Porlock Weir. Through West Porlock, signed right.

	Kim & Helen Youd
tel	01643 862338
fax	01643 863338
e-mail	info@porlockvale.co.uk
web	www.porlockvale.co.uk

Hotel

Whites Hotel & Restaurant

Church Road, North Hill, Minehead, Somerset TA24 5SB

Perched above Minehead town centre and on the fringe of Exmoor National Park this Edwardian family hotel has had new life and energy breathed into it. The Walfords took over in October 2002 transforming the place; it now has a fresh, more contemporary feel: pale, but tough, carpeting, subtle paintwork, good modern paintings (some by local artists, and for sale), decent lighting and deep sofas in bold ethnic prints. Tony's in charge of the jaunty Oyster Yacht Bar; Linda, who's vegetarian, loves cooking. She buys as much meat, fish and vegetables seasonally and locally as she can, and keeps things simple but imaginative. Try her scrambled eggs with fresh garden herbs for breakfast in the conservatory dining room. The garden, too, is having a makeover; there are plenty of childrens' games and an inviting swimming pool. Newly-decorated bedrooms are unfussy with the odd designery touch, such as carpet hangings and local stones. Some rooms have sea views, others original fireplaces and balconies; the two-room family suites are colour-themed and bathrooms are perfectly functional. Nice people, good value.

rooms	10: 8 doubles, 2 family.
price	From £60. Singles from £42.
meals	From £12.50 for two courses. Restaurant open Thursdays - Saturdays, or by arrangement.
closed	January & February (after New Year break).
directions	From Minehead town centre follow signs to North Hill & St Michael's church. 200m up Church Road.

	Tony & Linda Walford
tel	01643 702032
fax	01643 704905
e-mail	info@whites-hotel.co.uk
web	www.whites-hotel.co.uk

Hotel

map 2   entry 154

Luttrell Arms

36 High Street, Dunster, Somerset TA24 6SG

A sleepy hotel on the only street in Dunster, the 15th-century building was once used as a guesthouse by the Abbots of Cleeve. Walk through a magnificent stone porch with coat of arms above to find a proper traditional inn with horsey prints, open fires, dark wood doors and a monks' courtyard in the centre complete with minstrels' gallery. Eat at the bar, or by candlelight in the smart restaurant with striped wallpaper, cream curtains and tall-backed, upholstered chairs. The bedrooms are all big, not swish or sophisticated but with good furniture and linen. Bathrooms are white and spotless. There is a lovely garden at the back with mature trees and a pergola with climbers; treat yourself to a cream tea out here while you gaze at glorious views of Dunster Castle and Somerset's green hills. There's an old-fashioned feel but the staff are young and friendly and as this is a new venture for Martin and his partner (both local lads returned) there's an infectious enthusiasm about the place — especially for local traditions like 'Dunster by Candle Light' when every villager turns their lights out and puts a candle in the window. Magic!

rooms	28: 14 doubles, 9 twins, 5 four-posters.
price	£85–£130. Singles from £65.
meals	Lunch from £9.95. Dinner from £20.
closed	Rarely.
directions	A39 to Dunster. Turn south towards Tiverton on A396. This is the Steep, which becomes High Street. Hotel on left-hand side.

Martin Tarr

tel	01643 821555
fax	01643 821567
e-mail	info@luttrellarms.fsnet.co.uk
web	www.luttrellarms.co.uk

Inn

Glencot House

Glencot Lane, Wells, Somerset BA5 1BH

Jacobean elegance spills from this beautiful late-Victorian mansion into its 18-acre parkland setting. Inside, it's just as you would expect: four-poster beds, carved ceilings, walnut panelling, magical hallways filled with ancient furniture and bric-a-brac, plants and flowers everywhere. The drawing room is the magnet of the house; you'll meet the other guests here, all staring at the carved ceiling and the inglenook fireplace with open chimney flue the size of a room; in winter the flames leap six feet high. Hard to believe it has all mod-cons, too. Glencot was rescued from a state of dilapidation by Jenny and her husband; long hours of toil have brought it back to life. Don't miss the garden: a magnificent terrace with stunning stone balustrade and wide, gracious steps which sweep you down to the River Axe. There are fountains, a waterfall (planned to provide hydro-electric power) and an old stone bridge to take you over to the cricket pitch where the village team plays in summer. *Pets by arrangement.*

rooms	13: 2 doubles, 3 twins, 3 singles, 5 four-posters.
price	£92–£120. Singles £72–£85.
meals	Dinner from £26.50. Packed lunch from £3.50.
closed	Rarely.
directions	From Wells, follow signs to Wookey Hole. Sharp left at finger post, 100m after pink cottage. House on right in Glencot Lane.

	Jenny Attia
tel	01749 677160
fax	01749 670210
e-mail	relax@glencothouse.co.uk
web	www.glencothouse.co.uk

Hotel

map 2   entry 156

The George

Norton St Philip, Bath, Somerset BA3 6LH

Once an ostler would have calmed your snorting steed after its urgent canter across the Downs, directing you under the massive stone arch, across the cobbled courtyard and into the snug bar where logs crackled and ale was poured under darkened oak beams... The George must have been like that. The building is one of Somerset's finest, brilliantly converted, a 13th-century inn in continuous use – reputed to be an English record. During the English Civil War it sided with the rebels, harbouring the Duke of Monmouth, Charles II's illegitimate son; the Duke was later defeated at the Battle of Sedgemoor in 1685. There are restored 15th-century wall paintings, timber and stone everywhere, an ancient balconied corridor, and rear views across the cricket pitch to the church. The village street passes in front, but quietly at night. Eat well in a large beamed dining room, or a snug alcove; the bar bench is a 700-year-old monk's writing table – not often do you see the legs of the person serving your beer! Bedrooms are magnificently redone with reproduction beds and furniture, bare floorboards in some, luxury in all...

rooms	8: 5 doubles, 3 four-posters.
price	£80–£110. Singles from £60.
meals	Bar meals from £3.95. Dinner about £18.
closed	Christmas Day & Boxing Day.
directions	From Bath, A36 south, then A366 west for 1 mile. Inn in village.

	David & Tania Satchell
tel	01373 834224
fax	01373 834861
e-mail	georgeinnnsp@aol.com
web	www.thegeorgeinn-nsp.co.uk

Inn

The Bell Inn
Ferry Road, Walberswick, Suffolk IP18 6TN

A tiny summer-soft, winter-bleak Suffolk fishing village central to the 1920s Craft Movement (Charles Rennie Mackintosh was here) and still a refuge for artists. The ferry across the tiny boat-tangled river has been rowed by the same family for five generations. Swim, sail, fish for crabs, paint, walk the beach to Dunwich. The Bell is 600 years old and has ancient beams and flagstones, wooden settles and open fires. Time has also given it a few nooks and crannies in which to hide out for a drink. The country-style bedrooms are on the small side as you'd expect of an ancient inn, but full of comforts and some have blissful views. Sue is welcoming and attractive and has poured huge amounts of energy into making it such a happy place. Outside, soak up the sun in the large garden and look out on beach huts, dunes and the sea. It is also a perfect place for families, bird watchers (Minsmere is here) and East Anglian architecture buffs.

rooms	6: 4 doubles, 1 twin, 1 family.
price	From £70. Singles from £60.
meals	Lunch from £3.50. Dinner, Friday & Saturday, from £16.
closed	Rarely.
directions	From A12, B1387 to Walberswick. Inn on right, at far end of village near river.

	Sue Ireland-Cutting
tel	01502 723109
fax	01502 722728
e-mail	bellinn@btinternct.com
web	www.blythweb.co.uk/bellinn

Inn

map 8   entry 158

The Dolphin

Peace Place, Thorpeness, Aldeburgh, Suffolk IP16 4NA

Thorpeness is a one-off, the perfect antidote to 21st-century holidays. The village was the turn-of-the-century brainchild of G S Ogilvie, who set out to create a holiday resort for children, free of piers and promenades, with safety assured. His master stroke is the Meare – a 64-acre lake, never more than three feet deep, inspired by Ogilvie's friend, J M Barrie, creator of *Peter Pan*. Children can row, sail and canoe their way up creeks and discover islands that may have a lurking (wooden) crocodile round the corner. The Dolphin – in the middle of the village – is a great little inn. It has three very good bedrooms in cottage style with old pine furniture, soft colours and spotless bathrooms. There are two lively bars, open fires and wooden floors in the dining room and, outside, a terrace and lawn for barbecues and *al fresco* dinners. Choose between tennis at the Country Club, a great golf course, an unspoilt sand and pebble beach, a summer theatre company and even a "house in the clouds". A paradise for families and excellent value for money.

rooms	3 twins/doubles.
price	£75. Singles £55.
meals	Selected dishes for lunch and dinner from £4.50.
closed	Rarely.
directions	From A12 at Farnham, A1094 to Aldeburgh seafront. Left & follow coast road for 2 miles into Thorpeness. Inn on right, signed.

Tim Rowan-Robinson

tel	01728 454994
fax	01728 453868
e-mail	info@thorpeness.co.uk
web	www.thorpeness.co.uk

Inn

The Old Rectory

Campsea Ashe, Nr Woodbridge, Suffolk IP13 0PU

In summer you eat in the conservatory, gazing admiringly over the 2.5 acres of lawns, herb garden, shrubs and orchard. But the dining room is not to be missed; it has plum silk curtains, a wooden floor with rugs, white-clothed tables with candles and silver cutlery. Fresh flowers add colour to every room. The bedrooms have been lavishly cared for: one is Victorian, with period bath, basin, taps and fireplace; another is in the attic, up a spiral stair. It's a subtly, classily decorated place – modern country house style with oriental touches. There's an honesty bar, a sitting room with deep sofas and garden views and a delightful, welcoming mood. Sally has run her own design shop and pours her heart into this; she cooks, too. The menus are irresistible: Moroccan chicken, monkfish, hot smoked salmon salad, Italian trifle, local fish galore. Breakfasts are as home-made (sausages, bread and marmalade) and locally-sourced as possible. You are close to the best of Suffolk – Snape Maltings, Orford, Adeburgh, Southwold, Woodbridge, Sutton Hoo – in a delightfully ungrand yet lovely house with owners fired up with enthusiasm.

rooms	7: 3 doubles, 2 twins, 1 four-poster, 1 single.
price	£75–£95. Singles £37.50–£55.
meals	Dinner, 3 courses, £20. Restaurant closed Sunday evenings.
closed	Over Christmas.
directions	North from Ipswich on A12 for 15 miles, then right onto B1078. In village, over railway line; hotel on right, just before church.

	Michael & Sally Ball
tel	01728 746524
fax	01728 746524
e-mail	mail@theoldrectorysuffolk.com
web	www.theoldrectorysuffolk.com

Hotel

map 4   entry 160

Pipps Ford
Needham Market, Suffolk IP6 8LJ

Richard Hakluyt, the Elizabethan chronicler, once had the 'Manor at Pipps'. It is still a fine Suffolk house, beamed and whitewashed and now with a conservatory – a riot of vines and other climbing plants, like a smart greenhouse and an entertaining place to dine. And you dine well – on tiger prawns in coconut with coriander and lemon, or bream, partridge, lamb... even talapia. The atmosphere in this easy-going and cosy house encourages conversation. Once through the narrow hall you are into a big sitting room with some fine furniture and a grand piano (another sitting room is sometimes used for private parties or meetings). The dining room is dark red, low-beamed and wooden floored. The bedrooms in the main house – there are some in a barn – are full of fabric and chintz, floral patterns and plain carpets: traditional and endearingly cottagey. The floors are characterfully crooked and rooms have very English views over the lovely garden. The house stands on its own, with walks along the old canal and so much of lovely Suffolk to see beyond. *Children over five welcome.*

rooms	7 doubles.
price	£65–£85. Singles £52.50.
meals	Dinner from £22.50. No dinner on Sundays.
closed	2 weeks over Christmas & New Year.
directions	From Ipswich, A14 north to roundabout where A140 joins A14. 1st left at roundabout down private track, signed to house.

	Raewyn Hackett-Jones
tel	01449 760208
fax	01449 760561
e-mail	b+b@pippsford.co.uk
web	www.pippsford.co.uk

Other Place

Ounce House

Northgate Street, Bury St Edmunds, Suffolk IP33 1HP

An extremely handsome 1870 red-brick townhouse minutes from the heart of one of England's prettiest ancient towns. Bury St Edmunds has a rich history; the Romans were here, its Norman abbey attracted pilgrims by the cartload, and the wool trade made it rich in the 1700s. A gentle, one-hour stroll takes you past 650 years of architectural wonder – special indeed. Ounce House is more house than hotel, pristine and full of fine antiques. Enjoy sumptuous breakfasts around a mighty-sized mahogany dining table and slump in leather armchairs around an ornate carved fireplace. Light floods in all day through the double doors between the drawing and dining rooms. Elsewhere, a snug library has an honesty bar, while three fine, homely bedrooms are packed with books, mahogany furniture, local art and piles of magazines; the one at the back of the house has a pretty view of the garden. The Potts can arrange tickets to the Theatre Royal, pick you up from the train station, or help you decide between the 35 restaurants within five minutes of the house.

rooms	3: 2 doubles, 1 twin.
price	£85–£95. Singles £60–£70.
meals	Restaurants in Bury St Edmunds.
closed	Rarely.
directions	A14 north, then central junction for Bury, following signs to historic centre. At 1st r'bout, left into Northgate St. On right at top of hill.

Simon & Jenny Pott

tel	01284 761779
fax	01284 768315
e-mail	pott@globalnet.co.uk
web	www.ouncehouse.co.uk

Other Place

map 4   entry 162

The Great House
Market Place, Lavenham, Suffolk CO10 9QZ

A little pocket of France in a pretty corner of England, The Great House pulls off that rare trick of being a hotel that feels like a home. Régis and Martine are charming, as are their French staff. The house is authentic, too, with an 18th-century front and a 15th-century interior that is utterly lovely and full of surprises. The bedrooms have antique desks and chests of drawers, fresh flowers and superb marble in perfect bathrooms. One has a big Jacobean oak four-poster, like an island in a sea of rugs; another in the roof has sofas and armchairs from which to marvel at the huge beamed timbers. Most have their own private sitting area and some have views over this bustling, historic market town. It's simply impossible to escape the generosity and good taste of it all, and that's never more true than in the restaurant – essence of France in the middle of Suffolk. The sheer splendour of the food brings guests back again and again; the cheese board alone is a work of art. Catch the early sun in the courtyard for breakfast, or eat supper *al fresco* on warm and lazy summer nights. *Leisure break prices available during the week.*

rooms	5 doubles.
price	£90–£150. Half-board from £68.95 p.p. Singles from £70.
meals	Lunch from £11. Dinner from £22.95. Restaurant closed Sunday nights & Mondays.
closed	January.
directions	From Sudbury, A134 towards Colchester for about 2 miles, then left, signed Lavenham. Hotel in market place.

	Régis & Martine Crépy
tel	01787 247431
fax	01787 248007
e-mail	info@greathouse.co.uk
web	www.greathouse.co.uk

Restaurant with Rooms

entry 163   map 4

The White Hart Inn

High Street, Nayland, Colchester, Suffolk CO6 4JF

Michel Roux's 'other place' is exquisite on all counts; the way things are done here is second to none. The service is remarkable. Staff here do have a sense of pride in their work – something of a rarity in Britain these days (although not in this book, of course…). The inn dates from the 15th century and has kept its timber-framed walls and beams. Inside has been opened up a bit, not enough to lose its rambling feel, but just enough to make it light and airy. Feast on "scrumptious food", to quote an enraptured guest, and sup from a vast collection of New World wines. "People like to travel when they drink," says Michel. Exemplary bedrooms have a striking yet simple country-style elegance: yellow walls and checked fabrics, crisp linen and thick blankets, excellent bathrooms, angled beams (two rooms almost have vaulted ceilings), piles of cushions, sofas or armchairs, and wonderful art; some have wildly sloping floors and one has original murals that may be the work of Constable's brother. Superb.

rooms	6: 5 doubles, 1 twin.
price	£82–£95. Singles £69–£75.
meals	Lunch from £9.95. Dinner about £24. Restaurant closed Mondays.
closed	Rarely.
directions	Nayland signed right 6 miles north of Colchester on the A134 (no access from A12). In village centre.

Michel Roux
tel	01206 263382
fax	01206 263638
e-mail	nayhart@aol.com
web	www.whitehart-nayland.co.uk

Restaurant with Rooms

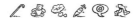

map 4   entry 164

Bailiffscourt Hotel

Climping, Sussex BN17 5RW

Everything about Bailiffscourt is exhilarating. It is beautiful to the eye, too, the architect having searched high and low for its soft, golden Somerset sandstone. The gardens and grounds are a simple paradise and as you stroll in peace from barn to coach house you feel as if you are walking around an ancient monastery. Inside, rooms are big and have a perfect medieval atmosphere, set off brilliantly by bold colours, rich fabrics and large tapestries on the walls. There are mullioned windows, heavy, ancient beams, even an entire ceiling of wood in the restaurant. Bedrooms are perfect, with carved four-posters, oak chests, waterfalls of cushions, 600-year-old doors, fabulous bathrooms and decanters of sherry. Best of all is the truth – Bailiffscourt, incredibly, is a 'genuine fake', built in the 1930s from innumerable medieval bits and bobs. One of the buildings was moved here brick by brick; only the 13th-century chapel is authentic. It is quite magnificent; there's even a beach at the end of the garden. Come and revel in it all.

rooms	40 doubles.
price	From £160. Singles from £140
meals	Lunch from £15.50. Dinner, 4 courses, £43.50.
closed	Rarely.
directions	From Littlehampton, A259 west. At brown sign for Bailiffscourt, left into Climping Street & up lane to hotel. Entrance last on right.

Sandy & Anne Goodman

tel	01903 723511
fax	01903 723107
e-mail	bailiffscourt@hshotels.co.uk
web	www.hshotels.co.uk

Hotel

The Royal Oak Inn

Pook Lane, East Lavant, Chichester, Sussex PO18 0AX

There's a comfortable, cheery, wine-bar feel to the Royal Oak; locals and young professionals come here, with their children, as often as not, yet it's as rural as can be. Inside, a modern-rustic look with traditional touches prevails: stripped floors, wooden tables, exposed brickwork, a dark leather sofa, racing pictures on the walls – the inn was once part of the Goodwood estate. The dining area is big, light and airy, with a conservatory, and you can spill out onto the front patio, warmed by outdoor lamps on summer nights; you face a road but this one goes nowhere. Five chefs serve up excellent salmon and chorizo fishcakes, honey and clove roasted ham, fillet steak. Bedrooms have a contemporary feel. Two are in a nearby barn, the rest are at the back of the pub, up the stairs; ask for one with a view. All have CD players and plasma screens, retro fans and top toiletries – the best of modern – along with excellent lighting, brown leather chairs and big comfy beds. Staff are friendly and attentive, breakfasts are good and fresh, and you are brilliantly placed for Chichester Theatre and Goodwood.

rooms	5 + 1: 5 doubles, 1 cottage for 4.
price	£70–£100. Singles £60–£70.
meals	Lunch & dinner, £13.50–£24.50, à la carte.
closed	Rarely.
directions	From Chichester, A286 towards Midhurst. At 1st mini r'bout, 1st right into East Lavant. Down hill, pass village green, over bridge, pub 200 yds on left. Car park opposite.

Nick Sutherland

tel	01243 527434
fax	01243 775062
e-mail	nickroyaloak@aol.com
web	www.sussexlive.co.uk/royaloakinn

Inn

map 3   entry 166

Ockenden Manor

Ockenden Lane, Cuckfield, Sussex RH17 5LD

If some hotels flatter to deceive, Ockenden Manor does the reverse, its handsome Tudor front providing no clue to the awesome cathedral proportions of inside. The change of scale is so sudden and surprising, it feels as if you've walked into a different building. In a way, you have, because what you see was rebuilt after a fire burnt down most of the original Tudor house in 1608. Enter a long hall that leads to an even grander drawing room with impossibly high ceilings. The dining room has original oak panelling from the floor up to a ceiling of carved floral motifs; stained-glass windows depict family crests and look onto well-loved gardens, small but perfect for a cream tea. Back inside, Sandy and Anne have filled the giant spaces with exquisite good taste: stunning furniture, vases of fresh flowers, decanters of port, cut-glass crystal and antique prints in the bar. Smart bedrooms, named after the children of previous owners, are decorated with Colefax & Fowler and Zoffany; some are in the house, the rest are in a 1990 addition. Close to Gatwick, but much more than an airport stopover.

rooms	22: 11 doubles, 4 twins, 1 single, 6 four-posters.
price	£160-£330. Singles from £105.
meals	Lunch from £12.95. Cream tea £7.50. Dinner, à la carte, £38.
closed	Rarely.
directions	A23 south from M23, then B2115 south-east to Cuckfield. In village, right, opp. Talbot Inn, into Ockenden Lane. Signed.

	Sandy & Anne Goodman
tel	01444 416111
fax	01444 415549
e-mail	ockenden@hshotels.co.uk
web	www.hshotels.co.uk

Hotel

The Griffin Inn

Fletching, Nr Uckfield, Sussex TN22 3SS

The Griffin is the sort of inn worth moving house to be near; perfect almost because of the occasional touch of scruffiness. The Pullan family run it with gentle passion as a true local inn: regulars were queuing up before opening time when we arrived on a chilly Tuesday in January. Inside, six open fires, obligatory 500-year-old beams, oak panelling, settles, red carpets, black and white photos on the walls... this inn has been allowed to age. There's a small club room for racing on Saturdays and two cricket teams play in summer. Bedrooms are perfect, tremendous value for money and full of uncluttered country-inn elegance: uneven floors, lots of old furniture, rag-rolled walls, free-standing Victorian baths, huge shower heads, crisp cotton linen, thick bathrobes. Rooms in the coach house, recently renovated, are quieter. Good food is guaranteed – the inn was voted best dining pub in Sussex. Over the summer months, jazz bands play in the garden against the backdrop of a 10-mile view across Ashdown Forest to Sheffield Park... and they lay on a spit-roast barbecue as well. Wonderful.

rooms	8: 1 twin, 7 four-posters.
price	£70–£120. Singles (Sun-Thurs) £50–£70.
meals	Lunch from £8. Dinner £20.
closed	Christmas Day.
directions	From East Grinstead, A22 south, then right at Nutley, signed Fletching. Straight on for 2 miles into village.

Bridget, Nigel & James Pullan

tel	01825 722890
fax	01825 722810
e-mail	thegriffininn@hotmail.com
web	www.thegriffininn.co.uk

Inn

map 4 entry 168

Stone House

Rushlake Green, Heathfield, Sussex TN21 9QJ

One of the bedrooms has a bathroom with enough room for a sofa and two chairs around the marble bath – but does that make it a suite? Jane thought not. The bedroom is big, too, has a beautiful four-poster, floods with light and, like all the rooms, has sumptuous furniture and seemingly ancient fabrics, all typical of the generosity of both house and owners. Stone House has been in the Dunn family for a mere 500 years and Peter and Jane have kept the feel of home. Downstairs, amid the splendour of the drawing room, there's still room for lots of old family photos; across the hall in the library, logs piled high wait to be tossed on the fire. Weave down a corridor to ancient oak panelling in the dining room for Jane's cooking – she's a Master Chef. Having eaten, walk out to the superb, half-acre walled kitchen garden and see where it's all grown – they're 99% self-sufficient in summer. There are 1,000 acres to explore and you can fish for carp. Indulgent picnic hampers for Glyndebourne, including chairs and tables, can be arranged.

rooms	6: 3 twins/doubles, 2 four-posters, 1 suite.
price	£115–£225. Singles £80–£115.
meals	Lunch, by arrangement, £24.95. Dinner £24.95.
closed	Christmas & New Year.
directions	From Heathfield, B2096, then 4th turning on right, signed Rushlake Green. 1st left by village green. Hotel on left, signed.

	Peter & Jane Dunn
tel	01435 830553
fax	01435 830726
web	www.stonehousesussex.co.uk

Hotel

Little Hemingfold Hotel
Telham, Battle, Sussex TN33 0TT

The south-east of England is much underrated in terms of rural beauty; drive up the bumpy track that leads to Little Hemingfold and you could be miles from the middle of nowhere. People who want to get away to the simplicity of deep country will like it here. It's comfortably rustic, a little like renting a remote country cottage, though here you don't have to cook or clean; open fires, *bergère* sofas and armchairs, books and games, lots of flowers and floods of light. Breakfast in the yellow dining room is under beams; at night the candles come out for delicious home-cooked dinners. The bedrooms are all over the place, some in the main house, others across the small, pretty courtyard. They are fairly earthy, four having woodburning stoves   again that feel of deep country – with a four-poster perhaps, maybe a sofa, glazed-brick walls and simple bathrooms. Outside, a two-acre lake to row and fish or swim in, a grass tennis court (the moles got the better of the croquet lawn), woodland to walk in and lots of peace and quiet.

rooms	12: 10 twins/doubles; 2 family with separate bath.
price	£90-£98. Singles £55-£85. Half-board £62-£69.50 p.p.
meals	Dinner, 4 courses, £26.50.
closed	January–12 February 2004.
directions	From Battle, A2100 for Hastings for 1.5 miles. Hotel signed left by 'sharp left' road sign, 0.5 miles up bumpy farm track.

Allison & Paul Slater

tel	01424 774338
fax	01424 775351
web	www.littlehemingfoldhotel.co.uk

Hotel

map 4   entry 170

Jeake's House
Mermaid Street, Rye, Sussex TN31 7ET

Rye, one of the Cinque Ports, is a perfect town for whiling away an afternoon; wander aimlessly and discover the tidal river, old fishing boats, arts and crafts shops and galleries. Jeake's House is in the middle of old Rye on a steep, ancient cobbled street. The house has a colourful past as wool store, school and home of American poet Conrad Potter Aiken. The galleried dining room, once an old Baptist chapel, is now painted deep red and is full of plants, busts, books, clocks and mirrors – perfect for those who like to make a grand entrance at breakfast! Jenny is engagingly easy-going and has created a lovely atmosphere. Rooms full of beams and timber frames are pretty, generously draped and excellent value. Some have stunning old chandeliers, others four-posters, and a mind-your-head stairway leads to a big attic room with views over roof tops and chimneys to open country. Downstairs, a small library keeps away the rainy day blues, the hearth is lit in winter and musicians will swoon at the working square piano. Relax into it all with a drink from the honesty bar. A super little hotel. *Children over 12 welcome.*

rooms	11: 7 doubles, 2 suites; 1 double, 1 single, sharing bath.
price	£84–£116. Singles £37–£77.
meals	Restaurants in Rye.
closed	Rarely.
directions	Enter Rye & follow signs to town centre under arch into High St, then 3rd left at Lloyds Bank & 1st right into Mermaid St. House on left. Parking nearby, £3 a day.

	Jenny Hadfield
tel	01797 222828
fax	01797 222623
e-mail	jeakeshouse@btinternet.com
web	www.jeakeshouse.com

Hotel

The Howard Arms

Lower Green, Ilmington, Warwickshire CV36 4LT

Once upon a time Robert and Gill ran the Cotswold House Hotel in Chipping Campden with a mix of flair, quirkiness and professionalism. After a deserved sabbatical, they decided to cast their fairy-dust over this old inn, with magical results. The Howard buzzes with good-humoured babble, as well-kept beer flows from the flagstoned bar. An irresistible dining room at the far end has unexpected elegance for a pub, with great swathes of bold colour and some noble paintings. Gorgeous bedrooms are set discreetly apart from the joyful throng, mixing period style and modern luxury beautifully: the double oozes olde worlde charm; the twin is more folksy, with American art and patchwork quilts; and the half-tester is almost a suite, full of antiques. All are individual, all huge by pub standards. The village is a surprise, too, literally tucked under a lone hill, with an unusual church surrounded by orchards and an extended village green. Round off an idyllic walk amid buzzing bees and fragrant wild flowers with a meal at the inn — folk come a long way to sample the food. Stratford and the theatre are close. *All bedrooms are no smoking.*

rooms	3: 1 twin, 2 doubles.
price	£98-108. Singles from £57.
meals	Lunch & dinner £8.50-£20.
closed	Christmas Day.
directions	From Moreton-in-Marsh, north on A429 for about 5 miles, then left, signed Darlingscott & Ilmington. Pub in village centre. From Stratford, south on A3400 for 4 miles, right to Wimpstone & Ilmington.

Robert & Gill Greenstock

tel	01608 682226
fax	01608 682226
e-mail	howard.arms@virgin.net
web	www.howardarms.com

Inn

map 3   entry 172

The Fox and Goose

Armscote, Nr Stratford-upon-Avon, Warwickshire CV37 8DD

Sue is young, clever and fun – one of those irrepressible innkeepers with an instinctive feel for what works. She also knows how to get, and keep, great staff – even chefs who don't have tantrums. It's obvious that she's popular with the locals who crowd the bar to do a bit of trading and get a glimpse of her and the lovely manager, Michelle. The walls and floors aren't half bad either – 17th-century beams and flagstones with 21st-century style and Farrow & Ball colours. Eat in the quieter dining room from a blackboard that changes every day – local, seasonal, fresh and rustled up by the very calm Dean. Sunday lunch is goose, beef or lamb, all roasted to perfection. Bedrooms are small, but bathrooms are big with claw-footed baths. The colours are very bold and there's not a whiff of chintz – instead find stripped wooden floors, good Egyptian cotton sheets and padded 'jester' headboards. Don't expect quiet until after 11.30 so join in the fun downstairs, or grab a disc from reception for your CD player, light the candles in the bathroom, fill the tub, and take in your glass of wine.

rooms	4 doubles.
price	£80. Singles £40.
meals	Lunch & dinner £4.50–£25.
closed	Christmas Day & New Year's Day.
directions	From Stratford A3400 south for 8 miles, then right for Armscote just after Newbold-on-Stour. In village.

	Sue Gray
tel	01608 682293
fax	01608 682293
web	www.foxandgoose.co.uk

Inn

The Red Lion

High Street, Lacock, Wiltshire SN15 2LQ

The dashing Mr Darcy was sensible enough to stop here during the BBC's filming of *Pride and Prejudice* – and how comforted he was by the inn's warm, beamed embrace. The Red Lion dates from the early 1700s, and may well have been known to the impressionable Jane Austen; big open fires, tankards hanging above the bar, rugs on flagstones, bare wooden floors – not a lot has changed. Order a drink and sit down to fine home-cooked food, amid timber frames, old settles, a row of branding irons and hanging Victorian birdcages; you may have to ask about the more bizarre farming tools on display. Climb the shallow tread of the stairs to small but excellent bedrooms in a Georgian style; old oak dressers, half-testers, crowns above beds, antique furniture, a beam or two. In summer, eat outside in the atmospheric courtyard garden, with country views. This beautifully preserved National Trust village was built around the 13th-century Abbey and on the old cloth route between London and Bristol. Fabulous walks from the pub, Lacock Abbey and the Fox Talbot Museum of Photography just down the road.

rooms	6: 5 doubles, 1 single.
price	£65–£75. Singles from £45.
meals	Lunch from £6. Dinner about £15.
closed	Rarely.
directions	Lacock, off A350 between Chippenham & Melksham. Inn on High Street.

Chris & Sarah Chappell

tel	01249 730456
fax	01249 730766

Inn

map 3   entry 174

The Angel Inn

Hindon, Wiltshire SP3 6DJ

It's impossible not to eat well at The Angel. The robust, modern English cooking draws folk from far and wide. Penny's latest venture at this 1750 coaching inn in the middle of beautiful Wiltshire countryside follows a wonderful Georgian conversion in Oxfordshire; she seems much more at home in her present surroundings. Over lunch, watch a mixed crowd of retired-military and likeable loafers file in for their medicinal pint. There's a great atmosphere: you might be asked to help with the crossword – that is, if Penny can't help. She's the first port of call for most things here: hands on, ever-present and a smiling stickler for things to be done just right, and why not! Downstairs, she's cast her magic wand over bar and restaurant; upstairs is next. We expect great things of the bedrooms, judging by the jazzy red walls and wooden floors of the bar. Further on, under the bust of a plaster angel, the linear and more formal restaurant is softened by impressively large black and white photographs of scenes taken within five miles of the inn – the tree surrounded by wild garlic is beautiful. Terrific.

rooms	7: 4 doubles, 1 twin, 1 family, 1 four-poster.
price	£50-£75. Singles from £50.
meals	Lunch, à la carte, about £14. Dinner, à la carte, about £22. Restaurant & bar closed Sunday evenings.
closed	Rarely.
directions	From A303, Hindon signed left about 7 miles after main A36 Salisbury turn-off. Inn at x-roads in village.

	Penny Simpson
tel	01747 820696
fax	01747 820869
e-mail	eat@theangel-inn.co.uk
web	www.theangel-inn.co.uk

Inn

Howard's House

Teffont Evias, Nr Salisbury, Wiltshire SP3 5RJ

Howard's has been a favourite of ours for years – luxurious without boasting, modest in its success, the sort of place where the sun shines, even in January. With one toe in deep country, this attractive 1623 stone house is the last building in a quiet village of soaring church spire and gently rising hills. Step inside the warm flagstoned entrance hall to beautiful mullioned windows of odd shapes and sizes, masses of space, flowers everywhere and bold colours throughout. Mustard and red walls draw you into the sitting room to relax by a huge stone fireplace – you'll find *Tatler*, *The Economist* and *Classic Car* on the table. Strong yellows and blues lift the crisp, modern dining room, and pastel hues dominate faultless bedrooms with floral fabrics, fresh fruit, home-made biscuits, bathrobes and big towels. French windows lead to patios with tables and chairs. The quintessentially English garden has clipped hedges, croquet lawns, a fountain, a pond and vegetable and sensory herb patches; some of the produce ends up on your table and the modern British cooking is consistently good. Beautiful Wiltshire starts right outside.

rooms	9: 6 doubles, 1 twin/double, 1 family, 1 four-poster.
price	£145–£165. Singles from £95.
meals	Dinner, £23.95; à la carte about £27.
closed	Christmas.
directions	From Salisbury, A350, then B3089 east to Teffont. In village, right at sharp left-hand bend, following brown hotel sign. Entrance on right after 0.5 miles.

Noele Thompson

tel	01722 716392
fax	01722 716820
e-mail	enq@howardshousehotel.co.uk
web	www.howardshousehotel.co.uk

Restaurant with Rooms

map 3   entry 176

The Compasses Inn

Lower Chicksgrove, Tisbury, Wiltshire SP3 6NB

The first impression on arriving at Compasses is of having found the perfect English pub; so is the second. In the middle of a lovely village of thatched and timber-framed cottages, this inn seems so content with its lot it could almost be a figment of your imagination. Over the years, 14th-century foundations have gradually sunk into the ground. Its thatched roof is like a sombrero, shielding bedroom windows that peer sleepily over the lawn. Duck instinctively into the sudden darkness of the bar and experience a wave of nostalgia as your eyes adjust to a long wooden room, with flagstones and cosy booths divided by farmyard salvage: a cartwheel here, some horse tack there; at one end is a piano, at the other, a brick hearth. The pub crackles with Alan's enthusiasm; he's fairly new to the trade, but his genuine hospitality more than compensates. People come for the food as well: figs baked in red wine, topped with goat's cheese and chorizo, or grilled fish from the south coast. Bedrooms have the same effortless charm and the sweet serenity of Wiltshire is all around. Modest, ineffably pretty, and great value.

rooms	4: 2 doubles, 2 twins/doubles.
price	From £55. Singles £40.
meals	Lunch from £4. Dinner, à la carte, about £20.
closed	Mondays except Bank Holidays, then closed Tuesdays.
directions	From Salisbury, A30 west, 3rd right after Fovant, signed Lower Chicksgrove, then 1st left down single track lane to village.

	Alan Stoneham
tel	01722 714318
fax	01722 714318

Inn

The Cottage in the Wood

Holywell Road, Malvern Wells, Worcestershire WR14 4LG

Walk along a path through the woods, dappled with light, and emerge in a clearing in this very English jungle. There, The Cottage gazes across the wide, flat Severn Valley to the distant Cotswolds. Walk all the way to the breezy top of the Malvern Hills – England's oldest rock and a forgotten corner much loved by Elgar. It is enough just to be here, but to find such an endearingly friendly, book-lined and log-fired country-house hotel is heart-warming. Furniture, curtains, carpets and wallpapers are polished, swagged, patterned and lined, and distinctly pre-modern. The service is magnificent, the sort you only get when a large and talented family is at the helm. Dominic's cooking is as good as his father's hotel-keeping, and his brother-in-law is front of house. Local produce is used in an eclectic, modern and imaginative way and portions are unusually generous: try poached pear with rocket and Cashel blue cheese, then baked salmon with a soft horseradish crust. Relax in the main house, drink in the views and John's well-chosen wines, play basketball from your bath. There's lots of humour as well as old-fashioned professionalism.

rooms	31: 21 doubles, 8 twins/doubles, 2 four-posters.
price	£99–£170. Half-board (min. 2 nights) £70–£117 p.p. Singles £79–£99.
meals	Lunch from £12.95. Packed lunch £8.50. Dinner, à la carte, £35.
closed	Rarely.
directions	M50, junc. 1, A38 for Worcester. After 3 miles on A4104, left for Upton upon Severn. Right after bridge on B4211, left 1.5 miles on, on B4209.

	John & Sue Pattin
tel	01684 575859
fax	01684 560662
e-mail	reception@cottageinthewood.co.uk
web	www.cottageinthewood.co.uk

Hotel

map 3   entry 178

The Endeavour

1 High Street, Staithes, Yorkshire TS13 5BH

A hidden treasure in the small fishing village of Staithes. Named, like so many things along this stretch of coast, after Captain Cook's ship – built at nearby Whitby – the little fish restaurant with rooms has been successfully squeezed into four storeys of an old terraced house. Elegantly-laid tables occupy two floors, and look onto a narrow, cobbled street leading to the harbour. Bedrooms are equally comfortable and great value; one looks over the herb garden, one to the sea, another over rooftops to Cowbar's cliffs. The menu is stuffed full of fish dishes from today's catch, perfectly prepared by owners/chefs Charlotte and Brian: hake, crab, lobster, brill, turbot, mullet, halibut, shark, squid, wild salmon... some of the best seafood in Britain is landed here, and at Whitby. Meat and vegetarian dishes are also on the menu and puddings are an absolute treat. Walk to Cook's museum or round the exquisite, boat-bobbed harbour – waves crash, seagulls screech: little has changed since Cook gazed out to sea. Book well ahead – the secret is out! *Private parking spaces reserved for guests.*

rooms	3 doubles.
price	£60-£70. Half-board Tues-Thurs (min. 2 nights) £100-110 p.p.
meals	Dinner, à la carte, £30 with wine. Restaurant closed Sunday & Monday.
closed	Rarely.
directions	From Whitby, A174 for about 8 miles, then right, signed Staithes. Head right down into old village. Restaurant on right about 100 yds before quayside.

Charlotte Willoughby & Brian Kay

tel	01947 840825
e-mail	theendeavour@ntlworld.com
web	www.endeavour-restaurant.co.uk

Restaurant with Rooms

Simonstone Hall

Hawes, Yorkshire DL8 3LY

Drool over the picture of Simonstone, knowing it's just as good inside. This is a glorious country house, built in the 1770s as a shooting lodge for the Earl of Wharncliffe. The drawing room is magnificent – gracious and elegant – with a wildly ornate fireplace, painted panelled walls and a flurry of antiques. Its triumph is the huge stone-mullioned window through which Wensleydale unravels – a place to stand rooted to the spot. Elsewhere, find stone-flagged floors, stained-glass windows and old oils and trophies. There's a big warm traditional bar – almost an inn – with hanging fishing nets, clocks and mirrors, where you can eat well; or pull out all the stops and dine in the lovely, cream-panelled dining room on cream of celery soup, perhaps, and noisette of lamb. Bedrooms are superb. It's well worth splashing out and going for the grander ones – they indulge you completely: four-posters, mullioned windows, stone fireplaces, oils – the full aristocratic Monty. Breakfast on the terrace with those fabulous views, then stride off into the hills… preferably with a champagne picnic.

rooms	20: 9 doubles, 4 twins/doubles, 5 four-posters, 2 suites.
price	£120–£240. Singles from £60.
meals	Lunch from £5. Dinner about £35.
closed	Rarely.
directions	From Hawes, north for Muker for about 2 miles. Hotel on left, at foot of Buttertubs Pass.

	Jill Stott
tel	01969 667255
fax	01969 667741
e-mail	e-mail@simonstonehall.demon.co.uk
web	www.simonstonehall.com

Restaurant with Rooms

map 6   entry 180

Waterford House

19 Kirkgate, Middleham, Yorkshire DL8 4PG

In a lively village dominated by Middleham Castle — northern stronghold of Richard III — is this comfortable Georgian-house hotel. Martin and Anne arrived here a year ago; they are exceptional hosts, easy and delightful. Settle into the sitting room where antiques and sofas jostle, chat to Anne by the Aga as she stirs a strawberry coulis. After canapés in the drawing room with guests, prepare for a memorable meal and ambrosial wines — the list is long. On summer evenings dine *al fresco* in the country garden with its trickling stream. Bedrooms, up narrow — in some parts steep — stairs have bags of old-fashioned comfort: wrought-iron beds, William Morris wallpaper, pictures, books, magazines, sherry, home-made cakes... the panelled four-poster with blue bedspread and bolsters is a treat. Middleham is a racing village and has 14 stable yards — horses clop by in the morning on their way to the gallops. Breakfast, served on fine china and white linen, is a feast of produce from Anne's parents' farm. Linger as long as you like — it's that sort of place; then pull on your hiking boots and unravel the Dales.

rooms	5: 2 doubles, 1 twin/double, 2 four-posters.
price	£75-£100. Singles £50-£60.
meals	Dinner from £29.
closed	Rarely.
directions	Southbound from A1 at Scotch Corner via Richmond and Leyburn; house at top of hill on right, on entering village square. Northbound from A1 on B6267 via Masham; in right-hand corner of square.

	Martin Cade & Anne Gardener
tel	01969 622090
fax	01969 624020
e-mail	info@waterfordhousehotel.co.uk
web	www.waterfordhousehotel.co.uk

Restaurant with Rooms

The Blue Lion

East Witton, Nr Leyburn, Yorkshire DL8 4SN

The Blue Lion has a big reputation locally; so big it followed our inspector round Yorkshire – "you must go there," everyone said. Paul and Helen came here several years ago, mixing the traditions of a country pub with the elegance of a country house. This is a bustling, happy place and no-one seems in a hurry to leave – add superlative food and it's not hard to see why it's such a favourite with locals. Aproned staff, polished beer taps, stone-flagged floors, open fires, newspapers on poles, big settles to sit at, huge bunches of dried flowers hanging from beams, splashes of fresh flowers. The two restaurants have boarded floors and shuttered Georgian windows, two coal fires, gilt mirrors and candles everywhere. Bedrooms are comfortable rather than luxurious: those in the main house have bold dashes of colour, padded headboards and wooden beds; in the stables, exposed beams, old pine, regal colours, velux windows, maybe a brass bed. East Witton has an interesting plague tale to tell, Jervaulx Abbey is a mile away, there's tennis next door and a lush, enclosed garden at the back that's safe for children.

rooms	12: 9 doubles, 2 twins, 1 family.
price	£69-£89. Singles £54.
meals	Bar meals from £7. Dinner from £25.
closed	Rarely.
directions	From Leyburn, A6108 for 3 miles to East Witton.

Paul & Helen Klein

tel	01969 624273
fax	01969 624189
e-mail	bluelion@breathemail.net
web	www.thebluelion.co.uk

Inn

map 6   entry 182

The Yorke Arms

Ramsgill-in-Nidderdale, Nr Harrogate, Yorkshire HG3 5RL

It takes a lot of nous to establish one of the best restaurants in Britain, let alone one up a small country lane in the middle of the Yorkshire Dales. The Yorke Arms is near perfection; exquisite food, wonderful rooms and beautiful countryside make it irresistible. The oldest part was built by monks in the 11th century, the rest added in 1750 when it became a coaching inn. The interior is absolutely charming, with polished flagstone floors, low oak beams, comfy armchairs, open fires and antique tables; in summer, eat under a pergola near a burbling beck. Classy rooms continue the theme; attention to detail is guaranteed. Bill, affable and considerate, is a natural host, while Frances scintillates the palette in the kitchen, using fish from the east and west coasts and meat and game from the Dales. Wander from the hamlet of Ramsgill to nearby Gouthwaite reservoir – formed during the Industrial Revolution to supply the city of Bradford with water – or work up an appetite visiting Brimham Rocks or Stump Cross Caverns. *Kennels for pets £5 per night.*

rooms	14: 7 doubles, 3 twins/doubles, 3 singles, 1 cottage suite.
price	Half-board only £90-£160 p.p.
meals	Lunch about £25. Dinner included; non-residents about £35-£40. Restaurant closed Sunday evenings to non-residents.
closed	Occasionally in Jan & Nov.
directions	From Ripley, B6165 to Pateley Bridge. Over bridge at bottom of High St; 1st right into Low Wath Road to Ramsgill (4 miles).

Bill & Frances Atkins

tel	01423 755243
fax	01423 755330
e-mail	enquiries@yorke-arms.co.uk
web	www.yorke-arms.co.uk

Restaurant with Rooms

The Red Lion
By the Bridge at Burnsall, Nr Skipton, Yorkshire BD23 6BU

Family-run and family-friendly, The Red Lion is an inn for all ages, full of olde-worlde charm and fun. Even the resident ghost in the 12th-century cellars has a sense of humour, amusing itself by turning off the beer taps from time to time! Elizabeth keeps a matriarchal eye on things, ensuring spirits a floor above don't get out of hand either, while son-in-law Jim cooks seriously good food. The net result is cosy, unpretentious, thoroughly comfortable, and humming with happy locals. The sitting room, with comfy sofas and a woodburning stove, has books for all, from guides to kids' adventure stories. Bedrooms above the inn are small but have bags of character with wooden beams, low slanting ceilings and big brass beds. Rooms in a next-door courtyard barn annexe are larger and two have an open fire. Originally a ferryman's inn, it was made redundant by the beautiful stone bridge that spans the wide and shallow river; its gentle meander matches the pace of this small, sleepy village set in a glorious English landscape. The Burnsall fell race – eight minutes up, four minutes down – starts outside the front door.

rooms	11: 5 doubles, 4 twins/doubles, 1 family, 1 single.
price	£95–£120. Singles from £55. Half-board £80 p.p.
meals	Brasserie lunch & dinner from £7.50. Dinner in restaurant £28.95.
closed	Rarely.
directions	From Harrogate, A59 west to Bolton Bridge; B6160 to Burnsall. Hotel next to bridge.

Elizabeth & Andrew Grayshon

tel	01756 720204
fax	01756 720292
e-mail	redlion@daelnet.co.uk
web	www.redlion.co.uk

Inn

map 6   entry 184

The Boar's Head Hotel

Ripley Castle Estate, Harrogate, Yorkshire HG3 3AY

When the Ingilbys decided to reopen The Boar's Head, the attic at the castle got a shakedown and the spare furniture was sent round. The vicar even came to bless the beer taps – you'll find them in Boris's bar, Boris being the eponymous head. Elegant fun is the net result and there's something for everyone. Lady Ingilby has done a brilliant job with the décor. The sitting rooms and hall have crisp yellow Regency wallpaper, big old oils, roaring fires and gilt mirrors. The restaurant is a deep, moody crimson, candlelit at night, and you drink from blue glass. There are games to play, newspapers to peruse, menus to drool over and a parasoled garden where you can sip long summer drinks. Up the staircase, past more ancestors, to bright, smartly done bedrooms, with floral fabrics, antique furniture, fresh flowers, sofas, tumbling crowns above big beds and rag-rolled bathrooms; those in the coachman's loft in the courtyard have the odd beam and pretty pine panelling. Visit the castle gardens as a guest of the hotel; umbrellas and wellies are there for you on rainy days.

rooms	25: 4 doubles, 21 twins/doubles.
price	£120. Half-board (min. 2 nights) from £80 p.p. Singles £99-£120.
meals	Dinner, à la carte, £18.50-£30. Lunch & dinner in bistro from £9.95.
closed	Rarely.
directions	From Harrogate, A61 north for 3 miles, then left at r'bout, signed to Ripley & castle.

Sir Thomas & Lady Emma Ingilby

tel	01423 771888
fax	01423 771509
e-mail	reservations@boarsheadripley.co.uk
web	www.boarsheadripley.co.uk

Inn

Hotel du Vin & Bistro

Prospect Place, Harrogate, Yorkshire HG1 1LB

That wise bunch at the Hotel du Vin have picked the Georgian spa town of Harrogate as the latest outpost in a string of city successes. Overlooking 200 acres of urban greenery known as the Stray, the old Harrogate Spa Hotel has been transformed into a busy, bustling bistro and bar with beautifully chic and wickedly comfortable rooms. Beds are made to while away most of the morning in (breakfast is served until 11am), linen is luscious, duvets are duckdown, there are showers that drench and free-standing baths big enough to swim in. 'Feel free to take the toiletries home,' reads the sign: it's that sort of place – informal, easy, where children (by arrangement) can sleep in your room. The bistro has antique tables, bright leather banquettes, murals of famous nudes – a heady mix; there's a great buzz, fabulous food and a French sommelier to help you choose from 600 wines, many sold by the glass. The package is contemporary but not off-puttingly cool, and staff get the balance right between friendliness and formality. Harrogate is charming and stylish, the legendary Betty's Tea Rooms comfortingly close.

rooms	43: 39 doubles, 4 suites.
price	£95–£115. Suites £145–£225.
meals	Breakfast £9.50–£13.50. Lunch & dinner £22–£30.
closed	Rarely.
directions	Follow city centre signs to Prince of Wales r'bout. 3rd exit off r'bout for 'town centre', stay in right-hand lane & pass West Park Church. 1st right into James St & right again into Prospect Place.

	Robin Hutson
tel	01423 856800
fax	01423 856801
e-mail	info@harrogate.hotelduvin.com
web	www.hotelduvin.com

Hotel

 map 7 entry 186

The Abbey Inn

Byland Abbey, Coxwold, Yorkshire YO61 4BD

The monks of Ampleforth who built this farmhouse would surely approve of its current devotion to good food; whether they'd be as accepting of its devotion to luxury is another matter. But one monk's frown is another man's path to righteousness. The Abbey Inn is a delightful oasis next to a ruined 12th-century abbey – lit up at night – that indulges the senses. They measure success in smiles up here; Jane loves to see the look on people's faces as they enter the Piggery restaurant, a big flagstoned space, lit by a skylight, full of Jacobean-style chairs and antique tables, that demands your joyful attention. Bedrooms are jaw-dropping, too. Abbot's Retreat has a huge four-poster while a bust of Julius Caesar in the gorgeous black and white tiled bathroom strikes a nice, decadent note – order a bottle of bubbly and jump in the double-ended bath. Priors Lynn has the best view – right down the aisle of the abbey; all have bathrobes, aromatherapy oils, fruit, home-made biscuits and a 'treasure chest' of wine. Come to enjoy it all.

rooms	3 doubles.
price	£80–£120.
meals	Light lunch from £5. Dinner, à la carte, about £16. Restaurant closed Sunday nights & Monday lunchtimes.
closed	Rarely.
directions	From A1 junc. 49, A168 for Thirsk for 10 miles, then A19 for York at r'bout. Left after 2 miles, to Coxwold. There, left to Byland Abbey. Opposite abbey.

	Jane & Martin Nordli
tel	01347 868204
fax	01347 868678
e-mail	jane@nordli.freeserve.co.uk
web	www.bylandabbeyinn.co.uk

Inn

The Star Inn

Harome, Nr Helmsley, Yorkshire YO62 5JE

You know you've 'hit the jackpot' as soon as you walk into The Star – it ticks over with such modest ease and calm authority. Andrew and Jacquie arrived in 1996, daughters Daisy and Tilly not long after, and the Michelin star in 2002. It's been a formidable turnaround given this 14th-century inn had an iffy local reputation when they took over, yet there's no arrogance; the brochure simply says: "He cooks, and she looks after you"… and how! Andrew's food is rooted in Yorkshire tradition, refined with French flair and written in plain English on ever-changing menus: try dressed Whitby crab, beef from two miles away, Ryedale deer, or maybe Theakston ale cake. Fabulous bedrooms, all ultra-modern yet seriously rustic, are just a stroll away. Thatched and 15th-century, Black Eagle Cottage has three suites; the rest of the rooms are in Cross House Lodge, a breathtaking new barn conversion; the largest room has its own snooker table. There's also the Mousey Thompson bar, the roof mural, the deli and the Coffee Loft   just possibly the most enchanting attic in the world. Brilliant.

rooms	11: 6 doubles, 2 doubles/twins, 3 suites.
price	£120–£195.
meals	Lunch from £3.50. Dinner, à la carte, £25.
closed	Mondays (incl. bank holiday Mondays) & Christmas Day (call to confirm).
directions	From Thirsk, A170 for Scarborough. Through Helmsley, then right, for Harome. Inn in village.

Andrew & Jacquie Pern

tel	01439 770397
fax	01439 771833

Inn

map 7   entry 188

The White Swan

Market Place, Pickering, Yorkshire YO18 7AA

Mix the boundless energy of a former futures trader with the magical beauty of the North Yorkshire Moors and amazing things can happen. Victor gave up a job in the City to take over this old coaching inn from his parents and it's obvious wandering round that he and Marion left the stress behind and brought a lot of style. They've refurbished the place throughout with simple good taste. Duck in through the front door to find cosy tap rooms that nicely contrast: the lounge with deep burgundy walls and open fire and the light dining room, with porthole mirrors and plaques from champagne cases on each table. Further on, the sitting room and formal restaurant add more indulgence. Bedrooms are elegantly clutter-free: good fabrics, Penhaligon smellies, antique beds, maybe a comfy armchair and a view of the pretty courtyard. The food is just as good – the head chef has been with the Buchanans for years; breakfast inspired one traveller to write a poem, now framed. Rievaulx Abbey is close, the steam railway even closer and a local pub has a tombstone in its roof. Full of surprises. *Pet surcharge, £7.50 per pet.*

rooms	12: 5 doubles, 5 twins/doubles, 2 suites.
price	From £110. Singles from £70. Suites from £130.
meals	Lunch about £15. Dinner about £25.
closed	Rarely.
directions	From Thirsk, A170 to Pickering. Entering town, left at r'bout, then 1st right up Market Place. On left.

Victor & Marion Buchanan

tel	01751 472288
fax	01751 475554
e-mail	welcome@white-swan.co.uk
web	www.white-swan.co.uk

Inn

The Grange Hotel

1 Clifton, York, Yorkshire YO30 6AA

Half a mile from the city wall where the ancient Minster stands, this lovely hotel casts its spell immediately. The Grange is everything a big townhouse hotel should be: gracious, elegant, sumptuously grand, with a warmth that will unravel the tightest knot. Jeremy and Vivien rescued the Georgian building from years of municipal neglect. Effortless style runs throughout: stone floors, Doric columns and urns erupting with flowers greet you in the hall. Deep comfy sofas in the morning room ask to be worn in some more, and the gorgeous vaulted brasserie in the old cellars with red banquettes in snug corners is an unexpected surprise. The formal dining room has a mural covering wall and ceiling showing a race scene through the open flaps of a blue-and-white-striped pavilion. The horse-racing link is apropos: York's course is considered one of the most exciting in Britain. The hotel is always full on race days – it's said the optimists meet here! Bedrooms are also full of flair: bold greens and reds, a silky purple four-poster, writing paper on the desks and rich fabrics. Those after history need only step outside.

rooms	30: 8 doubles, 16 twins/doubles, 3 singles, 2 four-posters, 1 suite.
price	£140–£200. Singles from £110. Suite £240.
meals	Lunch from £12.75. Dinner from £28.
closed	Rarely.
directions	From York ring road, A19 south into city centre. Hotel on right after 2 miles, 400 yds from city walls.

	Jeremy & Vivien Cassel
tel	01904 644744
fax	01904 612453
e-mail	info@grangehotel.co.uk
web	www.grangehotel.co.uk

Hotel

map 7   entry 190

Weaver's

15 West Lane, Haworth, Yorkshire BD22 8DU

If you don't know what a Clun or a Lonk is, use it as an excuse to make a trip to this unusual restaurant with rooms – the answer is somewhere on the walls. The rambling eccentricity here is superb; nothing has a place, yet everything is exactly where it should be. The front bar has the intimate feel of an old French café, with heavy wood, marble-topped tables, atmospheric lighting and comfy chairs, while the lively restaurant at the back seems in step with the Charleston era. None of this was intended, of course. Eat the best and most unpretentious food imaginable – smoked haddock soup, Pennine pie, home-made ice cream... even Yorkshire feta. It's outstanding value and people come back time and again. Bedrooms are as full of surprises and understated originality: French beds, dashes of bright colour, the odd bust, antique furniture – everything is just right. Rooms at the back overlook the Brontë Parsonage. Colin runs front of house – from the kitchen – with true Yorkshire sass: straight-talking, down-to-earth, and blessed with a wicked sense of humour. Worth a long detour, for the organic breakfast alone.

rooms	3 twins/doubles with separate bath.
price	£80. Singles £55.
meals	Dinner £12.50-£25; à la carte about £25; bar supper about £12.50. Dinner Tuesdays to Saturdays. Lunch Wednesdays, Thursdays, Fridays & Sundays.
closed	26 December-9 January.
directions	A6033 to Haworth, follow signs to Brontë Parsonage Museum. Use museum car park. Restaurant near passageway to high street.

Colin & Jane Rushworth

tel	01535 643822
fax	01535 644832
e-mail	weavers@amserve.net
web	www.weaversmallhotel.co.uk

Restaurant with Rooms

The Weavers Shed Restaurant with Rooms

Knowl Road, Golcar, Huddersfield, Yorkshire HD7 4AN

Stephen's reputation for producing sublime food goes from strength to strength at this restaurant with rooms, firmly fixed on the wish lists of foodies all over the country. His passion stretches as far as planting a one-acre kitchen garden; it now provides most of his vegetables, herbs and fruit. You may get warm mousse of scallops, Lunesdale duckling and warm rhubarb tartlet – the latter home-grown, of course – and edible flowers from Stephen's wildflower garden in the salad. The old mill owner's house sits at the top of the hill, with cobbles in the courtyard and a lamp by the door. Inside, whitewashed walls are speckled with menus from famous restaurants, a small garden basks beyond the windows and, at the bar, malts and eaux de-vie stand behind a piece of wood that looks as if it came from an ancient church, but actually is from the Co-op. Earthy stone arches and plinths in the Sardinian-tiled restaurant give the feel of a Tuscan farmhouse. Elsewhere, gilt mirrors, comfy sofas and big, bright, brilliantly priced bedrooms that hit the spot with complimentary sherry, dried flowers, bathrobes and wicker chairs.

rooms	5: 3 doubles, 1 twin/double, 1 four-poster.
price	£65–£80. Singles £50–£65.
meals	Lunch from £9.95. Dinner about £29. Restaurant closed Saturday lunchtimes, Sundays & Mondays.
closed	Christmas & New Year.
directions	From Huddersfield A62 west for 2 miles, then right for Milnsbridge & Golcar. Left at Kwiksave; signed on right at top of hill.

Stephen & Tracy Jackson

tel	01484 654284
fax	01484 650980
e-mail	info@weaversshed.co.uk
web	www.weaversshed.co.uk

Restaurant with Rooms

map 6   entry 192

Guernsey Tourist Board

channel islands

La Fregate Hotel

Les Cotils, St Peter Port, Guernsey GY1 1UT

Christopher, a larger-than-life Yorkshireman, has brought a whoosh of fresh air to Guernsey. The restaurant, dazzling with light, is semi-circular with cream walls, navy carpet, modern paintings and a pretty terrace overlooking the harbour – it all feels so French. Bedrooms are charming, very plain with thick cream and beige curtains, big beds with crisp white sheets and white bathrooms with wooden floors. There are four ground floor bedrooms and most upstairs rooms have glorious views to the harbour and the fort from little balconies with pots of flowers. The décor may be modern but the food is a mixture of styles with a classic twist – a flambé trolley still exists here and you can have lobster, proper Châteaubriand, carving at the table and formal service. Christopher's gardener grows 'the most cherished vegetables on the island' on an immaculate, terraced plot surrounded by little lawns and formal beds. Stunning beaches are close, the harbour is in front of you with boats to Sark and Hern and there are glorious gardens to wander through. A 50s style holiday in state-of-the art comfort.

rooms	13: 9 twins/doubles, 4 singles.
price	£135–£175. Singles from £85.
meals	Dinner, 2 courses from £13.95; à la carte from £21.
closed	Rarely.
directions	2 minutes' walk from the centre of town.

Christopher Sharp

tel	01481 724624
e-mail	01481 720443
web	www.lafregatehotel.com

Hotel

La Sablonnerie

Little Sark, Via Guernsey, GY9 0SD

If you tell Elizabeth which ferry you're arriving on, she'll send down her horse and carriage to meet you. "Small, sweet world of wave-encompassed wonder," wrote Swinburne of Sark. The tiny community of 500 people lives under a spell, governed feudally and sharing this magic island with horses, sheep, cattle, carpets of wild flowers and birds. There are wild cliff walks, thick woodland, sandy coves, wonderful deep rock pools, aquamarine seas. No cars, only bikes, horse and carriage and the odd tractor. In the hotel – a 400-year-old farmhouse – there is no TV, no radio, no trouser press… just a dreamy peace, kindness, starched cotton sheets, woollen blankets and food to die for. Eat in the lovely dining-room or in the prettiest of well-tended gardens with gorgeous colourful borders. The Perrées still farm and, as a result, the hotel is almost self-sufficient; you also get home-baked bread and lobsters straight from the sea. Elizabeth is Sercquaise – her mother's family were part of the 1565 colonisation – and she knows her land well enough to point you to the island's secrets.

rooms	22: 5 doubles, 6 twins, 6 family, 1 suite; 2 doubles, 2 twins, sharing 2 baths.
price	£95–£155. Half-board £59.50–£75.50 p.p.
meals	Dinner, 5 courses, £30.
closed	2nd Monday in October-Wednesday before Easter.
directions	Take ferry to Sark and ask!

Elizabeth Perrée

tel	01481 832061
fax	01481 832408

Hotel

map 3   entry 194

Atlantic Hotel

St Brelade, Jersey JE3 8HE

Perfect peace, perfect luxury – and sunsets across a golden sea will be your lasting memory of The Atlantic. It may look big, modern, almost brashly confident, but enter and you'll find the virtues we consider so important: warmth, personality and individual attention. In the past few years, Patrick has given the hotel built by his father in the early 70s an impressive makeover, creating the 21st-century equivalent of those grand old hotels of the Edwardian age. It is bold, beautifully run by loyal and friendly staff, irrepressibly comfortable, and understated. Classic and contemporary blend well, balancing antiques, urns, fountains, a wrought-iron staircase and specially commissioned furniture upholstered in warm, rich fabrics. The bedrooms are big, modern, pale and cool, with bathrooms of white marble, pale oak and polished chrome; many have sliding doors to balconies with ship-style balustrading and lovely sea views. Dine on smoked salmon parcels filled with fresh crab, tomato and saffron and then, perhaps, roast beef on potato rosti, wild mushrooms and shallot marmalade. Full of style – and the sound of the sea will hypnotise.

rooms	50: 48 twins/doubles, 2 suites.
price	£185–£270. Singles £140–£170. Suite £260–£445.
meals	Lunch £13.50. Dinner, 3 courses, £30; à la carte also available.
closed	5 January–5 February.
directions	From Jersey airport, B36 for St Brelade for 1.5 miles. Right at lights onto A13, for St Ouen's Bay, for 1 mile, then right into La Rue de la Sergente. Hotel signed at top of hill.

Patrick Burke

tel	01534 744101
fax	01534 744102
e-mail	info@theatlantichotel.com
web	www.theatlantichotel.com

Hotel

Eulah Country House

Mont Cochon, St Helier, Jersey JE2 3JA

Eulah Country House is a rare and wonderful treat, designed for hedonists, perfectionists, stressed business people who still need to plug in and for elegant weddings. Sink in, soak up and let this beautifully restored Edwardian house take the strain. Generous sofas tumble with cushions, flowers brim from vases, there's a curvaceous pool... of all the luxuries here, none is as engagingly self-mocking as the four-poster bath. Tables and chairs are attractive and chunky; the long, lovely sitting room has unexpected beams. Bedrooms are enormous, each carpeted with a meadow of rich, plain pile, each with its own breakfast 'nook'. Colours are bold and classic – swathes of material swoop up from behind headboards and over pillows to the ceiling. Few of us imagine having such impressive beds at home; the bathroom fittings are the ones you dare not buy for yourself. Long, lush views stretch across St Helier and St Aubin's Bay, and Penny runs the place with easy good humour. Whether you're in the sauna or the pool, you may wonder if it's a home or a hotel... in spite of the luxury, we found it hard to tell the difference.

rooms	9: 6 doubles, 3 twins/doubles.
price	£160–£230. Singles £100–£180.
meals	Restaurants locally.
closed	Rarely.
directions	From St Helier, A2 west, then right at lights on B27. Through next lights up Mont Cochon. Entrance 100 yds on right.

	Penny Clarke
tel	01534 626626
fax	01534 626600
e-mail	eulah@jerseymail.co.uk
web	www.eulah.co.uk

Hotel

map 3   entry 196

photograpy by Murray Carden, Knoyd.Art,The Pier House entry no 228

scotland

Raemoir House Hotel

Raemoir, Banchory, Aberdeenshire AB31 4ED

Grand it is – but not intimidating: the staff are lovely. The 1750 mansion, with east and west wings added, is built of granite and slate; the original House of Raemoir, known as the Ha' Hoose (Hall House), is older and makes a historically significant 'annexe'. (Mary Queen of Scots was a guest.) Raemoir is majestic on the outside, resplendent within. Vases burst with flowers, log fires glow, sofas tumble with cushions; stags' heads line the Morning Room and velvet brocade the dining room – an oval room, entirely lit by candles at night and with a fireplace big enough to take a small tree. Bedrooms are Old Scottish, or Italian, or Pine, the French Room is filled with Louis XV *ormolu*; each room is different, opulent, awash with modern comfort; the best look south to the hills. Splash in a large tub after a day's fishing, stalking or golf… bathrooms range from Edwardian to 21st-century spa. Food is modern classical – "Scottish with French flair" – and if you catch a fish they'll cook it. Three thousand acres of parkland and forest envelop you, the scenery is stunning, there are salmon in the River Dee and castles by the hatful.

rooms	21: 9 doubles, 6 twins, 3 singles, 3 suites.
price	£80–£110. Suites £130.
meals	Lunch from £4.75. Dinner from £24.50.
closed	Rarely.
directions	A597 into Banchory. Right at Raemoir Rd junction. On for 3-4 miles to entrance across the cross-roads. Take care on crossing!

	Peter Ferguson
tel	01330 824884
fax	01330 822171
e-mail	relax@raemoir.com
web	www.raemoir.com

Hotel

Darroch Learg

Braemar Road, Ballater, Aberdeenshire AB35 5UX

The Royal Family escapes to the fir district of Deeside in summer; the Franks family stays all year welcoming those in search of genuine Scottish hospitality. They have been here 40 years and know how to run a good hotel; nothing is too much trouble. Darroch Learg is Gaelic for 'an oak copse on a sunny hillside' and this turreted 1888 granite building is in a raised position on the outskirts of the pretty village of Ballater. Views stretch across the Dee Valley to Lochnagar, snow-capped for much of the year. The main part of the hotel is a baronial Victorian manor house, with a twist of Scottish grandeur thrown in for good measure. Regency-style bedrooms are split between here and a next-door annexe: all are subtly different, with warm colours, local watercolours, fresh flowers, thick curtains to keep out the nip of winter and modern bathrooms with spoiling touches; most rooms have the view. An intimate conservatory-style dining room, with lamps at each table, draws in the view as well. Chef David Mutter's modern Scottish cooking has won various awards, supported by a good wine list. You'll feel good staying here.

rooms	17: 5 doubles, 9 twins/doubles, 1 single, 2 four-posters.
price	£128-£158. Half-board (May to September) £93-£108 p.p.
meals	Dinner £36. Sunday lunch £19.50.
closed	Christmas week & last 3 weeks in January.
directions	From Perth, A93 north to Ballater. Entering village, hotel 1st building on left above road.

Nigel & Fiona Franks

tel	01339 755443
fax	01339 755252
e-mail	nigel@darroch-learg.demon.co.uk

Hotel

map 13 entry 198

The Manor House

Gallanach Road, Oban, Argyll & Bute PA34 4LS

A 1780 dower house for the Dukes of Argyll – their cottage by the sea – built of local stone, high on the hill, with long views over Oban harbour to the Isle of Mull. A smart and proper place, not one to bow to the fads of fashion: sea views from the lawn, cherry trees in the courtyard garden, a fire roaring in the drawing room, a beautiful tiled floor in the entrance hall and an elegant bay window in the dining room that catches the eye. Compact bedrooms are pretty in blues, reds and greens, with fresh flowers, crisp linen sheets, radios, padded headboards and piles of towels in good bathrooms; those that look seaward have pairs of binoculars to scour the horizon. Sample Loch Fyne kippers for breakfast, sea bass for lunch and, if you've room, duck in redcurrant sauce for supper; try their home-baking, too. Ferries leave for the islands from the bottom of the hill – see them depart from the hotel garden – while at the top, overlooking Oban, watch the day's close from McCaig's Folly; sunsets here are really special. *Children over 11 welcome.*

rooms	11: 8 doubles, 3 twins.
price	Half-board £60–£85 p.p.
meals	Lunch £7–£13. Dinner, 5 courses, £29.50.
closed	Christmas.
directions	In Oban, follow signs to ferry. Hotel on right 0.5 miles after ferry turn-off, signed.

	Gabriella Wijker
tel	01631 562087
fax	01631 710378
e-mail	manorhouseoban@aol.com
web	www.manorhouseoban.com

Hotel

Lerags House

Lerags, By Oban, Argyll & Bute PA34 4SE

A rare touch of city chic on the beautiful west coast, Lerags is a stylish old building with a contemporary country-house feel. Charlie, a sail maker, and Bella, a cook, both in their late thirties and originally from Australia, came for six months, stayed for nine years, and now own their place by the sea – they absolutely love it here. Built in 1815, the house is large, with gardens that run down to tidal mud flats: watch the ebb and flow from the dining room. Cool interiors mix natural colours and light pine surfaces with pale olive sofas, fresh lilies, straight lines and a deliberate lack of clutter. Charlie and Bella represent an emerging generation of hoteliers: more style, less formality, good prices, great service and exceptional food – guinea fowl in a gin and juniper sauce with crème fraîche and spring onion mash caught the eye. Don't think you have to be young to enjoy it either. At the end of the road – a brisk stroll of less than a mile – is a beach for uninterrupted walks, or a constitutional dip. Day trips to Mull, Crinan and Glencoe are all easy. There's Fingal the dog, too.

rooms	8: 4 doubles, 1 twin, 1 single, 2 suites.
price	£88. Half-board £64–£79 p.p. Singles from £33. Suites £98.
meals	Packed lunch £6. Dinner, 3 courses, £25.
closed	Christmas.
directions	From Oban, south on A816 for 2 miles, then right, signed Lerags for 2.5 miles. Hotel on left, signed.

Charlie & Bella Miller

tel	01631 563381
e-mail	stay@leragshouse.com
web	www.leragshouse.com

Hotel

map 9   entry 200

The High and Dry

Landlubber Lane, Droughtville, Argyll & Bute NOS EA1

If you are old enough to have read *Orlando the Marmalade Cat* you will remember the old black wooden boat in which the family lived – 'Peggotty'. A generation of English readers will therefore be thrilled that the concept has been brought up to date in this imaginative way. Why leave the boat in the water or on the mud when you can bring it ashore and put it conveniently in the nearest car park? A hop up the ladder and you are aboard within seconds of arriving. Space is precious, so bring very little baggage. (Head space, too, so bring some aspirin.) The advantages of a place like this are obvious, though you may not have considered the relief for the children of not having to go aloft, and to experience on-board life without the terror of falling into the sea. The role of 'skipper' will give the average man an excuse to bark at the rest of the family. We should, perhaps, mention that there will be a coming-and-going of cars at all hours as the supermarket in whose car park this is based is open 24 hours a day. But there again, your shopping is a doddle and you can eat as exotically as you will sleep – afloat on a sea of fantasies.

rooms	4 bunks sharing facilities.
price	Charter only in high season.
meals	Basic - avoid.
closed	1st January - 31st December, most years.
directions	Take coast road away from coast. Keep driving until all sign of sea has been left behind. Then take first right.

Jonathan Livingstone

tel	01700 222 444
e-mail	captain@dundriftin.co.uk
web	www.dundriftin.co.uk

Hotel

Ardanaiseig

Kilchrenan, By Taynuilt, Argyll & Bute PA35 1HE

It's enough to make you believe in fables... "All you need to stay in love," was how one guest described this seductive place. The pleasures of the journey to Ardanaiseig unfold with lingering suspense: from the village of Kilchrenan, an even smaller single track road leads into a mighty landscape of loch and mountain. Wind through heath and ancient woodland, then down an avenue of beech trees, through a collection of rare and exotic rhododendron, to a baronial 1834 house right on the shores of Loch Awe. Celtic legend says the lake has magical properties after Bheithir, goddess of ageless beauty, accidentally let the well of eternal youth on neighbouring Ben Cruchan spill over. Guests enthuse about the light here – over breakfast, watch mists swirl over the soft silhouettes of islands out on the lake. The hotel is impeccable inside, full of the eclectic style of its art dealer owner. Bedrooms have lots of flair; Tervine is wonderfully over the top; others are more restrained. Enchanting.

rooms	16: 8 doubles, 8 twins/doubles.
price	£78–£250. Half-board (min. 3 nights) £59–£148 p.p. Singles £69–£155.
meals	Light lunch from £3.75. Afternoon tea £2–£10. Dinner, 5 courses, £39.50.
closed	January-mid-February.
directions	A85 to Taynuilt. Left for Kilchrenan on B845. Left in village at Kilchrenan pub down track for 3.9 miles. Hotel at end down drive.

Peter Webster

tel	01866 833333
fax	01866 833222
e-mail	ardanaiseig@clara.net
web	www.ardanaiseig.com

Hotel

map 9   entry 202

The Lodge

Loch Goil, Argyll & Bute PA24 8AE

A lodge on the west shore of Loch Goil – a serene place caressed by the lake with mountains rising behind. It was built in 1863, a modest summer house for a Glasgow plumber... today, with its atmosphere of warm indulgence, soothing colour schemes, bowls of fresh flowers, heavenly views, it is *the* place for a private party. Come to celebrate a birthday, a wedding, Christmas – or to mix business with pleasure. Each bedroom is different, each named after a Scottish isle: a big wrought-iron bed, a white rug on a glowing floor, perfect linen. Television is delightfully absent and music plays, there are no clocks and your mobile won't work. Perfect. Dining plays a big part here and the food (much of it organic) is fresh and delicious: guinea fowl with roast parsnips and braised lentils, rhubarb creme brulée, a lochside picnic with fresh lobster from the loch. Walk the hills, cycle, canoe; return to a soak in the large tub, a massage, chess by the fire. You are surrounded by fir trees, red squirrels and deer, gardens run down to the jetty, there's no one to rush you and the staff are lovely. *Only open to groups of 8 or more; min. stay 2 nights weekends.*

rooms	8 doubles.
price	Half-board only, £150 p.p.
meals	Breakfast, dinner & afternoon tea included.
closed	Rarely.
directions	From Glasgow, A82 to Tarbet, then A83, then B828 to Lochgoilhead. Right just before bridge over a small river. After Ministry of Defence base the house is 3rd opening on left.

	Alice Gill
tel	01301 703173
fax	01301 703103
e-mail	enquiries@thelodge-scotland.com
web	www.thelodge-scotland.com

Other place

Royal Hotel
Tighnabruaich, Argyll & Bute PA21 2BE

In that never-ending search for a tourist-free destination, Tighnabruaich is near the top of our list, an end-of-the-road village, lost to the world and without great need of it. The Royal is its relaxed and informal hub. Yachtsmen tie up to the moorings and drop in for lunch, the shinty team pops down for a pint after a game, and fishermen land fresh mussels and lobster straight from the sea for Roger to cook. Roger and Bea – ex-pat Scots – returned from London with an eye to "buying something run-down so they could..." run it up? Which is exactly what they've done: stripped wooden floors and a roaring fire in the brasserie, tartan carpets and leather sofas in the restaurant. Claire, their daughter, has joined the team, and now cooks. Food is a big pull: masses of fresh seafood, and local venison, as stalked by Winston Churchill of Dunoon. Big views of the Kyles of Bute are getting bigger as conservatories are being added. Bedrooms are big and warm, homely and comfy, and most have sea views. Play tennis on a nearby tennis court where you can lose balls in the sea, or take a short ferry ride to Bute.

rooms	11: 9 doubles, 2 twins.
price	£94–£124. Half-board from £65 p.p. Singles £74.50.
meals	Dinner, à la carte, about £30. Meals in brasserie from £10.
closed	Christmas.
directions	From Glasgow, A82 north, A83 west, A815 south, A886 south, A8003 south, then B8000 north into village. Hotel on seafront.

	Roger & Bea McKie
tel	01700 811239
fax	01700 811300
e-mail	info@royalhotel.org.uk
web	www.royalhotel.org.uk

Hotel

map 9 entry 204

Culzean Castle

The National Trust for Scotland, Maybole, Ayrshire KA19 8LE

Few places to stay in the world come close to Culzean, pronounced 'Cullane' – Scotland's sixth most popular tourist destination defies overstatement. Built into solid rock a couple of hundred feet above crashing waves, the castle is considered to be architect Robert Adam's final masterpiece. It was presented to the Scottish people in 1945 by the 5th Marquess of Ailsa and the Kennedy family. General Eisenhower was given use of the top floor during his lifetime – Scotland's thank you for his contribution to the war effort. You stay on the same floor where every room is a delight; Ike's bed is always popular. The rest is awe-inspiring: hundreds of portraits, including one of Napoleon, the round drawing room that juts out over the sea, the central oval staircase with two galleries and 12 Corinthian columns, and the Armoury, with 713 flintlock pistols and 400 swords – a good reminder to pay the bill. Tour the castle before the tourists invade at 11am, take a stirring cliff walk in 560 acres of idyllic coastal scenery, and dine together country-house style. All guaranteed to multiply your wildest dreams to the power of ten.

rooms	6: 1 double, 3 twins/doubles, 1 four-poster; 1 twin with separate bath.
price	£225–£375. Singles from £140.
meals	Dinner, 4 courses with wine, £50 by arrangement.
closed	Rarely.
directions	From A77 in Maybole, A719 for 4 miles, signed.

Jonathan Cardale

tel	01655 884455
fax	01655 884503
e-mail	culzean@nts.org.uk
web	www.culzeancastle.net

Other Place

Minmore House

Glenlivet, Banffshire AB37 9DB

Driving up from Balmoral in the late afternoon sun, you could be forgiven for thinking the colour green was probably created here. The east of Scotland often plays second fiddle to its 'other half' in the west, but this lush cattle-grazing land is every inch as beautiful. Amid it all is Minmore, a great wee pad run with breezy good cheer by Victor and Lynne. They used to run a restaurant in South Africa and once cooked for Prince Philip; their food continues to win rave reviews. Their kingdom stretches to 10 spotless bedrooms and a suite that Lynne describes as "very zoosh". Guests swap highland tales in a pretty sitting room or, best of all, in a carved wooden bar, half-panelled, with scarlet chairs, a resident Jack Russell, the odd trophy and 104 malts. The garden is a birdwatcher's paradise, with lapwing, curlew and a rare colony of oyster-catchers. Free-range chickens wander about and those with an iron constitution may fancy the unheated swimming pool! Visit the famous Glenlivet distillery, or cycle deep into the Ladder Hills where buzzard, falcon and even eagles soar. An Indian head massage, or some reflexology unwinds, too.

rooms	11: 4 doubles, 4 twins, 2 singles, 1 suite.
price	£130. Singles £55. Suite £240. Half-board £90 p.p.
meals	Light lunch £12–£15. Full picnic £10. Dinner, 4 courses, £35.
closed	February; one week in October.
directions	From Aviemore, A95 north to Bridge of Avon, then south on B9008 to Glenlivet. House at top of hill, 400 yds before distillery.

Victor & Lynne Janssen

tel	01807 590378
fax	01807 590472
e-mail	minmorehouse@ukonline.co.uk
web	www.minmorehousehotel.com

Hotel

map 13 entry 206

Churches

Albert Road, Eyemouth, Berwickshire TD14 5DB

As an introduction to hospitality north of the border, this fabulous restaurant with rooms is anything but traditional and we applaud it for that. Sure, Scotland wouldn't be Scotland without its tartan and thistles but it's always a pleasure to celebrate anywhere that's trying to be a little different. Marcus and Rosalind are a young couple doing just that. He's the exceptional chef, with experience in America and Europe and she, with a degree in law, manages front of house superbly. As for setting, it couldn't be better: an old manse, overlooking the pretty harbour at Eyemouth – the name alone should be enough to tempt you. The place looks good and you'll eat well. Watch the catch unloaded, then eat it later: local monkfish with Chinese leaves, Berwickshire crab with a sweet chilli dressing and fresh North Sea lobster. Meat is special too; Northumbrian lamb and fresh game in season. Inside, the hotel has a classy, modern feel, with lots of style, wooden floors, wrought-iron beds, the odd luxurious four-poster... there's even a moongate in the garden.

rooms	6: 3 doubles, 1 twin, 1 family, 1 four-poster.
price	£80-£125. Singles £60-£90.
meals	Dinner, à la carte, £30.
closed	22 Dec-10 Jan. 3pm Sun-10am Tues, every week.
directions	From Berwick, A1 north for 7 miles, then right, signed Eyemouth. Follow brown signs to hotel.

Marcus Lamb & Rosalind Dryden

tel	01890 750401
fax	01890 750747
e-mail	info@churcheshotel.co.uk
web	www.churcheshotel.co.uk

Hotel

Beechwood Country House Hotel

Harthope Place, Moffat, Dumfries & Galloway DG10 9HX

Once an Adventure Boarding School for Young Ladies, now an atmospheric country-house hotel. The whole place breathes an air of well-being, thanks to Stavros and Cheryl, so proud of their new venture and generous with treats: Penhaligon lotions in the bathroom, malt whiskies in the bar (Stavros's delight) and Loch Fyne kippers for breakfast. Beechwood walks – 12 acres of them – start from the door, and there are wellies in case you've forgotten yours. Even clean towels for muddy dogs: the attention to detail amazes. Sitting rooms have books, games and magazines, there's a smoking bar for cigars, hot cocoa for bed. The place hums with warmth and welcome: a cheerful mix of antiques and *objets* from far-flung places, family paintings on mellow yellow walls, kilims on polished pine, lilies from Edinburgh. Bedrooms are simply lovely, with white linen on big beds and wooden shutters to help you lie in. And in the dining room: fresh, colourful food from a singing chef, served on starched linen, and views over the gentle valley. Beyond, the old spa town of Moffat bustles with restaurants, shops and bars.

rooms	7: 3 doubles, 3 twins, 1 family.
price	£90. Half-board £69 p.p. Singles £62.
meals	Packed lunch £12. Dinner £24.
closed	23 December-14 February.
directions	Exit M74 at junc.15, signed Moffat; through town centre, then right between church and school. Hotel signed.

Stavros Michaelides

tel	01683 220210
fax	01683 220889
e-mail	enquiries@beechwoodcountryhousehotel.co.uk
web	www.beechwoodcountryhousehotel.co.uk

Hotel

 map 10 entry 208

Cavens Country House Hotel

Kirkbean, By Dumfries, Dumfries & Galloway DG2 8AA

Angus and Jane have painstakingly restored – are restoring still – this 1752 house built by a tobacco baron whose estates stretched the length and breadth of Dumfries. It's hard to appreciate the extent of their labours, but easy to enjoy the fruits... next to an open fire in the Green Room, wee dram in hand. The Fordyces are friendly professionals who put in a huge amount of effort to ensure guests will want to come back, and they do. Angus is chef and does good home cooking with a Scottish-French twist, four courses that change every day. A highlight are the cheeses from Loch Arthur Farm – worth leaving home for. Jane does the décor and no two bedrooms are alike; all have comfort, elegance, rich colours, wide beds, padded bedsteads, chintz with swags and tails, books in glass-fronted cases. Splendid views reach to the Solway Firth in one direction, acres of mature gardens in the other. This neck of the woods is a haven for wildlife and a twitcher's dream; go birdwatching in summer, shooting in winter, riding, walking or golfing. Or simply treat this as your own place in the country and revel in doing absolutely nothing.

rooms	7: 5 doubles, 1 twin, 1 family.
price	£80–£110. Singles from £65.
meals	Dinner, 4 courses, £25. Packed lunch available.
closed	Rarely.
directions	From Dumfries, A710 to Kirkbean (12 miles). Hotel signed in village.

	Jane & Angus Fordyce
tel	01387 880234
fax	01387 880467
e-mail	enquiries@cavens.com
web	www.cavens.com

Hotel

Knockinaam Lodge

Portpatrick, Wigtownshire, Dumfries & Galloway DG9 9AD

The lawn runs down to the Irish sea, sunsets streak the sky red and roe deer amble down to eat the roses. An exceptional 1869 shooting lodge with unremitting luxuries: a Michelin star in the dining room, 150 malts in the bar, and a level of service that you don't expect in such far-flung corners of the realm. And history. Churchill once stayed, and you can sleep in his big elegant room, where copies of his books wait to be read, and where you need steps to climb into an ancient bath. It remains very much a country house: plump cushions on a Queen Anne sofa in an immaculate morning room where the scent of fresh flowers mixes with the smell of burnt wood, invigorating cliff walks (hills on three sides), curlews to lull you to sleep, nesting Peregrine falcons, and a rock pool where David keeps lobsters for the pot. In storms, waves crash all around – bracing stuff. Trees stand guard high on the hill, their branches buffeted by the wind. Remote, beguiling, utterly spoiling – Knockinaam is worth the detour. John Buchan knew the house and described it in *The Thirty-Nine Steps* as the house to which Hannay fled.

rooms	9: 7 doubles, 2 twins.
price	Half-board or full-board only. Half-board £97.50–£170 p.p. Full-board £125–£170 p.p. Singles from £145.
meals	Lunch £3.50–£30. Dinner, 5 courses, included; non-residents £40.
closed	Rarely.
directions	From A77 or A75 follow signs for Portpatrick. 2 miles west of Lochans, left at smokehouse. Follow signs to Lodge for 3 miles.

David & Sian Ibbotson
tel	01776 810471
fax	01776 810435
e-mail	reservations@knockinaamlodge.com

Hotel

map 9   entry 210

Greywalls

Muirfield, Gullane, East Lothian EH31 2EG

It is gracious, stately and hugely impressive, yet you could curl up on a sofa and feel perfectly at home. Sir Edwin Lutyens built the house in 1901 for a golfer determined to be within a 'mashie niblick' shot of the 18th green; two gate lodges were added for staff, then a nursery wing. Now it's half hotel, half private home – held in equal affection by family and guests. Greywalls is discreet, peaceful, welcoming and unpompous – one guest said staying here was "like breathing silk". Enter a charmed world of log fires, French windows, family portraits, and views that sail over golf course to sea. There's a panelled library, a cosy bar, chintz in the bedrooms, jackets and ties for dinner and a dedicated team in the kitchen – the food is sublime. Bedrooms – four in the lodges, more in the house – have everything you could wish for, and there's the Colonel's House for a private group. The walled garden was designed by Gertrude Jekyll: a tapestry of arbours, arches, peonies, lavender and the most immaculate lawns. Sandy beaches, castles and Edinburgh by day; by night, the gentle click of backgammon die and the crackle of the fire.

rooms	23: 19 twins/doubles, 4 singles.
price	£240. Singles £120.
meals	Dinner £40.
closed	Mid-October–mid-April.
directions	A198 from A1 & take last road at east end of Gullane village.

	Giles Weaver
tel	01620 842144
fax	01620 842241
e-mail	hotel@greywalls.co.uk
web	www.greywalls.co.uk

The Witchery by the Castle

Castlehill, Royal Mile, Edinburgh EH1 2NF

Ornately Gothic in style and grandly exuberant, this glorious restaurant with rooms should really be a theatre – it's such a magical and passionate setting. Described as "one of the seven wonders of the world", it might best suit a Jacobean drama – there are enough drapes and alcoves to conceal a medium-sized cast of conspirators and lovers. The Witchery is the inspiration of James Thomson. He has trawled the flea-markets of Europe to fill two 16th-century tenements next to the gates of Edinburgh Castle with sumptuous architectural bric-a-brac, from the medieval to the quasi-Byzantine... the spiral staircase, the candles, the stone floors, the tapestries, even the shadows delight. The suites are incredible: the Inner Sanctum has one of Queen Victoria's chairs, the pillars in the Old Rectory came from London's Trocadero, and the red, black and gold Vestry has a fabulous *trompe l'œil* swagged bathroom. A bottle of champagne is included, as is continental breakfast in bed   superb home made pastries. The three restaurants excel   one fills a rooftop – and if you can drag yourself away, Edinburgh's not bad either.

rooms	7 suites.
price	From £225.
meals	Lunch £9.95. Dinner, à la carte, about £30.
closed	Christmas Day & Boxing Day.
directions	Find Edinburgh Castle. Witchery 20 yds from main castle gate.

	Mark Rowley
tel	0131 225 5613
fax	0131 220 4392
e-mail	mail@thewitchery.com
web	www.thewitchery.com

Restaurant with Rooms

map 10   entry 212

The Point Hotel

34 Bread Street, Edinburgh EH3 9AF

According to a local, the building was right on the point where fresh water came in to the city in the 1800s – hence the name. Those who prefer not to be hurtled into the 21st century will not appreciate what has happened to the old Co-op building, but come if you want to be dazzled by space, light, bright colours and clean lines. Italian ceramic floor tiles cool the gallery-space entrance; a glass wall dominates. An open plan restaurant shimmers on the ground floor with a curved chrome bar in the centre, an acid yellow glass wall and a burgundy lino floor. Bedrooms are minimalist: huge windows show off walls laminated to waist height, no pictures, more smoked glass in vivid colours lit from behind, sensible thick curtains, plain beds and immaculate, white bathrooms. Upper rooms have long views over the city roof tops to the Castle and the suites are large, art-filled and jacuzzi'd. Modern design enthusiasts will adore it. Heat sensors, technology and space to sit will thrill workaholics; shoppers will find Harvey Nics around the corner and if you need an old-time fix there are still canons and pipers galore up on Princes Street.

rooms	140: 136 twin/doubles, 4 suites, all with bath/shower.
price	£95-£200.
meals	2 or 3 course lunch from £8.90. 3-course dinner £14.90.
closed	Rarely.
directions	From Princes Street down Lothian Road. Bread Street on left. Short walk from Waverley station.

Andrew Doolan

tel	0131 221 5555
fax	0131 221 9929
web	www.point-hotel.co.uk

Hotel

Prestonfield

Priestfield Road, Edinburgh EH16 5UT

A long drive winds through parkland, Highland cattle contentedly graze, peacocks shriek to announce your arrival. Strange, then, that you are just five minutes by car from the centre of Edinburgh. Prepare to be impressed and to marvel at wonderful architectural features: decorative, ornate plasterwork, a 300-year-old ceiling, a drawing room panelled with leather and marble floors. When we went to press the new owner, James Thomson, was working frantically to transform the traditional country house to something altogether more 'wow'. We've been told to expect massive helpings of opulence: gilded tassel chandeliers, black and gilt regency banquettes, velvet upholstery, white marble, rich reds and the same wallpaper suppliers as the Lord Chancellor! It might not surprise you to know that Thomson owns and operates The Witchery, another sybaritic Edinburgh paradise, but there will be no breathless chasing of Michelin stars – his style is too assured for that kind of thing. He is simply confident that he can lure local foodies to his 'destination restaurant'. RIP the residents' dining room? Hurrah!

rooms	30 twins/doubles.
price	From £150.
meals	Lunch from £19. Dinner from £28.
closed	Rarely.
directions	10 minutes by car from centre of Edinburgh.

	Mark Rowley
tel	0131 668 3346
fax	0131 668 3976
e-mail	info@prestonfield.com
web	www.prestonfield.com

Restaurant with Rooms

map 10   entry 214

The Inn at Lathones

Lathones, St Andrews, Fife KY9 1JE

Once upon a time in the Kingdom of Fife, two people fell in love, married and lived happily ever after in this old inn; beer flowed, food was plentiful, customers burst into song, even a dwarf highwayman dropped in after work. Legend says when the landlady died in 1736, the wedding stone above the fireplace in the lounge cracked, so strong was their love. Today, she and her horse haunt the wonderful Stables, the oldest part of the inn, with its garlands of hops and bottle-green ceiling – but in the friendliest way. Lathones could charm the most cantankerous ghost: superb food, the draw of an open fire, leather sofas to sink into, and a warm, Scottish welcome. Walk into the bar to find bottles of grappa and eau-de-vie asking to be sampled, while Marc Guibert's menu is mouthwatering: try local grilled sea bass followed by a clootie dumpling served with fresh strawberry. Comfortable, traditional-style bedrooms are split between a coach house and an old blacksmith's house either side of the inn. Historic St Andrews and the East Neuk of Fife fishing villages are close.

rooms	14: 12 twins/doubles, 2 singles.
price	£120–£160. Singles £65–£85.
meals	Lunch £9.50. Packed lunch from £5. Dinner, à la carte, from £20.
closed	2 weeks in January.
directions	From Kirkcaldy, or St Andrews, A915 to Largoward. Inn 1 mile north on roadside.

Nick White

tel	01334 840494
fax	01334 840694
e-mail	lathones@theinn.co.uk
web	www.theinn.co.uk

Inn

Brunswick Merchant City Hotel

106-108 Brunswick Street, Glasgow G1 1TF

Stephen and Michael are simply gorgeous and bouncing with vim – indeed, they seem to create gentle mayhem wherever they go! The bar/brasserie is bold and clean with a black zebra stripe along the wall, graceful curved cream tiles and pretty lighting. A lift zooms you straight up to the bedrooms, all colour-themed in two tones and niftily designed so that only the white-cotton-sheeted beds stick out. Small rooms are not for partying (take the penthouse, with three bedrooms and sauna, instead) but if you want to sleep they're fine; bathrooms are tiled and lino'd in fun colours. At breakfast you might be sitting next to a famous actor, a local musician or a lorry driver, it's an egalitarian place – 'the boys' will be flitting hither and thither brewing up mind-blowing coffee and warming croissants, and the lovely Celia, front of house, will be calming things down. Art galleries, museums, clubbing and shopping (Versace and Cruise a minute's walk) are on the doorstep if you want them, Edinburgh is a short hop on the train, and when you've run out of funds, or your feet are killing you, limp back to a large G&T and a slice of TLC.

rooms	19: 18 doubles, 1 penthouse suite for 6.
price	£55–£95. Suite £395.
meals	Brasserie open noon–8pm. Main courses about £6.50. Closed Sunday.
closed	Rarely.
directions	10-minute walk from Queen Street or Central stations. Airport bus stop round the corner in George Square. Metred parking outside, NCP near.

Stephen Flannery & Michael Johnson

tel	0141 552 0001
e-mail	enquiry@brunswickhotel.co.uk
web	www.brunswickhotel.co.uk

Hotel

map 9   entry 216

St Jude's

190 Bath Street, Glasgow G2 4HG

If you loathe the corporate feel of many large hotels but don't value the intimacy of a B&B then St Jude's is perfect: an elegant, early-Victorian townhouse on a wide street, intelligently converted into a fuss-free place to stay with no pomposity, great food and super staff. The wide hall is dominated by an ornate cast-iron and mahogany staircase lit by the huge glass cupola above. Big, unfussy bedrooms have good sound systems (and access to other electronic joys), exciting finds in the fridge, bathrooms to linger in and fluffy blankets with designer spots. The restaurant is crisp and contemporary, yet still cosy, with excellent lighting, gleaming floors, well-designed furniture and a mixed, imaginative menu – try slow-roasted sticky pork salad or fresh figs wrapped in prosciutto. If you want to drink seriously first, the downstairs bar is humming. Bobby, an ex-musician, loves flowers and arranges them with flair, the art on the walls is original, there's a sky-lit club room for private parties, and shops, restaurants, galleries and museums are a short hop. But perhaps the best part of St Jude's is the calm, friendly people who work there.

rooms	6: 2 doubles, 3 twins/doubles, 1 suite.
price	From £115. Singles from £90. Suite £185.
meals	Dinner, 2 courses from £11.50, 3 from £14.50; à la carte, main courses from £11.50.
closed	Rarely.
directions	Exit 19 from M8 for city centre. 20 minutes from airport, 10 minutes from station.

Paul Wingate & Bobby Patterson

tel	0141 352 8800
fax	0141 352 8801
e-mail	info@saintjudes.com
web	www.saintjudes.com

Restaurant with Rooms

The Arthouse

129 Bath Street, Glasgow G2 2SY

Chances are that you've already seen the award-winning Arthouse — as a backdrop in a film, maybe, or in the odd ad. Glaswegians in the know and, now, heaps of others flock there not just for the stylish surroundings but to get a fix of the atmosphere and the great food, too. Built in 1911, the hotel's classic listed architecture is the perfect backdrop for Paul Cassidy's innovative interior design. An antique elevator whisks you upstairs to individually-designed guestrooms, each with a Queen size bed, brilliant bathrooms, robes and in-room entertainment systems...: 40 digital movies, CDs, a video jukebox, even! A tour of them all would leave you confused as to which to plump for. If you ascended via the lift, descend via the magnificent stairwell, past the 20-foot interior waterfall to The Arthouse Grill. Daily deliveries of oysters, scallops and lobster make their way onto the menu along with contemporary Scottish dishes made with local farm produce. Glasgow's first Teppan-Yaki grill is here, too, presided over by a Japanese chef, so authenticity is guaranteed. With an art gallery on the third floor, it's a fascinating package with that dash of originality that we've come to expect from Glasgow.

rooms	65: 44 doubles, 21 suites.
price	From £110.
meals	Available at award-winning Arthouse Grill.
closed	25 December and 1 January.
directions	5-minute taxi ride from station, 20 minutes from airport.

Paul Cassidy

tel	0141 221 6789
fax	0141 221 6777
e-mail	info@arthousehotel.com
web	www.arthousehotel.com

Hotel

map 9   entry 218

Rab Ha's

83 Hutcheson Street, Glasgow G1 ISH

Big, noisy, smoky and battered – that's the bar: a huge square room with stone walls, wooden floorboards, candles burning on rough wooden tables, a bright fire, nudes on the walls and the most eclectic mix of locals – students, housewives with buggies and some old fellas seriously staring into a pint, all rub shoulders with backpackers and suited businessmen. You can eat old favourites like mince and tatties or cod and chips with mushy peas in the bar from lunch-time till late or go a bit posher in the restaurant from 5.30 p.m. Bedrooms are modern and spruce – crisp white linen, yellow walls – with good bathrooms and claw-foot baths. Don't expect peace and quiet until late, the atmosphere here is not hushed. Continental breakfast can be delivered to your room or there's full Scottish in the bar. Exploring Glasgow from here is easy: shops, museums, galleries, theatres, clubs and good transport are all near, but you may just want to stay and join in the fun.

rooms	4: 3 doubles, 1 twin.
price	£50–£75.
meals	Bar menu from £10 for 2 courses & à la carte.
closed	Rarely.
directions	5-minute walk from Queen Street station.

	Sheri & Hamish McLean
tel	0141 572 0400
fax	0141 572 0402

Other place

Tigh an Eilean
Shieldaig, Highland IV54 8XN

Tigh an Eilean is the Holy Grail of the west coast – when you arrive you realise it's what you've been looking for all these years. A perfect place in every respect, from its position by the sea in this very pretty village, to the magnificence of the Torridon mountains that rise all around... this area is one of the wonderlands of the world, an undisputed heavyweight champion of natural beauty. And Sheildaig itself is an exceptionally friendly village with a strong sense of community, the hub of which is the pub – like the shop, owned by the hotel – where locals come to sing their songs, play their fiddles, drink their whisky, and talk. Most surprising of all is the hotel. Christopher and Cathryn, two ex-London lawyers, now run an immaculate bolt hole, a faultless place, airy and stylish, with tartan cushions on window seats, sensational views, home-made shortbread, and bedrooms that elate. No TVs, no telephones, but kind, gentle staff who chat and advise. Relax in sitting rooms with plump sofas, an honesty bar and an open fire. Eat in the smart restaurant, or try the pub – fewer frills but lots of fun. Exceptional.

rooms	11: 4 doubles, 4 twins, 3 singles.
price	£115. Half-board from £74 p.p. Singles £52.50.
meals	Bar meals from £5. Dinner in restaurant from £30.
closed	November–March.
directions	On loch front in centre of Shieldaig.

Christopher & Cathryn Field

tel	01520 755251
fax	01520 755321
e-mail	tighaneileanhotel@shieldaig.fsnet.co.uk

Hotel

map 12 entry 220

Glenelg Inn

Glenelg, By Kyle of Lochalsh, Highland IV40 8JR

There are two routes in: the tiny Kyle Rhea ferry from Skye or the road over Mam Ratagan from Loch Duich. Given that both are spectacular in their own right, it's not a bad idea to take one in, the other out, and get the best of both worlds. Your reward is the view across the sea to the mountains of Skye. The inside is split between bar, restaurant and bedrooms. The bar is a Highland institution: an ancient fireplace, stone-flagged floors and piles of old fish boxes on which you sit (more comfortable than you'd imagine). There's music, too: pipers, fiddlers and folk musicians. If the bar is earthy, then the bedrooms are smart: rugs and books, old pine dressers, waffle blankets, soothing bathrooms. Light floods in, one room has two balconies, the suite its own garden, and most have sea views. Great food – crab, mussels, venison, lamb – all local, all cooked with flair and eaten in a bright room with great pictures. Residents have the run of a private drawing room (logs under window seats, a fender by the fire, cosy sofas). There are 10 Glenelg's around the world, all named after this one. Christopher will tell you why.

rooms	7: 3 doubles, 3 family, 1 suite.
price	Half-board only £89-£99 p.p.
meals	Bar lunch from £8. Dinner, 4 courses, £29.
closed	Rarely.
directions	West off A87 at Sheil Bridge. Keep left into village & inn on right. Kylerhea ferry from Skye is a beautiful alternative.

Christopher Main

tel	01599 522273
fax	01599 522283
e-mail	christophermain@glenelg-inn.com
web	www.glenelg-inn.com

Inn

The Dower House

Highfield, Muir of Ord, Highland IV6 7XN

Neither a restaurant, nor a hotel, this historic house in the cottage-*orné* style happily defies attempts to label it. It's a must for anyone who enjoys good food in an intimate country house setting but that only partly does it justice; maybe better to compare it to the small, reliable and quite adorable Mini that Robyn somehow coaxed into transporting several of the larger artefacts up here. Mena describes Robyn's eclectic brand of no-frills cooking as "gutsy and colourful", which could just as well describe the chef himself, a broad presence dressed in bold mediterranean colours; his enthusiasm and eye for the extraordinary fill the house, as much as your plate. Impeccable rooms are full of surprises: a working organ, a magnificent Victorian half-tester and *trompe l'œil* of wisteria curling up one of the bathrooms – what better way to work up an appetite than a lazy soak. Dinner starts in a graceful dining room, with a piano at one end, and finishes with home-made truffles and coffee by an open fire in the cosy sitting room. You may wonder what you've done to deserve all this... a gem of a place.

rooms	5: 2 doubles, 2 twins/doubles, 1 suite.
price	£110–£130. Singles £65–£85. Suite £150.
meals	Dinner £35.
closed	Rarely.
directions	A9 north of Inverness to Tore r'bout, then left on A832 for Muir of Ord. In village, A862, for Dingwall. Entrance 1 mile on left.

Robyn & Mena Aitchison

tel	01463 870090
fax	01463 870090
e-mail	stay@thedowerhouse.co.uk
web	www.thedowerhouse.co.uk

Other Place

map 12 entry 222

The Cross

Tweed Mill Brae, Kingussie, Highland PH21 1LB

If anyone knows their food, David does: in his previous life he was a senior food inspector. So what did the poacher buy when he turned gamekeeper? One of his favourite restaurants, of course. The Cross, an old tweed mill, is a fusion of Scottish and Scandinavian styles. There are stone walls, old beams and whitewashed interiors downstairs, then clean lines, windows in the eaves and an open-plan sitting room one floor up. Bedrooms are stylishly simple, with Egyptian cotton linen, tongue and grooved bathrooms, halogen spotlighting and a clean crisp elegance. There are wicker chairs, canopied beds, a sofa if there's room, and you can fall asleep to the sound of the river in rooms that face south. Most important at The Cross is dinner, with chef Becca Henderson at the helm. Expect the freshest local ingredients, perhaps scallops, cauliflower purée and basil oil, then rack of lamb, aubergine and dauphinoise potatoes, finally poached pear, chocolate sauce and caramel ice. There's also one of the best wine lists in Scotland. The river Gynack falls down a mountain right outside and a short circular walk crosses the river. *Children over eight welcome.*

rooms	8: 6 doubles, 2 twins.
price	£90–£160. Singles from £80. Half-board £80–£110 p.p.
meals	Dinner, 3 courses, included. Restaurant open Tuesday–Saturday. Dinner, 2 courses, £28.50 for non-residents.
closed	Christmas & January.
directions	At the only traffic lights in Kingussie, right up hill (if coming from north); signed left.

Katie & David Young

tel	01540 661166
fax	01540 661080
e-mail	relax@thecross.co.uk
web	www.thecross.co.uk

Restaurant with Rooms

Old Pines Restaurant with Rooms

Spean Bridge, By Fort William, Highland PH34 4EG

Sukie's cooking is an undisputed highlight of the highlands; her star has risen so high that even those journalists who rarely venture north of Islington are queuing up to dine at her table. Honours roll in: she was recently voted 'Rural Chef of the Year' by her peers; no big surprise given that her food — maybe roast local venison with a wild fungi sauce and caramelised rhubarb flan — continues to elate. Old Pines remains fundamentally down to earth, a model of relaxed informality, where guests' children are free to play with the Barbers', and where dinner is eaten communally in a chalet-style dining room at eight. Stone walls, flagged floors, loads of books and maps, the best advice, and Ben Nevis looming large through the window. Bedrooms are spotless, with pine-clad walls, fine linen, good bathrooms, the occasional sofa. Sukie and Bill are social energisers and always find time for a chat, to introduce guests, to get the ball rolling. Nothing is too much trouble, and while Old Pines is one of Scotland's gastronomic jewels, it's the way that the Barbers do things here that makes the place so special. Don't miss it.

rooms	8: 2 family, 2 doubles, 2 twins, 1 single; 1 single with separate bath.
price	Half-board from £85 p.p.
meals	Dinner, 5 courses, afternoon tea included; non-residents £22–£32. Restaurant closed Mondays.
closed	Rarely.
directions	On A82, 1 mile north of Spean Bridge left just after Commando Memorial onto B8004 to Gairlochy. Old Pines 300 yds on right.

Bill & Sukie Barber

tel	01397 712324
fax	01397 712433
e-mail	specialplaces@oldpines.co.uk
web	www.oldpines.co.uk

Restaurant with Rooms

map 9   entry 224

Ballachulish House

Ballachulish, Highland PA39 4JX

For today's traveller, seeing this charming Scottish laird's house come into view after a long day's trek in the mountains must surely be as special as it was for clansmen of yore – only for different reasons! Once a refuge from hostile neighbours, now a sanctuary from the capricious elements of nature, Ballachulish appears part fortress, part country house, tucked at the foot of mighty Glencoe mountain, scene of the 1692 massacre of the recalcitrant MacDonald clan. Flop into a comfortable chair by an open fire and savour the warm glow of more peaceful endeavours. The McLaughlins have altered little of the house's 18th-century origins, retaining its elegant simplicity. Bedrooms have comfortable beds, the odd combed plaster ceiling and little touches like fresh fruit. Most have mountain views across a part-walled garden of herb beds, stone fountain, orchard and specimen trees; two at the front have loch views over a croquet lawn. Raise a smile and your glass to 'Lang may your lum reek', inscribed on a tiled iron range in the dining room. The welcome is generous and the food wonderful. *Children over 10 welcome.*

rooms	9: 4 doubles, 3 twins, 1 single, 1 family.
price	£90-£160. Singles £50-£60. Family £185.
meals	Dinner, 3-5 courses, £28-£37.50.
closed	Rarely.
directions	From Glasgow, A82, via Crianlarich and Glencoe, to Ballachulish, then A828 at r'bout, signed Oban. Under Ballachulish Bridge. Entrance 100 yds.

Marie & Michael McLaughlin

tel	01855 811266
fax	01855 811498
e-mail	mclaughlins@btconnect.com
web	www.ballachulishhouse.com

Hotel

Kilcamb Lodge

Strontian, Highland PH36 4HY

Kilcamb has all the ingredients of the perfect country house: A stupendous setting, with Loch Sunart at the end of the garden and Glas Bheinn rising beyond, a smart yellow drawing room with a roaring fire, a dining room that has won just about all the awards going and warmly-coloured bedrooms. New owners Sally and David are thrilled to have made the move up here from Devon and plan to buy a boat to take guests around the loch. The feel here is shipwreck-chic. There's a twelve-acre garden with half a mile of shore line by which guests often stroll after dinner (they mow paths in the lawn so you don't get lost). Wander at will and you'll come across stained-glass windows on the landing, a ship's bell in the drawing room, fresh flowers in bedrooms and great food in the dining room. Bedrooms have all the trimmings: super king size beds, padded headboards, big white towels and power-showered bathrooms. Ardnamurchan Point is up the road and worth a visit: it's the most westerly point in mainland Britain. There's wildlife, too: eagles, otters, deer and seals all visit. *Children over 12 welcome.*

rooms	11: 4 doubles, 7 twins/doubles.
price	£95–£170. Singles from £70.
meals	Lunch from £6. Dinner, 4 courses, £35.
closed	January.
directions	From Fort William, A82 south for 10 miles to Corran ferry, then A861 to Strontian. Hotel west of village on left, signed. From Fort William, via A830 & A861 takes an hour longer.

Sally & David Fox

tel	01967 402257
fax	01967 402041
e-mail	enquiries@kilcamblodge.com
web	www.kilcamblodge.com

Hotel

map 9   entry 226

Doune

Knoydart, Mallaig, Inverness-shire PH41 4PL

Ever imagined taking a boat from a tiny Scottish fishing village and landing in paradise? Doune might persuade you if you haven't. The boat collects you at Mallaig, then crosses Loch Nevis, with the mighty mountains of Knoydart rising to the east... and lands in a sacred place, with no roads, a friendly community and a glorious view of Skye and the Cullins across the Sound of Sleat. Straining an ear confirms your first thought – the only sounds you can hear are natural: water lapping, the call of a bird, a whistling wind... and the whoops of joy of other guests as the combination of solitude, beauty, comfort and hospitality triggers an overpowering happiness in all. Hike and see no one all day, dive and find your own supper, or stroll over to Inverie and the pub – a couple of hours' walk. For at least one day, though, we recommend you do absolutely nothing. Food is exceptional – maybe something from the sea in front, or from the hills behind – and the kindest people look after you. Lodge bedrooms, by the way, are perfect: wood, windows and cathedral roofs. Hard to find better value anywhere in Britain.

rooms	3: 2 doubles, 1 twin. Lodge sleeps 12.
price	Full board for 3 or 4 nights: £60 p.p. per night. 7 nights £360 p.p. Singles from £70.
meals	Dinner & packed lunch included.
closed	October-Easter.
directions	Park in Mallaig, the boat will collect you at an agreed time.

Martin & Jane Davies

tel	01687 462667
fax	08700 940428
e-mail	martin@doune-knoydart.co.uk
web	www.doune-knoydart.co.uk

Other Place

The Pier House Restaurant with Rooms

Inverie, Knoydart, Inverness-shire PH41 4PL

Inverie, population 60, is accessible only by water unless you prefer to stagger over a couple of mountains; many people do. But you should know that the overnight sleeper from Euston ends at Mallaig. You can decant into the ferry, arrive in time for an afternoon nap, then attend to the business of the day. dinner. There's a good choice, maybe moules marinières, or venison shepherd's pie, but for those that love seafood, the Pier House Seafood Platter is regarded by many as a culinary wonder of the world — you get a huge pile of Loch Nevis langoustines, smoked salmon, mussels and Orkney herrings. It is served in the most unpretentious room you can imagine, with locals popping in for a chat, an onion or the time: such is life in this far-flung enclave of mild eccentricity. Not a smart, designer place — if that matters, don't come — but if you dream of being shipwrecked at the foot of a big green hill with the sea 20 paces from the front door you'll be in heaven. Seaweed ales and fruit wines downstairs, hot water bottles and patchwork quilts in the bedrooms. The whole village seems to breakfast here. Oh, and you can walk for days.

rooms	4: 1 twin, 1 family; 1 twin, 1 double sharing bath & shower.
price	Half-board £45 p.p.
meals	Packed lunch £4.50. Dinner from £15.
closed	November-March unless by arrangement.
directions	A830 west, Fort William-Mallaig. Cars can be left in car park (on left as enter village). Ferry leaves 10.15 & 14.15 from the fishing quay (Mon, Wed, Fri only), £13 return.

Gwen Barrell & Murray Carden

tel	01687 462347
e-mail	info@thepierhouseknoydart.co.uk
web	www.thepierhouseknoydart.co.uk

Restaurant with Rooms

map 12 entry 228

Tomdoun Sporting Lodge

Glengarry, Invergarry, Inverness-shire PH35 4HS

The single track road that passes outside follows its nose upstream for 20 miles to Kinloch Hourn, but as so little traffic passes, they play tennis on it. Down in the valley, the river Garry jumps from one loch to another, while across the water Glas Bheinn rises from Glengarry Forest. Tomdoun is a landmark for hikers heading for Knoydart (this is the only road in). It's a place for the last good meal, the last sleep-easy bed (occasionally you're joined at breakfast by ravenous folk who have spent days walking over mountains). It's a stylishly unpretentious place, with old leather trunks in the hall, a roaring fire in the grate – a place with loads of rugs and ramble, communal dining, great wines and food that puts a smile on your face. Bedrooms are homely, well-priced and spotlessly clean, and those at the front have Glengarry views. There's loads to do: clay-pigeon shooting, white-water rafting, water-skiing, abseiling, mountain-biking, fishing and some of the best walking in Scotland. There's also 'green' stalking: you shoot with film, not bullets.

rooms	10: 3 doubles, 2 family; 1 single, 2 twins sharing bath; 1 double, 1 twin sharing bath.
price	£70–£100. Singles from £45.
meals	Packed lunch £5.95. Bar meals from £7. Dinner, 3 courses, from £18.95.
closed	24-25 December.
directions	A82 north from Fort William, then A87 west from Invergarry. After 5 miles, left for Glengarry. Hotel 6 miles up on right.

Michael & Sheila Pearson

tel	01809 511218
fax	01809 511300
e-mail	enquiries@tomdoun-sporting-lodge.com
web	www.tomdoun-sporting-lodge.com

Other Place

Argyll Hotel
Isle of Iona PA76 6SJ

Iona doesn't need much selling – a ferry that stops at six in the morning, azure seas, golden beaches, gentle ridges, glorious walks, an abbey, a drop of history and nothing between you and America. It's been firmly fixed on the tourist trail ever since St Columba landed on the island in AD563. Scottish kings, Viking warlords and Celtic warriors have all visited, though given that The Argyll didn't open its doors until 1867, they must have had to rough it. It's a pretty place, with views over the water to Mull. Daniel and Claire have kept the old, cosy island feel alive: open fires, loads of books, pretty bedrooms and a delightful conservatory where you can watch Iona life pass by. The hotel is virtually self-sufficient for salads and vegetables and there's an impressive one-acre organic garden that provides much for your plate: expect dinner to be a feast, maybe seafood chowder, organic venison, home-made ice cream. Seals and dolphins pass through the Sound of Iona, and Mark, maintenance man, friend and sailor, will take you under sail around the island. Walk west a mile for astounding sunsets. You may see the Northern Lights.

rooms	16: 5 doubles, 2 twins, 1 family, 6 singles, 1 suite; 1 double with separate bath.
price	£44–£86. Half-board from £55 p.p. Singles £39–£48. Suite from £152.
meals	Dinner, à la carte, about £20. Light lunch & cream tea available.
closed	December-January.
directions	Oban ferry to Craignure on Mull, then west to Fionnphort for Iona ferry. Cars not allowed on Iona but can be left safely at Fionnphort.

Claire Bachellerie & Daniel Morgan

tel	01681 700334
fax	01681 700510
e-mail	reception@argyllhoteliona.co.uk
web	www.argyllhoteliona.co.uk

Hotel

map 11 entry 230

Tiroran House

Pennyghael, Isle of Mull PA69 6ES

The drive to Tiroran takes you through some of the wildest and most spectacular scenery in Scotland, single track roads connecting the island through a magical landscape of rugged mountains and stepped silhouettes. Tiroran lies on the north shore of Loch Scridain, an arm of sea that separates the Ross of Mull from nearby Ben More, the only munro on the island. A stirring burn tumbles past the house through an enchanting garden and down to the sea; it's the dreamiest of walks. Colin and Jane used to run a bigger hotel on the mainland but they wanted something smaller, more intimate. Sit under the shade of a grape vine in the conservatory, or relax in one of two lounges, with log fires and nautical prints. Jane is an excellent cook, so meals are a special occasion, and Colin, ever helpful, is full of suggestions. Bedrooms are all different and most have garden views; binoculars are provided to spot grazing deer. As for wildlife: golden eagles and sea eagles have been seen soaring, otters and dolphins basking and leaping. The isle is a vast playground for lovers of the outdoors.

rooms	6: 3 twins, 3 doubles.
price	£104–£110. Singles £55–£70.
meals	Dinner from £26.
closed	November–March.
directions	From Craignure or Fishnish car ferries, A849 for Bunessan & Iona car ferry, right on B8035 for Gruline for 4 miles. Left at converted church. House 1 mile further.

	Colin & Jane Tindal
tel	01681 705232
fax	01681 705240
e-mail	colin@tiroran.freeserve.co.uk
web	www.tiroran.com

Other Place

Calgary Hotel & Dovecote Restaurant
Calgary, Nr Dervaig, Isle of Mull PA75 6QW

Talk to Muilleachs about their island and they all tip you the wink on Calgary Bay – a place for picnics, for cricket on the huge beach, sea-angling off the rocks and wind surfing in the bay. It's a fantastic spot, lost to the rest of Mull, and if you walk on the beach after 8pm you'll probably have it all to yourself. You can stroll back to the hotel through Matthew's latest venture, the woodland walk, a natural art gallery of sorts that stops you in your tracks: standing stones, tree art, living sculpture – mind-blowing stuff. Back at the hotel, free-range children, a tearoom, a gallery, a sparkling restaurant in the old dovecote, and a courtyard with a fountain. Calgary is a neat little homespun place that has an unmistakably mediterranean feel: family-run, no dress code, a slim rule book, a relaxed feel. Remarkably, Matthew renovated the whole place himself; walls were falling down, ceilings had disappeared. He also works in wood and much of what you see around the place is his workmanship. Bedrooms are lovely: farmhouse cosy with country fabrics and whitewashed walls. Book for one night only and you'll kick yourself.

rooms	9: 4 doubles, 2 twins, 1 single, 2 family.
price	£66–£80. Singles £33–£40.
meals	Lunch from £5. Dinner £20.
closed	December-February. Open weekends November & March.
directions	From Dervaig, B8073 west for 5.5 miles. House signed right before Calgary Bay.

Julia & Matthew Reade

tel	01688 400256
fax	01688 400256
e-mail	calgary.farmhouse@virgin.net
web	www.calgary.co.uk

Restaurant with Rooms

map 11   entry 232

Highland Cottage

Breadalbane Street, Tobermory, Isle of Mull PA75 6PD

A double first for Highland Cottage; this is clearly the loveliest place to stay in Tobermory, and the tastiest place to eat. Expect to be plied with treats from the kitchen: gallons of fresh orange juice served in crystal glasses, piping-hot coffee and the full cooked works. On one table, guests spoke glowingly of supper the night before: haddock risotto, saddle of venison, hot raspberries and ice cream – Highland Cottage is emerging as one of the jewels of Scottish cooking. Elsewhere, nothing disappoints. Bedrooms are exceptional: regal fabrics, crushed-velvet cushions, silk bedspreads, tartan tiles in fine bathrooms, Cadell prints, huge porcelain lamps, a French sleigh bed, even the odd sea view. In the sitting room, Tobermory light floods in, CDs wait to be played, pot-boilers (or *Kidnapped* – it's set on the island) wait to be read. If you can tear yourselves away, head to Iona, Fingal's Cave, or just wander around Tobermory, the prettiest town in the Western Isles, with its Highland games, art festivals, yachting regattas, and the daily to and fro of islanders stocking up on supplies. Marvellous. *Children over eight welcome.*

rooms	6: 2 doubles, 2 twins, 2 four-posters.
price	£110–£135. Singles from £85.
meals	Dinner, 4 courses, £28.50.
closed	Mid-October–mid-November, Christmas, January & February.
directions	From Oban ferry, A848 to Tobermory. Across stone bridge at mini-r'bout, then immediate right into Breadalbane St. On right opp. fire station.

	David & Jo Currie
tel	01688 302030
e-mail	davidandjo@highlandcottage.co.uk
web	www.highlandcottage.co.uk

Hotel

entry 233 map 11

Stein Inn

Stein, Waternish, Isle of Skye IV55 8GA

White cottages bob by the quay in this remote, tiny fishing village, the setting for Skye's oldest inn. Angus stocks 80 single malts, thirst-quenching ales and seasoned opinion behind the bar of this rough-hewn, fire-warmed hostelry. Stand under blackened joists and talk about anything with this affable rogue spirit. In good weather, sit out by the shore of the sea loch: across the water, the headland rises dramatically; to the north, a few low-slung islands lie scattered. Lose yourself with a pint watching locals potter about in their boats against a setting sun. With the sea being so close, the food is really good, too: from your window, watch the catch landed, hauled from the sea to your plate, impossibly fresh. If cosiness comes from contrast and setting, then the clean, closely-eaved, blue-carpeted and pine-panelled rooms above the bar are perfect. There are moorings for yachts — sailors can ring ahead to have provisions waiting — but far wiser to spoil yourselves with a couple of nights on land. A little paradise.

rooms	5: 2 doubles, 2 family, 1 single.
price	£49–£62. Singles £24.50–£30.
meals	Bar lunch from £4.50. Dinner about £13.
closed	Christmas Day & New Year's Day.
directions	From Isle of Skye bridge, A850 to Portree. Follow sign to Uig for 4 miles, left on A850 for Dunvegan for 14 miles. Hard right turn to Waternish on B886. Stein 3.5 miles along loch side.

Angus & Teresa McGhie

tel	01470 592362
fax	01470 592362
e-mail	angus.teresa@steininn.co.uk
web	www.steininn.co.uk

Inn

map 11   entry 234

Viewfield House

Portree, Isle of Skye IV51 9EU

A former factor's house with a genuinely relaxed country-house feel, Viewfield blends grandeur with odd touches of humour brilliantly. A family friend once placed notes by various of the house's belongings, detailing their history, all of which were fictional; one survives today. It's a fine ancestral seat, built in 1790, with huge windows in the sitting room, roaring fires, piles of wood, rugs on stripped wooden floors and some 100-year-old wallpapers upstairs. At 7.30 each evening a gong summons guests to dinner – Hugh and Linda take it in turns to cook. Meals are either taken communally around an enormous central table, or individually to one side; most who opt for the latter the first night, choose the former the second. Each night Hugh wears a kilt in the family tartan, while Linda, a Californian, remains delightfully unfazed by the splendour of the surroundings: ancestors on the walls – their portraits, that is – and beautiful period furniture. Bedrooms are exquisite: luxurious beds, pretty fabrics, crisp cotton linen… even polished stair rods. Climb through woods to Fingal's Seat for 360° views, or swim in a loch.

rooms	12: 4 doubles, 3 twins/doubles, 2 twins, 1 single; 1 double, 1 single sharing bath & shower.
price	£80–£100. Half-board £65–£75 p.p. Singles £40–£60.
meals	Packed lunch £4. Dinner, 4 courses, £25.
closed	Mid-October–mid-April.
directions	A87 onto Skye to Portree. On outskirts of town, opp. BP garage.

Hugh & Linda Macdonald

tel	01478 612217
fax	01478 613517
e-mail	info@viewfieldhouse.com
web	www.viewfieldhouse.com

Hotel

Hotel Eilean Iarmain

Eilean Iarmain, Sleat, Isle of Skye IV43 8QR

One of the prettiest spots on Skye – a shiny, whitewashed hamlet at the end of the road, with a pier. The Sound of Sleat wraps itself around the place and fishermen still land their catch 30 paces from the front door. Across the water Robert Louis Stevenson's lighthouse paddles in the shallows, while beyond the mountains of the mainland rise. Inside the hotel, the Hebrides of old survives, part shooting lodge, part gentlemen's club: tartan carpets, hessian on the walls, the papers by the fire in the morning room and a new Smuggler's Den where Gaelic whiskies can be savoured. Bedrooms, country-style, are split between the main house, the garden house and the stables, where sparkling new, two-storey suites sport crisp fabrics and new pine. Next door in the bar, the occasional ceilidh breaks loose and fiddles fly, but there's also a touch of refined culture in the art gallery round the corner. Sir Iain – born in Berlin, christened in Rome and schooled in Shanghai   is Skye through and through, and is deeply involved in regenerating the woodland terrain to the south of the island. He'll teach you the odd word of Gaelic, too. Bring your kilt.

rooms	16: 6 doubles, 6 twins, 4 suites.
price	£120–£160. Singles £85. Suites £200–£220.
meals	Bar meals from £7. Dinner, 4 courses, £31.
closed	Rarely.
directions	A87 over Skye Bridge (toll £5.50), then left after 7 miles onto A851, signed Armdale. Hotel on left after 8 miles, signed.

	Sir Iain Noble
tel	01471 833332
fax	01471 833275
e-mail	hotel@eilean-iarmain.co.uk
web	www.eileaniarmain.co.uk

Hotel

map 11   entry 236

The Pines

Woodside Avenue, Grantown-on-Spey, Moray PH26 3RJ

Michael and Gwen have created a retreat from the Highland elements full of soothing colours, exceptional art and sumptuous good taste. All is luxuriously welcoming, down to the two silky King Charles Cavaliers delighted to make your acquaintance. Though your hosts have only been here five years, there is an almost ancestral feel, as though they have been here for ever. Gwen cooks – brilliantly; Michael is 'mine host' with a passion for art. The jewels of his collection are paintings by David Foggie – the painter taught his great uncle – and the whole house is full of originals. Bedrooms welcome with soft lights, fresh flowers, fruit, books, magazines; dinner is a feast of traditional and modern Scottish cooking: wild venison from a local estate, smoked salmon from the smokehouse by the Spey. Enjoy the summer sunshine on the patio by one of the ponds, admire the courtyard with bonsai, alpines and ducks. The secluded garden and woodlands are a haven for wildlife and lead directly to the forest; keep going and you'll reach the River Spey for hikes, fishing and the odd whisky distillery. A wonderful port of call.

rooms	8: 4 doubles, 3 twins/doubles, 1 single.
price	£90-£120. Half-board £75-£90 p.p. Singles from £50.
meals	Dinner, 4 courses, £30. Packed lunch available.
closed	November-February.
directions	A95 north to Grantown-on-Spey. Right at 1st set of traffic lights onto A939 for Tomintoul, then 1st right into Woodside Ave. House 500 yds on left.

	Michael & Gwen Stewart
tel	01479 872092
fax	01479 872092
e-mail	info@thepinesgrantown.co.uk
web	www.thepinesgrantown.co.uk

Other Place

Woodwick House

Evie, Orkney KW17 2PQ

Poet George MacKay Brown's inscription in the garden of this quiet haven reads, "Drink here voyager, you are about to embark on the salt sound towards Eynhallow and the Kirk of Magnus". Trees are in short supply on Orkney but Woodwick sits in a wild sycamore wood fed by a burn that tumbles down to a small bay overlooking the Island of Gairsay; walk through wild flowers and hanging lichen, to the sound of rushing water and babbling crows – magical. Woodwick promotes "care, creativity and conservation", so come here to think, free of distraction. The house is nothing fancy, just clean and homely, friendly and peaceful. Built in 1912, it stands on the site of a larger building destroyed during the Jacobite rebellion; all that remains is a remarkable 'doocot'. There's a wisteria-filled conservatory, a candlelit dining room (food is organic where possible), two sitting rooms, an open fire, a piano, books and lots of old films you've been meaning to see. A nearby ferry takes you to some of the smaller islands, while the Italian Chapel and numerous ancient sites are an absolute must. *Cots available. Pets £7 for duration of stay.*

rooms	8: 2 doubles, 2 twins; 2 doubles, 1 twin, 1 single, all with basins, sharing 1 bath.
price	£56–£84. Singles £28.50.
meals	Lunch & packed lunch by arrangement. Dinner £24.
closed	Rarely.
directions	From Kirkwall or Stromness, A965 to Finstown, then A966, signed Evie. Right after 7 miles, just past Tingwall ferry turning, then left down track to house.

Ann Herdman

tel	01856 751330
fax	01856 751383
e-mail	mail@woodwickhouse.co.uk
web	www.woodwickhouse.co.uk

Other Place

map 13 entry 238

Killiecrankie Hotel

Pass of Killiecrankie, By Pitlochry, Perth & Kinross PH16 5LG

You're well-positioned here for all things Highland: the games at Braemar, fishing, walking, castles, golf... and whisky, about which Tim, once a big shaker in the wine trade, knows a thing or two. He and Maillie have come north of the border to cook great food, to serve good wines and to provide the sort of comfortable indulgence that caps a hard day's pleasure with rod, club or map. Food is top of the list, with an ever-changing menu of fresh, local produce, reasonably priced wine by the glass to complement each course, and a vegetarian menu that could convert the most ardent carnivore... for an evening at least; meat is available, too. Much is home-grown, thanks to a dedicated effort to bring the kitchen garden back to life: soft fruits, potatoes, asparagus, leeks, mangetout... and there are more edible plans for the future. Bedrooms are a good size, cosy and warm, with lashings of hot water and views down the Garry Valley. There's a small bar, a snug sitting room with books and games, and an RSPB sanctuary near the house that's home to buzzards. Set out with the binoculars.

rooms	10: 4 doubles, 4 twins/doubles, 2 singles.
price	Half-board only, £79-£99 p.p.
meals	Lunch from £2.95. Dinner, 4 courses, included; non-residents £33.
closed	January-mid-February.
directions	A9 north of Pitlochry, then B8079, signed Killiecrankie. Straight ahead for 2 miles. Hotel on right, signed.

Tim & Maillie Waters

tel	01796 473220
fax	01796 472451
e-mail	enquiries@killiecrankiehotel.co.uk
web	www.killiecrankiehotel.co.uk

Hotel

Loch Tummel Inn

Strathtummel, By Pitlochry, Perth & Kinross PH16 5RP

Listen to Michael. "When you get here, you can stop travelling... People need to be still and remember what their childhood senses are for – just look, listen, smell and let it all seep in." These wise sentiments sum up the simple pleasures in store at this lovely old coaching inn on a remote stretch of road overlooking Loch Tummel. Michael is in his element here; he and his wife Liz moved up from Sussex nine years ago. He's very much the consummate host orchestrating proceedings from behind the bar, and a firm believer in preserving the art of conversation; there's no piped music, your mobile won't work, and televisions are only provided on request. Idiosyncratic bedrooms have rustic charm, with checked bedspreads, china and good bathrooms; soak in a bath of soft hill water in one room next to a log fire and gaze at snow-capped mountains. There's also a sweet *bothy* room, with an open fire, where guests can retreat for some privacy. Breakfast is served in a converted hayloft with loch views, while the bar serves good local food, including home-smoked salmon. Perthshire in autumn is stunning.

rooms	7: 3 doubles, 2 family; 1 double, 1 twin, both with separate bath.
price	£70–£95. Singles £50.
meals	Bar lunch from £3.95. Dinner from £11.
closed	November–Easter.
directions	From Perth, A9 north, then turn off after Pitlochry, signed Killicrankie. Left over Garry Bridge onto B8019. Inn 8 miles on right.

Liz & Michael Marsden

tel	01882 634272
fax	01882 634272

Inn

map 9   entry 240

The Four Seasons Hotel
St Fillans, Perth & Kinross PH6 2NF

Andrew, an inveterate traveller, has scoured the Orient to furnish his hotel. You'll find Tibetan wall hangings, a Laotian rain drum, a Rajasthani window and a Chinese day bed. A Scot born "down south", he came back north for the obvious reasons: the seven-mile loch in front of the hotel and the hills that rise behind. It's a breathtaking spot. Those who wish to get close to nature can hunker down for a few nights in the forest cabins (lie in bed and gaze down the loch). Alternatively, hole up in this very relaxed hotel. Excellent Vietnamese art hangs on the walls of the sitting room, where a huge window frames Loch Earn. Food is a big pull here, so take to the hills by day and pay the penance before the feast. There are Arbroath smokies, Skye scallops, Angus beef and Lochaber lamb. Bedrooms are not luxurious, they're comfortable, homely and good value for money — so if plush feather pillows are your thing bring your own. Sip a sundowner under the cherry tree gazing down the loch, or find the fire for a nightcap. A great little base for a tartan tour — there's mountain biking and white-water rafting too.

rooms	12 + 6: 7 doubles, 5 twins. 6 family chalets for 4.
price	£70–£98. Singles from £35. Half-board from £59 p.p.
meals	Bar meals from £9.50. Dinner, 4 courses, £30.
closed	January–February.
directions	St Fillans on A85 at eastern tip of Loch Earn, 12 miles west of Creiff, 25 miles north of Stirling.

Andrew Low

tel	01764 685333
fax	01764 685444
e-mail	info@thefourseasonshotel.co.uk
web	www.thefourseasonshotel.co.uk

Hotel

Creagan House

Strathyre, Callander, Perth & Kinross FK18 8ND

We search high and low for places like Creagan; it brings to life all the ingredients that make a place special. Run with huge skill and passion by Gordon and Cherry, it is decorated not by numbers, nor by fashion, but by enthusiasm, evolving slowly and naturally. The welcome is second to none and the food magnificent – local Scottish produce, carefully sourced and cooked with great flair by Gordon. Expect some nice surprises, too, such as a small treatise entitled *The Iconography of the Creagan Toast Rack*; worth reading while waiting for eggs and bacon at a slab of polished oak in the baronial dining room. A small bar is stocked with 45 malt whiskies, with a guide to help choose; one of its ceiling beams was 'acquired' from the Oban railway line. No airs and graces, just the sort of attention you get in small, owner-run places. Bedrooms in the eaves have Sanderson wallpaper, old furniture and no TVs. "You don't come to Creagan to watch a box," says Cherry. Bag a munro instead – walking sticks at the door will help you up Beinn An T-Sidhein.

rooms	5: 4 doubles, 1 twin.
price	£95. Singles £57.50.
meals	Dinner £25.50.
closed	February.
directions	From Stirling, A84 north through Callander to Strathyre. Hotel 0.25 miles north of village on right.

Gordon & Cherry Gunn

tel	01877 384638
fax	01877 384319
e-mail	eatandstay@creaganhouse.co.uk
web	www.creaganhouse.co.uk

Restaurant with Rooms

map 9 entry 242

Monachyle Mhor

Balquhidder, Lochearnhead, Perth & Kinross FK19 8PQ

The position here is fabulous, with Loch Voil at the bottom of the hill, mountains rising all around you, and cars that pass at the rate of one an hour; the road ends two miles up the track. Monachyle is a great place to be, far prettier than it first seems, with a rambling old farmhouse feel spruced up into a funky factory of fun: bold colours, good food, dynamic people and excellent food cooked by Tom. Everything you see has evolved more by chance than design. They started here as farmers – and still are – then began doing B&B, and now, that has evolved too... Various members of the family are involved, the place is extremely relaxed, but standards are kept extremely high – a perfect combination. The old, tiny, panelled bar with its cosy wood fire is a great spot for a pint. Bedrooms are split between the house, barns and coach house. All are excellent: country-cosy, fairly big, with splashes of colour. Locals fill the place at weekends. And you pass Rob Roy's grave on the way in.

rooms	10: 5 doubles, 2 twins, 3 suites.
price	£95–£115. Singles from £55. Suites £115–£150.
meals	Dinner £35. Sunday lunch £19.50.
closed	January.
directions	M9, junc. 10, A84; left at Kings House Hotel, following signs to Balquhidder. Along Loch Voil. Hotel on right up drive, signed.

	Rob, Jean, Tom & Angela Lewis
tel	01877 384622
fax	01877 384305
e-mail	info@monachylemhor.com
web	www.monachylemhor.com

Restaurant with Rooms

entry 243   map 9

Glenmorangie, The Highland Home at Cadboll

Fearn, By Tain, Ross-shire IV20 1XP

Glenmorangie – glen of tranquillity – and so it is; this is heaven. Owned by the eponymous distillery, this 1700s farmhouse of thick walls and immaculate interiors stands in glorious country, with a tree-lined path down to the beach; see your supper landed by fishermen, or search for driftwood instead. A perfect place, a real find, with levels of service to surpass most others, where staff are attentive, yet unobtrusive, and where the comforts seem unending. Bedrooms are exceptional: decanters of whisky, *fleur de lys* wallpaper, tartan blankets and country views. Rooms flood with light, there are bathrobes and piles of towels, the best linen and blankets. Downstairs, the portrait of the Sheriff of Cromarty hangs on the wall, a fire crackles between plump sofas in the drawing room, and views of the garden – apple-blossom white, cherry-blossom pink – draw you out. Here you find a half-acre walled garden, both beautiful and productive, with much for your plate. Fields all around, absolute peace, delicious food, golf at Royal Dornoch, Tain and Brora. Exceptional.

rooms	9: 6 twins/doubles, 3 cottage suites.
price	Half-board only, £120-£185 p.p.
meals	Light lunch from £5. Dinner, 4 courses, included; non-residents £38.50 with wine.
closed	3-23 January.
directions	A9 north from Inverness for 33 miles to Nigg r'bout. Right on B9175, for Nigg, over r'way crossing for 1.5 miles, then left, following signs to house.

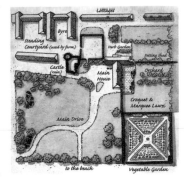

	Helen McKenzie-Smith
tel	01862 871671
fax	01862 871625
e-mail	relax@glenmorangieplc.co.uk
web	www.glenmorangie.com

Other Place

map 13   entry 244

The Old Mill Highland Lodge

Talladale, Loch Maree, Ross-shire IV22 2HL

Chris and Jo are a remarkable pair providing the sort of effortless hospitality that few hotels can match. Old Mill isn't plush, but it doesn't pretend to be, and it's great value. Here are delightful home comforts, relaxing company and extremely good nosh. We sent along two self-confessed foodies who can be highly critical. They found Chris's food fresh, flavoursome and imaginative. Praise indeed! Jo, a keen photographer, is good on detail, and remembers everyone's Christian names. Both are great travellers and the comfy living room is full of travel books, novels and photo albums charting the fortunes of this 1840 horse-driven mill since its rebuild in the 1970s. The best bedroom is upstairs; those downstairs are pet-friendly. The Honeysuckle room is gorgeous, with a sumptuous duvet, giant pillows and garden views – watch the tame pine marten being fed, and fall asleep to the sound of burns hurrying through two acres of garden to Loch Maree, regarded as one of, if not *the* best loch in Scotland. It's wider than most, with islands in the middle and Caledonian pine forests at the foot of Beinn Eighe. Bring walking boots.

rooms	6: 2 doubles, 3 twins; 1 double with separate bath.
price	Half-board only, £70 p.p.
meals	Packed lunch £4. Dinner included.
closed	20 October–15 March.
directions	Hotel on A832, 10 miles north of Kinlochewe & 10 miles south of Gairloch, signed.

	Chris & Jo Powell
tel	01445 760271
e-mail	jo.powell@bosinternet.com
web	www.theoldmillhighlandlodge.co.uk

Other Place

2 Quail Restaurant & Rooms

Castle Street, Dornoch, Sutherland IV25 3SN

One of the best restaurants in Scotland and in one of the few places in the Highlands that can be truly described as 'pretty'. Officially a county town in the Royal Burgh of Dornoch – granted by King Charles I in 1628 – it's really a village. The stone used in the buildings has a hint of the Cotswolds and this small and stylish restaurant is right in the middle of it all, a short stroll from the cathedral. Michael and Kerensa look after you impeccably, with contrasting styles: he, calm chef in control of superb ingredients; she, at front of house with energy and enthusiasm. Both keep you smiling. The dining room has beautiful Buchanan tartan carpets and tablecloths the colour of leaves just turning in the autumn. Settle into the book-filled sitting-room and dream about the meal to come, or have a drink there after dinner and recover. When you have, go upstairs, three pleasant bedrooms have a mixture of authentic Victorian and Edwardian furniture; all feels welcoming and comfortable. *Children over seven welcome.*

rooms	3: 1 double, 1 twin, 1 twin/double.
price	£70-£90.
meals	Dinner, 4 courses, £32.50.
closed	Christmas; 2 weeks in February/March.
directions	From Inverness, A9 north for 44 miles, then right on A949, for Dornoch. Restaurant on left before cathedral.

Michael & Kerensa Carr

tel	01862 811811
e-mail	stay@2quail.com
web	www.2quail.com

Restaurant with Rooms

map 13   entry 246

Applecross Inn

Shore Street, Applecross, Wester Ross IV54 8LR

No Highland fling would be quite complete without a visit to this simple little inn looking across the sands of Applecross; they extend about half a mile at low tide, and views go on for miles, to Rassay, then Skye beyond. Weather permitting, arrive by Bealach-Na-Ba, the highest mountain pass in Britain. The view at the top is magical, a 50-mile sweep of Hebridean heaven, of sea and mountain, of island and sky. Down at the inn, Judith continues to win rave reviews for her rooms and for her food. More renovation and redecoration will bring bright and breezy blues and yellows to the walls, and bathrooms to every room; all are great value. And so to the food: expect the freshest seafood, scooped from the water out front and cooked simply. The inn has become a magnet for foodies, a place of pilgrimage for those in search of dressed crab, squat lobster, queen scallops, or half a pint of fat prawns. Eat outside in good weather, but the down-to-earth bar is just as good; locals and visitors mix easily. As one guest wrote: "To be Applecrossed; a rare and wonderful experience." Don't miss it.

rooms	7: 1 double, 2 twins, 2 singles, 2 family.
price	£60–£70. Singles £25.
meals	Bar meals from £5. Packed lunch £5. Dinner about £25.
closed	New Year's Day.
directions	From Loch Carron, A896 north for 5 miles, then left over Bealach-Na-Ba pass for 11 miles to village. Inn on left. Use alternative route via Kenmore when snow closes pass.

	Judith Fish
tel	01520 744262
fax	01520 744400

Inn

Scarista House

Isle of Harris, Western Isles HS3 3HX

All you need to know is this: Harris is one of the most beautiful places anywhere in the world. Beaches of white sand that stretch for a mile or two are not uncommon. If you bump into another soul, it will be a delightful coincidence, but you should not count on it. The water is turquoise, and coconuts sometimes wash up on the beach. The view from Scarista is simple and magnificent: field, ridge, beach, water, sky. Patricia and Tim are the kindest people, quietly inspiring. Their home is island heaven: coal fires, rugs on painted wooden floors, books everywhere, old oak furniture, a first-floor drawing room, fresh flowers and fabulous Harris light. The golf club has left a set of clubs by the front door in case you wish to play (the view from the first tee is one of the best in the game). A corncrake occasionally visits the garden. There are walking sticks and Wellington boots to help you up the odd hill. Kind local staff may speak Gaelic. And the food is exceptional, maybe twice-baked cheese soufflé, hand-dived Harris scallops, tarte tatin and cinnamon ice cream. A perfect place.

rooms	5: 3 doubles, 2 twins.
price	£140. Singles from £75.
meals	Packed lunch £5.50. Dinner, 4 courses, £39.50.
closed	Occasionally in winter.
directions	From Tarbert, A859, signed Rodel. Scarista 15 miles on left, after golf course.

	Patricia & Tim Martin
tel	01859 550238
fax	01859 550277
e-mail	timandpatricia@scaristahouse.com
web	www.scaristahouse.com

Restaurant with Rooms

map 11   entry 248

photography by Plas Bodegroes entry no. 256

wales

The Big Sleep Hotel
Bute Terrace, Cardiff CF10 2FE

Cheap but chic and sure damn groovy, this novel and gutsy designer hotel is a perfect launch-pad from which to discover a regenerated Welsh capital. Retro 1970s style and 1990s minimalism blend to amazing effect inside a 10-storey former office block near Cardiff railway station. The building was converted to a hotel by a previous owner and then resurrected as The Big Sleep by two innovators with flair and a friend in the actor John Malkovich, who helped back the project. To keep costs down, Cosmo supplied the formica from his Bath-based factory – the first in Britain to bend the material – and Lulu sourced the fake teddy-bear fur to make full-length curtains and to carpet the fun penthouse suite. Swimming-pool blues and stark white walls were inspired by 1950s Italian architect Gio Ponti. So far, only rooms on the ninth floor, and the two suites on the tenth, have had the treatment; the rest will follow. Most have spectacular city views, especially at night. Elsewhere, modular seating re-upholstered in white PVC, a colourful lobby, and deep red 1960s wallpaper in the busy bar. Great value for a city hotel.

rooms	81: 42 doubles, 30 twins, 7 family, 2 suites.
price	£45–£99.
meals	Continental breakfast only.
closed	Christmas Day & Boxing Day.
directions	M4, junc. 29, A48(M), for Cardiff East. 3rd junc., A4232 to city centre. At 1st r'bout, 2nd exit, 1 mile past Lloyds TSB, left at lights on A4160. Right at 3rd set of lights, under bridge. On left.

Cosmo Fry & Lulu Anderson

tel	029 2063 6363
fax	029 2063 6364
e-mail	bookings@thebigsleephotel.com
web	www.thebigsleephotel.com

Hotel

Tŷ Mawr Country Hotel

Brechfa, Carmarthenshire SA32 7RA

Tŷ Mawr embraces all that is best about Wales, and John and Pearl fit perfectly, having returned to run a hotel in the valley where they met as teenagers. Full of kindness and chatty enthusiasm, they clearly love looking after you. Tŷ Mawr translates as 'big house' and this is a classic 15th-century Welsh building, with lots of exposed stone, low wooden beams, log fires and handsome sash windows. The list of guests who have stayed here over the years is impressive, and eclectic: a platoon of Dragoons during the 1843 Rebecca Riots, President Jimmy Carter on a fishing trip, Pavarotti and Shirley Bassey, separately... and Alexi Sayle; it was also a grammar school in the 1860s. Simple but attractive bedrooms have William Morris fabrics and wallpaper, claw-foot baths and handmade soap. The food is local and free-range from named sources. Dine *al fresco* in summer; the River Marlais runs through the lawned garden. Marlais was Dylan Thomas's middle name as his grandfather lived in the village. Big-hearted, open-minded, even the housekeeper joins in the fun, taking guests' pets for a walk.

rooms	8. 2 doubles, 1 twin, 1 family, 1 four-poster; 1 double with separate bath.
price	£82–£106. Half-board (for 2 nights) £130 p.p. Singles £55–£65.
meals	Sunday lunch £13.50. Packed lunch from £5. Dinner, 5 courses, £26.
closed	Rarely.
directions	M4 west onto A48, then B4310 exit, for National Botanic Gardens of Wales, north for 9 miles to Brechfa. In village centre.

John & Pearl Richardson

tel	01267 202332
fax	01267 202437
e-mail	info@tymawrhotel.co.uk
web	www.tymawrhotel.co.uk

Hotel

map 2   entry 250

Hurst House

East Marsh, Laugharne, Carmarthenshire SA33 4RS

Arriving at Hurst House is like falling off the end of the world onto a pillow of unadulterated style. This pocket of sophistication is miles from anywhere, isolated by windswept marshland that spreads endlessly in all directions; from a distance, the hotel looks half-crushed by the weight of the sky. The building is Georgian and older, with parquet floors, sash windows, stone fireplaces and exposed beams, but the interiors couldn't be more contemporary... bold colours, chic furniture, seductive lighting, pristine bathrooms and Bang & Olufsen stereos and laptops connected to the internet in every bedroom, all carefully designed with you in mind. Matt is a young, friendly Londoner who believes in good food, generous service and great parties – there's no stuffy pretension here. No need to worry about the neighbours either as they own 69 acres of marsh towards the coast. A pond created near the house is fantastic at night, lit by underwater fibre optics, and a spa is planned for derelict barns. Dion the chef is young, talented and changes the menu according to what's local and in season. Fabulous.

rooms	4 doubles.
price	£125. Deluxe double £175.
meals	Lunch £11.95. Dinner £22.95; à la carte, about £26.
closed	Rarely.
directions	From St Clears, A4066 for Pendine, through villages of Laugharne & Broadway. 0.5 miles past 2nd village, left down track towards marshes, signed. Follow signs.

Matt Roberts & Neil Morrissey

tel	01994 427417
fax	01994 427730
e-mail	info@hurst-house.co.uk
web	www.hurst-house.co.uk

Hotel

West Arms Hotel

Llanarmon Dyffryn Ceiriog, Denbighshire LL20 7LD

Come here if you dream of a traditional inn in a gorgeous village where the road ends and the real country begins. The smell of fresh bread may greet you, perhaps the scent of fresh flowers, or a crackling fire. Hear the sound of the River Cleriog through the open front door; sit in the half-glow of the dimly-lit bar, warm and cosy. It's as a 16th-century inn should be, of flagstone, beam, and leaded windows. Décor is simple, the layout all higgledy-piggledy, with old Welsh colours, traditional furniture, a few antiques and inglenook fireplace. Bedrooms are clean and modest, on different levels, some with oak beams and low ceilings; plainer ones at the back have pastoral views. The river runs through the peaceful garden, with the rolling Berwyn Hills beyond – for walks, wildlife and the Pistyll Rhaeder waterfall. Geoff and Gill are laid-back but dedicated, thoroughly at one with what they're doing. The chef is Welsh and superb – a local TV celebrity no less! – and backed by two gourmet chefs. All manner of country pursuits can be arranged, from painting to shooting, and sheepdog trials are held in the village.

rooms	15: 2 doubles, 2 twins, 9 twins/doubles, 2 suites.
price	£95–£138. Singles £52.50–£74.
meals	Bar lunch from £3.95. Packed lunch from £6. Dinner £26.75.
closed	Rarely.
directions	From Shrewsbury, A5 north to Chirk. Left at r'bout on B4500, signed Ceiriog Valley, for 11 miles to Llanarmon DC. Hotel in centre.

Geoff & Gill Leigh–Ford

tel	01691 600665
fax	01691 600622
e-mail	lford@www.thewestarms.co.uk
web	www.thewestarms.co.uk

Inn

map 6   entry 252

Tyddyn Llan
Llandrillo, Corwen, Denbighshire LL21 0ST

Everything is orchestrated superbly here. Your entry is into a smart country home – there's no reception desk – where new owners Bryan and Susan Webb greet you with the promise of deep comfort and excellent modern cooking. There are three sitting rooms, a log fire, carefully chosen antiques and a dining room almost colonial in feel, with blue-painted wooden panelling and yellow floral curtains. Dine at white-clothed tables on fresh, locally sourced produce lovingly cooked: grilled scallops, Welsh black fillet of beef *au poivre*, calves' sweetbreads with pancetta, whimberry creme brulée. Bedrooms vary in size but all are cosy and well-designed in a traditional style with quiet colours, CD players and every indulging extra. Treat yourself to tea on the veranda after a game of croquet on the lawn... or walk the Berwin Ridge which rises to 2,000 feet. Or come with rod and wellies to fish trout and grayling on the River Dee. Great comfort and fine food in an astonishingly beautiful Welsh valley.

rooms	12: 8 doubles, 4 twins.
price	£130–£210. Singles from £65. Half-board £95–£120 p.p.
meals	Lunch, 2 courses, £14.50; 3 courses, £19.50. Dinner, 2 courses £27; 4 courses £35 (included in half board).
closed	Rarely.
directions	From A5 west of Corwen, left on B4401 to Llandrillo. Go through village, entrance on right before tight bend.

	Bryan & Susan Webb
tel	01490 440264
fax	01490 440414
e-mail	tyddynllan@compuserve.com
web	www.tyddynllan.co.uk

Hotel

Penmaenuchaf Hall

Penmaenpool, Dolgellau, Gwynedd LL40 1YB

A long, windy road leads to the hall and it's worth taking for the views over the Mawddach estuary. You can stand at the front of the house, on the Victorian stone balustrade, and gaze down on the tidal ebb and flow, or walk around to the back to blazing banks of rhododendrons, azaleas and camellias, and a rising forest behind. Pass through the front door – all is equally delightful within. The house is pristine: rugs, wooden floors and oak panelling, flowers erupting from jugs and bowls, leather sofas and armchairs, open fires and seagrass matting and, everywhere, those views. Upstairs, bedrooms – more views, of course – come in different shapes and sizes, the big being *huge*, the small being warm and cosy. One room up in the eaves has a fine *bergère* bed. In the dining room, still white napery, a dress code and the best of modern British cooking. Fish in the hotel's 13 miles of river; back in the garden, they grow as much as they can. You'll warm to Mark's sense of humour, too. *Children over six welcome. Pets by arrangement.*

rooms	14: 7 doubles, 5 twins, 1 family, 1 four-poster.
price	£116–£176. Singles £75–£115.
meals	Lunch £3.50–£15.95. Afternoon tea from £4.95. Dinner, 4 courses, £28.50; à la carte also available.
closed	Rarely.
directions	From Dolgellau, A493 west for about 1.5 miles. Entrance on left.

Mark Watson & Lorraine Fielding

tel	01341 422129
fax	01341 422787
e-mail	relax@penhall.co.uk
web	www.penhall.co.uk

Hotel

map 6   entry 254

Llwyndû Farmhouse & Restaurant

Llanaber, Barmouth, Gwynedd LL42 1RR

It's a good mile down the steepish hill to the beach and the gracious sweep of Cardigan Bay, but it looks as though you could hurdle the wall and jump straight into it; an old stone wall frames the view perfectly. The beach is long and wide, a good place to walk, as are the Rhinog mountains which take to the skies behind. And walkers will enjoy Llwyndû. It's warm and earthy, simple and rustic, with ancient stone walls, spiral stone stairways that lead nowhere, a woodburner in the big inglenook and a likely priest's hole cupboard. Peter, an historian turned cook, has brought life to the simple, everyday story of the house and its past owners; you can read up on it. Old wills hang on the walls, the proof of fables. Bedrooms are split between the main house and the granary annexe; there are two four-posters, beams, bold Peter-painted stone walls, good bathrooms and bunk beds for children; don't expect frilly luxury. The farmhouse and restaurant are set in four pretty acres, with great views up and down, cats, dogs and a horse that comes home for the holidays.

rooms	7: 2 doubles, 1 twin, 2 family, 2 four-posters.
price	£70-£76.
meals	Packed lunch £4-£5. Dinner £18.95-£21.95 (restaurant closed Sunday evening).
closed	Christmas Day & Boxing Day.
directions	From Barmouth A496 north. Through Llanaber. Farmhouse signed right where street lights & 40mph limit end.

Peter & Paula Thompson

tel	01341 280144
fax	01341 281236
e-mail	intouch@llwyndu-farmhouse.co.uk
web	www.llwyndu-farmhouse.co.uk

Restaurant with Rooms

Plas Bodegroes

Pwllheli, Gwynedd LL53 5TH

Close to the end of the world and worth every single second it takes to get here. Chris and Gunna are inspirational, their home a temple of cool elegance, the food possibly the best in Wales. Fronted by an avenue of 200-year-old beech trees, this Georgian manor house is wrapped in climbing roses, wildly roaming wisteria and ferns. The veranda circles the house, as do the long French windows that lighten every room; open one up, grab a chair and sit out reading a book. Not a formal place – come to relax and be yourself. Bedrooms are wonderful, the courtyard rooms especially good; exposed wooden ceilings and a crisp clean style give the feel of a smart Scandinavian forest hideaway. Best of all is the dining room, almost a work of art in itself, cool and crisp with modern art and Venetian carnival masks on the walls – a great place to eat Chris's ambrosial food. If you can tear yourself away, explore the Lleyn peninsula: sandy beaches, towering sea cliffs, country walks. Snowdon is also close, and Gunna and Chris will direct you.

rooms	11: 7 doubles, 2 twins, 1 single, 1 four-poster.
price	£80–£150. Singles £40–£80. Half-board from £70 p.p.
meals	Dinner £35. Sunday lunch £16.50.
closed	December-February & Sunday/Monday.
directions	From Pwllheli, A497 towards Nefyn. House on left after 1 mile, signed.

Chris & Gunna Chown

tel	01758 612363
fax	01758 701247
e-mail	gunna@bodegroes.co.uk
web	www.bodegroes.co.uk

Restaurant with Rooms

map 5   entry 256

The Bell at Skenfrith

Skenfrith, Monmouthshire NP7 8UH

Indulge the senses at this swish gastro-pub in a 17th-century coaching inn on the banks of the River Monnow. Follow remote country lanes to a blissful village setting, with a ruined Norman castle and an ancient humpback bridge. Inside is smartly done but informal, and run with warmth – Janet treats staff like members of the family. Expect the best of everything: coffee comes from a proper cappuccino machine, food is mostly organic and the wine superb – there's even a 'Miniscoff' organic menu for children. Bedrooms, all different, are luxurious with Farrow & Ball colours and beds dressed in cotton piqué and Welsh wool; there are home-made biscuits, Molton Brown goodies, even a hi-tech console by the bed so you can listen to music in your bath. After an energetic day out on the hills – or on the river – treat yourself to Usk Valley lamb and tarte tatin in the restaurant overlooking the terrace. Toast the occasion with perry – English 'champagne' and much underrated – then flop into one of the big sofas next to a blazing fire.

rooms	8: 3 doubles, 1 twin, 2 four-posters, 2 attic suites.
price	£85–£150. Singles from £65.
meals	Bar lunch from £15. Dinner, à la carte, £27–£32.50.
closed	2 weeks Jan/Feb, and Mondays from November–March.
directions	From Monmouth, B4233 to Rockfield; B4347 for 5 miles; right on B4521, signed Ross-on-Wye. Skenfrith 1 mile. On right before bridge.

William & Janet Hutchings

tel	01600 750235
fax	01600 750525
e-mail	enquiries@skenfrith.com
web	www.skenfrith.com

Inn

Lake Vyrnwy Hotel

Llanwddyn, Montgomeryshire SY10 0LY

Lake Vyrnwy lives in a blissfully remote pocket of Wales, surrounded by pine forests and ancient grazing land. Both lake and hotel are man-made: the lake was completed in 1891 to provide Liverpool's water, taking two years to fill; the hotel was built shortly afterwards to allow civic dignitaries from the city to come and ogle the dam – they also came to fish the 400,000 trout that were released into the water. The view *is* stupendous, the lake stretching five miles into the distance, home to rolling mists and dramatic bursts of sunshine. Walk, or cycle around it, canoe, sail or fish here – all can be arranged; there's tennis and clay pigeon shooting, and birdwatchers will be in heaven. Once inside, a sense of old style splendour envelopes. The Bisikers have done a wonderful job restoring the hotel to its former glory, with wooden floors, a grand piano, heavy oak furniture, even a postbox in the entrance hall. Bedrooms are excellent and most have lake views, as do the award-winning restaurant, the yellow drawing room, the leather-chaired library, the new conservatory and the terraced bar. A place to return to again and again.

rooms	35: 32 twins/doubles, 2 four-posters, 1 suite.
price	£120–£190. Half-board £77.50–£110 p.p. Singles from £90.
meals	Bar meals from £8. Dinner £29.50.
closed	Rarely.
directions	A490 from Welshpool; B4393 to Lake Vyrnwy. Brown signs from A5 at Shrewsbury as well.

The Bisiker Family

tel	01691 870692
fax	01691 870259
e-mail	res@lakevyrnwy.com
web	www.lakevyrnwy.com

Hotel

map 6   entry 258

Penally Abbey

Penally, Nr Tenby, Pembrokeshire SA70 7PY

It's not often a hotel exceeds your expectations, but then there aren't many places like Penally. It's not a grand hotel and doesn't pretend to be. It just does well the simple things that make a stay memorable. Steve's gentle, unflappable manner suits front of house: chatting to guests one minute, taking orders and mixing a drink at a small bar the next – he makes it look so easy. There's an unhurried charm about the whole place; you won't feel rushed into doing anything. The building is a former 1790s abbey; there's also a ruined 13th-century church called St Diniel's – lit up at night – suggesting even earlier roots. A beautiful garden looks across Carmarthen Bay. The beach is a 10-minute walk and great for pebble collectors; beautiful coastal walks lead from here. Bedrooms are all different: most in the main house have gorgeous four-posters and antiques, while those in the Tuscan-style coach house are more cottagey. Elleen cooks in a self-taught French style, much of it picked up in the kitchen of a French château many years back. The Tenby sea bass was exquisite.

rooms	12: 3 doubles, 1 twin, 8 four-posters.
price	£126–£148. Singles £98. Half-board £90–£104 p.p.
meals	Dinner £30. Lunch by arrangement.
closed	Rarely.
directions	From Tenby, A4139 for Pembroke. Right into Penally after 1.5 miles. Hotel signed at village green. Train station 5-minute walk.

Steve & Elleen Warren

tel	01834 843033
fax	01834 844714
e-mail	info@penally-abbey.com
web	www.penally-abbey.com

Hotel

Twr-y-Felin

St David's, Pembrokeshire SA62 6QS

In this great, spiritual centre of Europe, lots of adrenaline is pumping for planet earth… and you're welcome to jump off a cliff and join in. Andy runs pulsating adventure holidays with a green slant from an old windmill that's been converted into a hotel. There's nothing preachy about his approach; he prefers to reverse widespread indifference to the environment by setting hearts racing: kayak, rock climb, sail, surf… even 'coasteer' with a wetsuit over cliff and rock — all overseen by qualified instructors. Pembrokeshire's rugged coastline and crashing surf is just as good to walk; or gaze out to sea past Ramsey Island from the top of the windmill. The hotel is carbon neutral (as is Alastair Sawday Publishing) it plants trees to offset the pollution it causes — you're charged a £1 tax for driving here! Andy is at the forefront of a local campaign to make St David's the first — and smallest — sustainable city in the world. Most of the food served is organic and locally produced. Bedrooms are clean with good linen and life downstairs is laid-back. Hands on, no frills, friendly and worth a modern day pilgrimage.

rooms	12: 1 twin/double, 1 single, 2 family; 1 twin/double with private shower; 1 double, 2 twins, 2 singles, 2 family, sharing 4 showers.
price	£80–£90. Singles £40–£45.
meals	Lunch £5–£9. Dinner £19.50.
closed	Rarely.
directions	From Haverfordwest, A487 to St David's. Entering city, 1st left after flagpoles, signed, then next left down lane. Entrance on right.

Andy Middleton

tel	01437 721678
fax	01437 721838
e-mail	stay@tyf.com
web	www.tyf.com

Other Place

map 1   entry 260

Three Main Street

Fishguard, Pembrokeshire SA65 9HG

A beautiful Georgian townhouse and restaurant with rooms, less than a minute's walk from Fishguard's busy market square. Marion and Inez have made quite a splash in Wales building a reputation for sublime food, served in style and with generosity. Rugs, stripped wooden floors, candles, hand-written menus and classical music or jazz all combine to give a warm and relaxed, slightly bohemian feel to the place. Big bedrooms have a hint of Art Deco and are homely with fresh flowers, rugs, sofas, good furniture, maybe a walnut bed. The whole place is extremely comfortable – superb value for money – but the pounding heart of Three Main Street is the kitchen whence comes exceptional food. Inez makes the pastries and puddings – try chilled dark chocolate praline, while Marion looks after the starters and main courses – maybe twice-baked crab soufflé with sweet chilli sauce and then succulent Milford turbot fillet on caramelised fennel. Take to the nearby coastal path and walk off your sins amid the divine Welsh landscape. Day trips to Ireland are also possible; it's only an hour-and-a-half away by Sea Lynx.

rooms	3: 2 doubles, 1 twin.
price	£70–£80. Singles £50.
meals	Dinner, 2 courses, £24; 3 courses, £30. Restaurant closed Sundays & Mondays.
closed	February.
directions	Main Street runs off town square in town centre. All roads lead to it.

Inez Ford & Marion Evans

tel	01348 874275
fax	01348 874017

Restaurant with Rooms

Cnapan

East Street, Newport, Nr Fishguard, Pembrokeshire SA12 0SY

The welcome here is immediate and wonderful — you'll feel like an old friend by the time you've walked through the front door! Locals love it here, too. Michael and Judith were on duty the Saturday afternoon we arrived, up to their eyeballs supervising a *cawl* lunch to raise money for the twinning committee, but they still made us feel our arrival was the best thing to have happened all day. Michael answered the door with a big, mischievous smile, while Judith immediately pulled her hands out of a mixing bowl in the kitchen, gave them a wipe and came over to shake our hands. Inside, bright rooms with traditional stone walls and lovely sea views have all you'll need to feel comfortable and cosseted: fresh flowers, comfy sofas and lots of books. Upstairs, past a photo album of family and friends that covers a whole wall, find homely bedrooms without a whisper of bad taste. Newport is a bustling town in the middle of Pembrokeshire National Park; walks to hill, moor, sea and cliff start from the door, with regular buses to bring you back to the best food around.

rooms	5: 1 double, 3 twins, 1 family, plus extra bath.
price	£64. Singles £38.
meals	Lunch from £6.50. Dinner from £21. Restaurant closed Tuesday evenings Easter to October.
closed	Christmas, January & February.
directions	From Cardigan, A487 to Newport. 1st pink house on right.

John & Elund Lloyd,
Michael & Judith Cooper

tel	01239 820575
fax	01239 820878
e-mail	cnapan@online-holidays.net
web	www.online-holidays.net/cnapan

Restaurant with Rooms

map 1   entry 262

Gliffaes Country House Hotel

Crickhowell, Powys NP8 1RH

Gliffaes is matchless: grandly comfortable but as casual and warm as home. It's a house for all seasons – not even driving rain could mask its beauty. Stroll along the rhododendron-flanked drive and wander the 33 acres of stunning gardens and woodland, or bask in the sun on the high, buttressed terrace as the River Usk cuts through the valley 150 feet below. In winter, curl up by fires burning in extravagantly ornate fireplaces – one looks like the Acropolis. Tea is a feast of scones and cakes laid out on a long table at one end of a sitting room of polished floors and panelled walls. The house could be a garden shed and you'd still love it – as long as the Suters remained at the helm, just as Susie's parents did. The clan has been welcoming guests for over 55 years – the fourth generation, aged eight and ten, are ready for some rope-learning, while the first generation, the "granny patrol", is still seen walking her dog; go and have a chat – she's amazing. Bedrooms are excellent, the cooking modern British, and membership of the Slow Food movement means local and seasonal food is used. Fisherfolk can cast to their heart's content.

rooms	22: 3 doubles, 13 twins/doubles, 6 singles.
price	£71.50–£180. Singles from £62.
meals	Light lunch from £3.50. Dinner £29.
closed	First 2 weeks in January.
directions	From Crickhowell, A40 west for 2.5 miles. Entrance on left, signed. Hotel 1 mile up windy hill.

	James & Susie Suter
tel	01874 730371
fax	01874 730463
e-mail	calls@gliffaeshotel.com
web	www.gliffaeshotel.com

Hotel

entry 263   map 2

The Felin Fach Griffin

Felin Fach, Brecon, Powys LD3 0UB

Add a dash of London to a liberal dose of the Brecon Beacons and you have The Felin Fach Griffin. This bold venture mixes the buzz of a smart city bistro with the easy-going pace of good old country living, and it's proving very popular. Full of casual elegance, downstairs fans out from the bar into several eating and sitting areas, with stripped pine and old oak furniture. Make for three giant leather sofas around a raised hearth and settle in. Dine at a smartly-laid table, or opt for the rustic charm of the small backroom bar – there's usually a nice chatty atmosphere. Breakfast is served around one table in the morning room; make your own toast on the Aga, as you like it – or as it comes, depending on how engrossed you are in the newspapers provided. Bedrooms are done in a modern Scandinavian style, clean and simple, with a few designer touches; cylindrical bedside tables and a carved antique four-poster came from India. Charles hosts with aplomb – he is young and ambitious, as are smiley staff who genuinely seem to be enjoying themselves. A cool place to relax. *Dogs welcome by arrangement.*

rooms	7: 2 doubles, 2 twins/doubles, 3 four-posters.
price	£82.50–£92.50. Singles from £57.50
meals	Lunch about £15. Dinner about £20. Restaurant closed Monday lunchtimes.
closed	Christmas Day, New Year's Day & occasionally.
directions	From Brecon, A470 for Builth Wells to Felin Fach (4.5 miles). On left.

	Charles Inkin
tel	01874 620111
fax	01874 620120
e-mail	enquiries@eatdrinksleep.ltd.uk
web	www.eatdrinksleep.ltd.uk

Restaurant with Rooms

map 2   entry 264

Llangoed Hall
Llyswen, Brecon, Powys LD3 0YP

One of the most refined hotels in Britain, Llangoed is a fond tribute to the late Laura Ashley, doyenne of the stylish floral print. It was always her long-held dream to do up this Clough Williams-Ellis house; she used to drive past it often. Sir Bernard saved it from certain demolition and took on the project in her memory. As a result, this magnificent Edwardian manor house has risen like a phoenix. Sir Bernard has decorated with brand new wallpaper, and fabrics from his own company Elanbach. There's something of the Victorian collector in him, too, with corridors and rooms full of remarkable artefacts and curios from around the world – from amazing model railway memorabilia to extremely rare Whistler lithographs in the breakfast room, from old Penguin editions to original Roberts radios. Bedrooms are big and beautiful, some with lovely views. There's a maze big enough to get lost in and a private path to the River Wye for picnics on a small beach. Afternoon tea served on a silver tray is sheer indulgence. It's all done in house-party style, and you're invited.

rooms	23: 20 twins/doubles, 3 suites.
price	£160–£295. Half-board (min. 2 nights) £230–£390 for two. Suite £320–£340.
meals	Lunch from £28.50. Afternoon tea £6–£12.50. Dinner from £48.
closed	Rarely.
directions	From Brecon, A470 for Builth Wells for about 6 miles; left on A470 to Llyswen. Left in village at T-junc. Entrance 1.5 miles further on right.

	Sir Bernard Ashley
tel	01874 754525
fax	01874 754545
web	www.llangoedhall.com

Hotel

Three Cocks Hotel

Three Cocks, Brecon, Powys LD3 0SL

You don't have to walk through it: "the house just creaks on its own," says Michael of this 500-year-old coaching inn built around a tree. Michael and Marie-Jeanne are exceptionally friendly, bringing energy and experience from Belgium, where they ran a restaurant for 10 years. They obviously know their Belgian onions. Michael, who is English, but Belgian by marriage, produces incredible Belgian dishes – i.e. French without the portion control – in the stone-walled restaurant that's peppered with some fine old Dutch oils. The house is hugely welcoming with a bright red carpet, stone walls, a crackling fire, heavy rugs and lots of lovely Belgian beer. It's a very sociable place; the warm and simple bedrooms are TV free, so people stay up late chatting in the limed-oak panelled drawing room downstairs. When you do make it to bed, you'll find beams, sloping floors, timbered walls, thick old eiderdowns and comfy beds. At breakfast, the feasting continues with home-baked bread that melts in the mouth.

rooms	7: 4 doubles, 2 twins; 1 twin with private bath.
price	£70. Singles £50-£70.
meals	Dinner, 4 courses, £30.
closed	December-14 February.
directions	On A438 Brecon-Hereford road. 27 miles from Hereford, 11 miles from Brecon, 4 miles from Hay-on-Wye.

Michael & Marie-Jeanne Winstone

tel	01497 847215
fax	01497 847339
web	www.threecockshotel.com

Hotel

map 2   entry 266

The Lake Country House
Llangammarch Wells, Powys LD4 4BS

Grand but not stuffy, and so cosseting, Lake House is the genuine article — a real country house. Afternoon tea is served in the drawing room where seven beautiful rugs warm a brightly polished wooden floor and five chandeliers hang from the ceiling. The hotel opened 100 years ago and the leather-bound fishing logs and visitors' books go back to 1894. A feel of the 1920s lingers. Fires come to life in front of your eyes, seemingly unaided by human hands, walking sticks wait at the door, grand pianos, antiques and grandfather clocks lie about the place and snooker balls clack in the distance. The same grandeur marks the bedrooms; most are suites: *trompe l'œil* wallpaper, rich fabrics, good lighting, stacks of antiques, crowns above the beds, a turndown service — the works. Jean-Pierre runs his home with gentle charm, happy to share his knowledge of this deeply rural slice of Wales. The grounds hold a lake to fish — you can hire rods — a nine-hole golf course, the River Ifron where kingfishers swoop, and acres of peace and quiet. Riding also can be arranged.

rooms	18: 8 twins/doubles, 10 suites.
price	£130–£198. Singles £90–£145. Suite £198–£260.
meals	Lunch, 3 courses, £18.50. Dinner £35.
closed	Rarely.
directions	From Builth Wells, A483 west for 7 miles to Garth. Signed from village.

Jean-Pierre Mifsud

tel	01591 620202
fax	01591 620457
e-mail	info@lakecountryhouse.co.uk
web	www.lakecountryhouse.co.uk

Hotel

Carlton House

Dolycoed Road, Llanwrtyd Wells, Powys LD5 4RA

A Welsh spa town – Wales's prettiest – with one of the most talented chefs in Britain. Mary Ann joined the cooking elite in 2002, winning a Michelin star; high time, said her legion of fans. They've been coming to this marvellously eccentric restaurant with rooms for years. Victorians flocked to Llanwrtyd Wells in the 1800s, drawn in the belief that the natural springs could cure everything from a troubled soul to a wart on the toe. The 1900 townhouse has a wonderful feeling of several black and white movies rolled into one as you walk up the gun-metal galleried staircase to rooms full of faded charm. The Gilchrists are old pro's, and great company. Alan, an ever engaging and unflappable host, orchestrates all in the ground-floor restaurant, full of blue and modern furniture and screened off by book shelves. Mary Ann is entirely self-taught and cooks with instinctive brilliance; she decides what to cook only hours before she puts on her apron. Their brasserie across the road is fun for a light meal, too. Pony-trekkers, cyclists and walkers fill the town in summer… Carlton suits all year.

rooms	6: 4 doubles, 2 twins/doubles.
price	£60–£80. Half-board (min. 2 nights) from £54.50 p.p. Singles £45.
meals	Packed lunch £3.50. Dinner £27–£37.
closed	Last 2 weeks in December (open for New Year).
directions	From Builth Wells, A483 to Llanwrtyd Wells. 1st right in town. House 50 yds on right.

Alan & Mary Ann Gilchrist

tel	01591 610248
fax	01591 610242
e-mail	info@carltonrestaurant.co.uk
web	www.carltonrestaurant.co.uk

Restaurant with Rooms

map 2　entry 268

The Talkhouse

Pontdolgoch, Nr Cearsws, Powys SY17 5JE

From the outside it looks like a nice, neat pub. Which is just what it used to be… Today it serves the best bottled beers and the most delicious wines. The Garratt brothers should have a winning formula in their newly acquired 17th-century drover's rest – special rooms, attentive service, marvellous food and wine. The bar has beams, log fire and sumptuous sofas; the claret-and-cream dining room has French windows that open to the garden in summer – and you can dine *en plein air*. The three bedrooms – soon to be five – are rich and relaxing: Tirion is a 'business man's room' with a nautical feel, its own vestibule, small desk and 1920s bathroom decorated in Moustier tiles; Tybie is for lovers, with a wonderful wrought-iron bed and a mosaic bathroom of Sicilian sandstone; Myfanwy has a corona over the bed and a shower of glass, stainless steel and African slate. Classical, seasonal cooking – the lightest sweet potato and butternut soup, the most delicately cooked Welsh lamb – is a treat, and breakfasts, accompanied by fresh orange juice and home-made jam, are memorable. A small, perfect find in the rolling wilderness of mid-Wales.

rooms	3 doubles.
price	£75-£95. Half-board, Friday & Saturday, from £55 p.p. Singles £65.
meals	Dinner, à la carte, about £25.
closed	Rarely.
directions	From Newtown, A489 west, then right before level crossing on A470, for Caersws & Dolgellau. Inn on left after 1 mile, under railway bridge.

Mark & Stephen Garratt

tel	01686 688919
fax	01686 689134
e-mail	info@talkhouse.co.uk
web	www.talkhouse.co.uk

Inn

Milebrook House Hotel

Milebrook, Knighton, Powys LD7 1LT

Your arrival at Milebrook is peculiarly comforting and understated, with no hidden surprises. The parquet floor in the hall smells of lavender floor wax, the clock ticks quietly, the flowers are fresh and Beryl is likely to come out of the kitchen in her apron to greet you. Fabrics are blended rather than matched; the furniture comfortable rather than remarkable; and the service is attentive and unobtrusive. Chickens that produce the eggs for your breakfast cluck contentedly in the walled kitchen garden where flowers and vegetables are grown for the table – a table to reckon with, for their chef trained in France and is eager to win recognition. He mixes classic French with the best of English, ably assisted by that garden. There's wild terrain, too, devoted to a mature arboretum and a wildlife pond. Elsewhere, terracing, a gazebo, a pergola with roses growing over obelisks, and still room for a croquet lawn. The River Teme runs along the bottom of the garden where you can fly-fish and the countryside belongs to a portion of Britain – sadly decreasing – that can still be called 'tranquil'. Come to rest completely.

rooms	10: 5 doubles, 4 twins, 1 family.
price	£86–£92. Half-board, 2 nights, £117–£126 p.p. Singles £56–£60.
meals	Dinner £23.50; à la carte about £28.50. Restaurant closed Monday lunchtimes.
closed	Rarely.
directions	From Ludlow, A49 north, then left at Bromfield on A4113 towards Knighton for 7 miles. Hotel on right.

Rodney & Beryl Marsden
tel	01547 528632
fax	01547 520509
e-mail	hotel@milebrook.kc3ltd.co.uk
web	www.milebrookhouse.co.uk

Hotel

map 6   entry 270

WHAT'S IN THE BACK OF THE BOOK?

A SHORT STORY:
NIGHT OF THE ARMY ANTS

By Mary Mackey

My sister and I picked a good hotel: a clean place with white-washed walls, a quaintly thatched roof, toilets that worked, and hot water. It was a far cry from the other places we had stayed at during our two weeks in Guatemala. The room in Chichicastenango had been windowless, smelled of urine, had two straw-stuffed pads instead of beds, and sported a family toilet planted neatly in the middle of the courtyard. In Flores we had made do with a tin roof that leaked, chattering bats in the rafters, and spoiled pork for dinner. I had spent a good part of the past six years living in the jungles of Costa Rica and I prided myself on traveling tough, but my sister — who was new to the tropics – had had it. She had a stomachache (soon to become amoebic dysentery that would ultimately land her in Intensive Care — but that's another story).

"For God's sake let's pay whatever it takes to get a toilet seat that doesn't fall off," she begged. She had been a great sport, but she was getting that glassy look in her eyes that meant she was about to crack. It was the same look she had given me when she was twelve, and I invited her to Mexico City, picked her up at the airport, and drove her through a riot, so I gave in.

That afternoon we checked into the nicest hotel in Tikal and spent the rest of the day in the park climbing the pyramids, watching the howler monkeys, and admiring the phosphorescent blue butterflies. At dusk, we even spotted a timid, deer-like agouti peering out of the brush. That night as we lay in our comfortable beds in our ever-so comfortable hotel, the jungle frogs sang us to sleep.

I woke in pitch blackness, some time around midnight with the distinct sensation I was not alone. Suddenly, like galley slaves rowing to the same beat, a host of little things all bit me simultaneously. With a howl, I catapulted out of bed, and staggered around the room, slapping randomly. Roused out of a sound sleep, my sister went for the lights, but there were no lights. The electricity had been turned off at ten – not an uncommon occurrence in the tropics where fuel for generators is expensive.

"Help!" I yelled as I continued my St. Vitus dance around the dark room, slapping, stumbling, tripping over the luggage, and generally doing a great imitation of someone who had lost her mind. Being a level-headed sort, my sister located a flashlight, turned the beam on me, and to our mutual horror we discovered I was covered from head to toe with ants. Snatching off my nightgown, she began to beat me with a towel, smashing the little suckers, while I went on hopping and screaming.

When I was de-antified and a few degrees calmer, she directed the flashlight toward my bed. It was seething like an anthill that had been kicked in. Thousands of ants were crawling across the pillow and sheets, but that wasn't the worst of it: There were more ants streaming down the wall of the room in a column four or five feet wide and several inches thick. In many tropical buildings, the walls don't go all the way up to the ceiling. The ants had located the ventilation space and were rushing through it in unbelievable quantities.

"Looks like a goddamned waterfall," my sister observed as the slick, black column poured down the wall. "In a few seconds they would have gotten to my bed. Thanks for sounding the alarm. I can just imagine our skeletons lying there, picked to the bone."

Summoning what little dignity I had left, I brushed the smashed ants off my naked body.

"Army ants don't eat people," I announced. My voice grew shrill. "There is nothing to fear."

"How do we make them go away?"

"We can't. When the army ants march, the local people gather up all their food and move out of their houses until they've passed. The ants are a kind of pest control service. By the time they're done there's not a snake, rat. Or bug left." I was always one for appreciating the balance of nature.

"Son of a bitch," my sister said. "You mean we're stuck with these things for the rest of the night?"

By now the guests in the hotel were all awake, and, convinced we were being murdered, they had all began to pound on our door.

"Are you two okay?" a voice called.

We dressed, went out, and explained the ant situation to our fellow tourists. There were perhaps fifteen of us altogether, from Germany, France, Canada, and the United States, mostly young, mostly experienced travelers, but no one had been through an army ant invasion before. Since the entire staff of the hotel had mysteriously disappeared, we were on our own.

Sleep being out of the question, we arranged ourselves on the sofas in the lobby, pulled up our feet so the ants wouldn't crawl over them, and waited. A few people tried to make ant jokes, but no one was in the mood.

"I have to go to the bathroom," a German woman announced. Several of us picked our way to the door with her, but by now the bathroom floor was a heaving mass of ants. It was clear they were going to troop through every room in the hotel.

We waited. Above us, the thatch began to make soft rustling noises. Suddenly there was a plop, and a scorpion about the size of a human hand hit the floor running. Fifteen tourists screamed simultaneously. No, make that fourteen. There was one guy who wouldn't have screamed if you'd put a red hot poker to his forehead.

"Scorpions!"

"Are they poisonous?"

You bet they were. The old hands insisted that little ones were even more poisonous – even fatal – but that was small consolation. These were big, their bites could land you in the hospital, and by now they were falling like hail, dozens at a time, driven out of the thatched roof by the ants.

"Umbrellas!" a guy from Chicago suggested.

We rose like one person, fled back to our rooms, seized our umbrellas, opened them to keep off the scorpions, and retreated to the lobby, where we sat, hunched up against one another, like people waiting for a bus in a rainstorm. Occasionally a large scorpion would hit one of the umbrellas, bounce to the floor, and scuttle away, but it never got far before the ants mobbed it. After two hours of this, we were so tired we could hardly sit upright. It was then that a man whose name I never knew, but whom neither I nor my sister will ever forget, made one of the most generous offers one human being has ever made to another: "The ants haven't made it to my room yet. If you and your sister would like to try to get some sleep in my bed, I'll hold an umbrella over you." We checked him out. He was perhaps twenty-eight, thin, with dark brown hair, and he had a face that inspired confidence. Reassured that this wasn't some crazy plot to seduce both of us in the middle of an ant invasion, we agreed.

For the next few hours, my sister and I lay side by side in his bed as he sat next to us, silently holding a large black umbrella over our bodies so we wouldn't get stung by falling scorpions. Somehow against all odds we fell asleep. When we we woke the umbrella was neatly furled, and the chair was empty. He was gone, and so were the ants.

Mary Mackey

Reprinted from *I Should Have Stayed Home*
(RDR Books: Oakland, California).

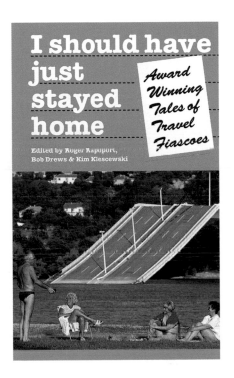

The trip of a lifetime or a life sentence?

I Should Have Stayed Home, I Really Should Have Stayed Home, I've Been Gone Far Too Long and *I Should Have Just Stayed Home* have brought travel literature to a new low. Easily surpassing the technicolor school of travel writing, this series shows you how innocents abroad can easily turn a dream vacation into a nightmare. Proof positive that misery loves company, this hilarious series is available from your favorite bookseller and distributed in the United Kingdom by Roundhouse Publishing. Or email to ***trouble@rdrbooks.com*** for more information. You can also submit stories for consideration in the next volume in this series.

A BIT OF FUN....

First five correct entries received by July '04 will win
2 books of their choice from our Special Places to Stay Series.

Across

1. A pheasant to be found in this county (7).

5. Mere water (4).

7. See 24.

8. He was muddled over time (6).

10. Rue this genus of plants (4).

11. Lion gait-not a cameo (8).

13. The Fox and the Acorn in this county (6).

14. Black boy, thrown overboard (6).

17. Look at the opening in this border town (8).

19. Scrutinise look (4).

21. Watch out for this, spy (6).

22. Late owing mixed - ooze (5).

23. A kiss for the French shaft (4).

24 & 7 Is this home to a sanitary engineer in Dorset? (7, 5).

Down

1. Felix is unique in this university town (9).

2. The pastor minus one can be found in York (7).

3. Rear - it's unusual (4).

4. You are, when you're away! (6)

5. At the ebb (3,5).

6. Not a likely settlement to find in our book (5).

9. Order ever to take over (10).

12. Remember to learn by heart (8).

15. Cub scum to capitulate (7).

16. Ta part to adorn (6).

18. Find the bell in a county twixt Durham and Gloucestershire (5).

20. One hopes for a good one in our hotels (4).

Compiled by coelacanth

WHAT IS ALASTAIR SAWDAY PUBLISHING?

Twenty or so of us work in converted barns on a farm near Bristol, close enough to the city for a bicycle ride and far enough for a silence broken only by horses and the occasional passage of a tractor. Some editors work in the countries they write about, e.g. France; others work from the UK but are based outside the office. We enjoy each other's company, celebrate every event possible, and work in an easy-going but committed environment.

These books owe their style and mood to Alastair's miscellaneous career and his interest in the community and the environment. He has taught overseas, worked with refugees, run development projects abroad, founded a travel company and several environmental organisations. There has been a slightly unconventional streak throughout, not least in his driving of a waste-paper-collection lorry, the manning of stalls at jumble sales and the pursuit of causes long before they were considered sane.

These books owe their style and mood to Alastair's miscellaneous career and his interest in the community and the environment

Back to the travel company: trying to take his clients to eat and sleep in places that were not owned by corporations and assorted bandits he found dozens of very special places in France — farms, châteaux etc — a list that grew into the first book, *French Bed and Breakfast*. It was a celebration of 'real' places to stay and the remarkable people who run them.

The publishing company grew from that first and rather whimsical French book. It started as a mild crusade, and there it stays — full of 'attitude', and the more appealing for it. For we still celebrate the unusual, the beautiful, the individual. We are passionate about rejecting the banal, the ugly, the pompous and the indifferent and we are passionate, too, about 'real' food. Alastair is a trustee of the Soil Association and keen to promote organic growing and consuming by owners and visitors.

It is a source of deep pleasure to us to know that there are many thousands of people who share our views. We are by no means alone in trumpeting the virtues of resisting the destruction and uniformity of so much of our culture — and the cultures of other nations, too.

We run a company in which people and values matter. We love to hear of new friendships between those in the book and those using it, and to know that there are many people — among them farmers — who have been enabled to pursue their decent lives thanks to the extra income our books bring them.

FRAGILE EARTH SERIES

The Little Earth Book

Now in its third edition and as engrossing and provocative as ever, it continues to highlight the perilously fragile state of our planet.
£6.99

The Little Food Book

Makes for a wonderfully stimulating read — one that may change your attitude to the food choices you make daily.
£6.99

The Little Money Book

Could make you look at everything financial — from your bank statements to the coins in your pocket — in a whole new way.
Available November 2003
£6.99

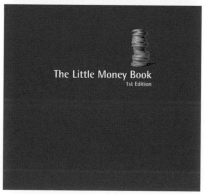

This fascinating series has been praised by politicians, academics, environmentalists, civil servants — and 'general' readers. It has come as a blast of fresh air, blowing away confusion and incomprehension.

www.fragile-earth.com

SIX DAYS

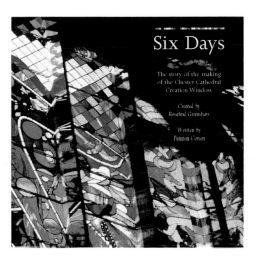

Celebrating the triumph of creativity over adversity.

An inspiring and moving story of the making of the stained glass 'Creation' window at Chester Cathedral by a woman battling with Parkinson's disease.

"Within a few seconds, the tears were running down my cheeks. The window was one of the most beautiful things I had ever seen. It is a tour-de-force, playing with light like no other window ..."
Anthropologist Hugh Brody

In 1983, Ros Grimshaw, a distinguished designer, artist and creator of stained-glass windows, was diagnosed with Parkinson's disease. Refusing to allow her illness to prevent her from working, Ros became even more adept at her craft, and in 2000 won the commission to design and make the 'Creation' Stained Glass Window for Chester Cathedral.

Six Days traces the evolution of the window from the first sketches to its final, glorious completion as a rare and wonderful tribute to Life itself: for each of the six 'days' of Creation recounted in Genesis, there is a scene below that is relevant to the world of today and tomorrow.

Extracts from Ros's diary capture the personal struggle involved. Superb photography captures the luminescence of the stunning stained glass, while the story weaves together essays, poems, and moving contributions from Ros's partner, Patrick Costeloe.

Available from Alastair Sawday Publishing £12.99

ORDER FORM UK

All these books are available in major bookshops or you may order them direct. **Post and packaging are FREE within the UK.**

		Price	No. copies
French Bed & Breakfast	Edition 8	£15.99	
French Hotels, Châteaux & Inns (Nov. 03)	Edition 3	£13.99	
French Holiday Homes (Jan. 04)	Edition 2	£11.99	
Paris Hotels	Edition 4	£9.99	
British Bed & Breakfast	Edition 8	£14.99	
British Hotels, Inns & Other Places	Edition 5	£13.99	
Bed & Breakfast for Garden Lovers	Edition 2	£14.99	
British Holiday Homes	Edition 1	£9.99	
London	Edition 1	£9.99	
Ireland	Edition 4	£12.99	
Spain	Edition 5	£13.99	
Portugal	Edition 2	£8.99	
Italy	Edition 3	£12.99	
Europe with courses & activities	Edition 1	£12.99	
India	Edition 1	£10.99	
Morocco (Dec. 03)	Edition 1	£10.99	
The Little Earth Book	Edition 3	£6.99	
The Little Food Book	Edition 1	£6.99	
The Little Money Book (Nov. 03)	Edition 1	£6.99	
Six Days		£12.99	

**Please make cheques payable to
Alastair Sawday Publishing**   Total £ _____ _____

Please send cheques to: Alastair Sawday Publishing,
The Home Farm Stables, Barrow Gurney, Bristol BS48 3R N.
For credit card orders call 01275 464891 or order directly
from our web site **www.specialplacestostay.com**

Title	First name		Surname

Address

Postcode		Tel	

If you do not wish to receive mail from other like-minded companies,
please tick here ☐

If you would prefer not to receive information about special offers on our books,
please tick here ☐

ORDER FORM USA

All these books are available at your local bookstore, or you may order direct. Allow two to three weeks for delivery.

		Price	No. copies
Europe (Spring 04)	Edition 1	$19.99	
Morocco	Edition 1	$15.95	
Spain	Edition 5	$19.95	
Ireland	Edition 4	$17.95	
French Bed & Breakfast	Edition 8	$19.95	
Paris Hotels	Edition 4	$14.95	
British Holiday Homes	Edition 1	$14.95	
British Bed & Breakfast	Edition 8	$19.95	
French Hotels, Châteaux and Inns	Edition 3	$19.95	
Portugal	Edition 2	$14.95	
London	Edition 1	$12.95	
Italy	Edition 3	$19.95	
French Holiday Homes (Mar 04)	Edition 2	$17.95	

Total $ _____ _____

Shipping in the continental USA: $3.95 for one book, $4.95 for two books, $5.95 for three or more books. _____ _____
Outside continental USA, call (800) 243-0495 for prices.
For delivery to AK, CA, CO, CT, FL, GA, IL, IN, KS, MI, MN, MO, NE, NM, NC, OK, SC, TN, TX, VA, and WA, please add appropriate sales tax.

Please make checks payable to: **Total $** _____ _____
The Globe Pequot Press

To order by phone with MasterCard or Visa: (800) 243-0495, 9am to 5pm EST; by fax: (800) 820-2329, 24 hours; through our web site: **www.GlobePequot.com**; or by mail: The Globe Pequot Press, P.O. Box 480, Guilford, CT 06437

Date _____

Name _____

Address _____

Town _____

State _____

Zip code _____

Tel _____

Fax _____

WWW.SPECIALPLACESTOSTAY.COM

Britain

France

Ireland

Italy

Portugal

Spain

Morocco

India...

all in one place!

On the unfathomable and often unnavigable sea of online accommodation pages, those who have discovered **www.specialplacestostay.com** have found it to be an island of reliability. Not only will you find a database full of trustworthy, up-to-date information about all the Special Places to Stay across Europe, but also:

- Links to the web sites of all of the places in the series
- Colourful, clickable, interactive maps to help you find the right place
- The opportunity to make most bookings by e-mail – even if you don't have e-mail yourself
- Online purchasing of our books, securely and cheaply
- Regular, exclusive special offers on books
- The latest news about future editions and future titles

The site is constantly evolving and is frequently updated with news and special features that won't appear anywhere else but in our window on the worldwide web.

Russell Wilkinson, Web Producer
website@specialplacestostay.com

If you'd like to receive news and updates about our books by e-mail, send a message to newsletter@specialplacestostay.com

REPORT FORM

Comments on existing entries and new discoveries

If you have any comments on entries in this guide, please let us have them. If you have a favourite house, hotel, inn or other new discovery, anywhere, please let us know about it.

Existing Entry:

Name of property: _____

_____

New recommendation:

Name of property: _____

Address: _____

_____

_____

_____

Tel: _____

Comments.

_____

_____

_____

_____

_____

_____

_____

_____

Your name: _____

Address: _____

_____

Tel & e-mail: _____

Please send the completed form to:

Alastair Sawday Publishing, The Home Farm Stables, Barrow Gurney, Bristol BS48 3RW
or go to www.specialplacestostay.com and click on 'contact'.

Thank you.

QUICK REFERENCE INDICES

QUICK REFERENCE INDICES

Horse Riding Fancy leaping into the saddle? You can here.
England
2 • 21 • 50 • 57 • 71 • 75 • 84 • 88 • 128 • 132 • 135 • 144 • 150 • 152 • 170 • 177
Scotland
205 • 209 • 221 • 223 • 233 • 234 • 238
Wales
263

Local Produce Like to support local farmers? Eat at these places.
England
2 • 20 • 23 • 24 • 31 • 33 • 41 • 46 • 50 • 55 • 57 • 62 • 63 • 66 • 69 • 71 • 75 81 • 83 • 84 • 87 • 88 • 92 • 94 • 107 • 110 • 116 • 117 • 122 • 128 • 132 • 134 • 135 • 144 • 145 • 150 • 152 • 162 • 163 • 170 • 173 • 177 • 180
Scotland
200 • 205 • 209 • 212 • 213 • 221 • 222 • 223 • 233 • 234 • 237 • 238 • 240 • 242 • 245 • 246 • 247
Wales
256 • 260 • 263 • 264 • 267

Meeting Room These places have quiet meeting rooms.
England
20 • 21 • 31 • 46 • 50 • 55 • 62 • 63 • 69 • 71 • 75 • 84 • 88 • 92 • 94 • 107 • 116 • 117 • 122 • 128 • 138 • 150 • 152 • 173 • 180 • 183
Channel Islands
196
Scotland
209 • 212 • 213 • 223 • 237 • 240 • 247
Wales
256 • 263 • 264

Midweek deals These places have week day reductions.
England
2 • 33 • 41 • 46 • 50 • 55 • 57 • 62 • 71 • 84 • 87 • 88 • 94 • 116 • 122 • 128 • 132 • 134 • 135 • 150 • 152 • 162 • 163 • 170 • 177 • 180
Channel Islands
196
Scotland
205 • 209 • 212 • 213 • 222 • 223 • 233 • 238 • 240 • 247
Wales
263 • 267

QUICK REFERENCE INDICES

Music System in the bedrooms

For all you disco divas.
England
2 • 20 • 24 • 31 • 62 • 75 • 92 • 94 • 107 • 113 • 138 • 145 • 173
Scotland
213 • 240 • 242
Wales
256 • 263

Quiet places

These places are particularly peaceful.
England
2 • 21 • 33 • 46 • 50 • 55 • 62 • 63 • 66 • 69 • 71 • 84 • 107 • 122
• 128 • 132 • 135 • 138 • 145 • 150 • 162 • 170 • 177 • 183
Channel Islands.
196
Scotland
200 • 205 • 209 • 213 • 223 • 234 • 237 • 238 • 240 • 242 • 247
Wales
256 • 263 • 264

Weekend deals

These places offer special deals.
England
33 • 46 • 50 • 55 • 57 • 71 • 84 • 87 • 88 • 113 • 116 • 122 • 128
• 135
138 • 150 • 152 • 162 • 170 • 177
Channel Islands
196
Scotland
205 • 212 • 213 • 222 • 223 • 233 • 238 • 240 • 247
Wales
263 • 267

INDEX - PROPERTY NAME

INDEX - PROPERTY NAME

INDEX - PROPERTY NAME

INDEX - PROPERTY NAME

INDEX - TOWN

INDEX - TOWN

INDEX - TOWN

HOW TO USE THIS BOOK

explanations

① rooms

Assume all rooms are 'en suite' unless we say otherwise.

If a room is not 'en suite' we say **with separate bath** or **with shared bathroom**: the former you will have to yourself, the latter may be shared with other guests or family member.

② room price

The price shown is for one night B&B for two people sharing a room. A price range incorporates room/seasonal differences. We say when the price is for two.

③ meals

Prices are per person. Meals in B&B's must be booked in advance. If breakfast isn't included we give the price.

④ closed

When given in months, this means for the whole of the named months and the time in between.

⑤ directions

Use as a guide; the owner can give more details.

⑥ map & entry numbers

Map page number; entry number.

⑦ type of place

sample entry

ISLE OF SKYE

Stein Inn
Stein, Waternish, Isle of Skye IV55 8GA

White cottages bob by the quay in this remote, tiny fishing village, the setting for Skye's oldest inn. Angus stocks 80 single malts, thirst-quenching ales and seasoned opinion behind the bar of this rough-hewn, fire-warmed hostelry. Stand under blackened joists and talk about anything with this affable rogue spirit. In good weather, sit out by the shore of the sea loch: across the water, the headland rises dramatically; to the north, a few low-slung islands lie scattered. Lose yourself with a pint watching locals potter about in their boats against a setting sun. With the sea being so close, the food is really good, too: from your window, watch the catch landed, hauled from the sea to your plate, impossibly fresh. If cosiness comes from contrast and setting, then the clean, closely-eaved, blue-carpeted and pine-panelled rooms above the bar are perfect. There are moorings for yachts – sailors can ring ahead to have provisions waiting – but... far wiser to spoil yourselves with a couple of nights on land. A little paradise.

rooms	5: 2 doubles, 2 family, 1 single.
price	£49–£62. Singles £24.50–£30.
meals	Bar lunch from £4.50. Dinner about £13.
closed	Christmas Day & New Year's Day.
directions	From Isle of Skye bridge, A850 to Portree. Follow sign to Uig for 4 miles, left on A850 for Dunvegan for 14 miles. Hard right turn to Waternish on B886. Stein 3.5 miles along loch side.

	Angus & Teresa McGhie
tel	01470 592362
fax	01470 592362
e-mail	angus.teresa@steininn.co.uk
web	www.steininn.co.uk

⑦ Inn

 ⑥ map 11 entry 234

⑧ symbols

See the last page of the book for fuller explanation:

wheelchair facilities	pets can sleep in your bedroom
easily accessible bedrooms	internet connection available
all children welcome	swimming pool
smoking restrictions exist	bike hire
cash & cheques only	walking nearby
vegetarians catered for with advance warning	tennis on the premises